GHOST
FRONT

GHOST FRONT

FRONT

The Ardennes
before the
Battle of the Bulge

CHARLES WHITING

DA CAPO PRESS

Published by
DA CAPO PRESS
A Member of the Perseus Books Group

Copyright © 2002 by Charles Whiting

ISBN 0-306-81148-0

PRINTED AND BOUND IN THE UNITED STATES OF AMERICA.

Contents

Maps

"To defend everything is to defend nothing."
—Napoleon

———————

"The only thing to do when a son of a bitch looks cross-eyed at you, is to beat the hell out of him right there and then."
—Patton

SEPTEMBER
1944

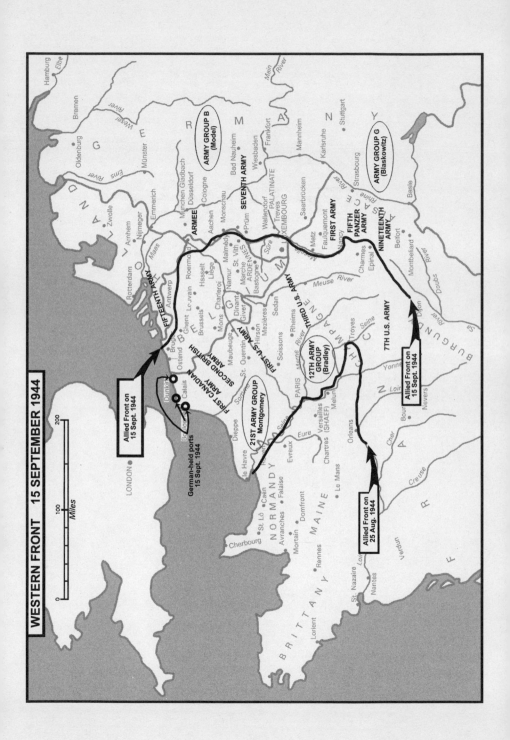

WESTERN FRONT · 15 SEPTEMBER 1944

ARMY GROUP B
(Model)

ARMY GROUP G
(Blaskowitz)

G E R M A N Y

SEVENTH ARMY

FIFTEENTH
ARMEE

FIRST ARMY

FIFTH
PANZER
ARMY

NINETEENTH
ARMY

Hamburg
Bremen
Oldenburg
Münster
Emmerich
Zwolle
Arnhem
Nijmeger
Rotterdam
Antwerp
Ostend
Bruges
Ghent
Dunkirk
Calais
Boulogne

H O L L A N D

FIFTEENTH ARMY
FIRST CANADIAN ARMY
SECOND BRITISH ARMY
FIRST U.S. ARMY
THIRD U.S. ARMY

München Gladbach
Düsseldorf
Cologne
Aachen
Monschau
Roermond
Hasselt
Liège
Namur
Charleroi
Mons
Brussels
Le Vrain
Maubeuge
St. Quentin
Hirson
Mézières
Sedan

ARDENNES
St. Vith
Malmédy
Marche
Bastogne
Dinant
Givet

C H A M P A G N E

Düren
Prüm
Wallendorf
Treves
LUXEMBOURG
PALATINATE
Saarbrücken
Faulquemont
Metz
Nancy
Charmes
Épinal

Frankfort
Bad Nauheim
Wiesbaden
Mannheim
Karlsruhe
Strasbourg
Stuttgart
Basle
Montbéliard
Belfort

21ST ARMY GROUP
Montgomery

12TH ARMY GROUP
(Bradley)

7TH U.S. ARMY

Meuse River

Rheims
Soissons
Soupre
PARIS
Melun
Versailles
(SHAEF)
Chartres
Orleans
Troyes
Dijon
Nevers
Bourg

B U R G U N D Y

Doubs River

Allied Front on
15 Sept. 1944

German-held ports
15 Sept. 1944

Allied Front on
15 Sept. 1944

Allied Front on
25 Aug. 1944

LONDON

Le Havre
Dieppe
Evreux
Caen
St. Lô
Cherbourg
Avranches
Mortain
Domfront
Falaise
Le Mans
Rennes
St. Nazaire
Lorient
Nantes

N O R M A N D Y
M A I N E
B R I T T A N Y

Elbe
Wesel River
Ems River
Main River
Rhine River
Maas
Meuse River
Marne River
Seine
Loire
Cher
Yonne
Loire
Creuse
Verdun

Miles
0   100   200

1

"But We All Thought You Were Dead"

At the end of August 1944, it was decided by the survivors of the SS divisions in France that they would attempt to break out from the trap. For days now, caught between the British Second and the American Third Armies, they had been relentlessly pounded by enemy artillery and aerial attacks. They had died by the scores, by the hundreds and, in the end, by the thousands. As SS General Kurt "Panzer" Meyer, acting commander of the 12th SS "Hitler Youth," put it: "There was no use even trying to take cover. We were helpless, stuck out in the open, presented to the enemy as if on a silver platter."

Viewed from the sky above the five German divisions of the corps to which "Panzermeyer" belonged, Wing-Commander "Johnnie" Johnson, the RAF ace, described the killing:

> When the Spitfires arrived over the small triangle of Normandy, bounded by Falaise, Trun and Chambois, the Typhoons were already hard at work. One of their favorite tactics against long streams of enemy vehicles was to seal off the front and rear of the column by accurately dropping a few bombs. This technique imprisoned the desperate enemy on a narrow stretch of dusty lane ... sometimes four abreast. Some of the armored cars and tanks attempted to escape by making detours across the fields and wooded country, but these were soon spotted by the Typhoons and were accorded the same treatment as their comrades on the highways and lanes.

As soon as the Typhoons were finished, in would zoom the Spitfires, machine guns chattering and cannons pounding away. Like flights of angry red hornets, the bullets and 20mm shells would hiss across the blue summer sky and slam into the packed German columns. Then, as Johnson described it afterwards, "as soon as the 'Spits' had fired all their ammo too, they flew back at high speed to their airfields where the ground crews worked flat-out in the hot sunshine to re-arm and re-fuel the aircraft in the shortest possible time."

Thus the brutal, impersonal killing continued that third week of August over half a century ago, with one excited twenty-year-old British pilot reporting over his radio: "One thousand plus [vehicles] ... very little movement ... packed bumper to bumper ... feeding main road from all sides like herring bones ..." By evening a comrade from the same fighter-bomber squadron was signaling back to Control, "Panic ...! Whole area burning."

On the evening of 23 August, the trapped Germans had had enough of what they called the "*Falaisekessel*" ("Falaise Pocket"). They were going to break out of that terrible killing ground at last. Huddled in a ditch, Panzermeyer and the other senior SS officers listened as "Papa Hausser," the SS commander of the Seventh German Army—what was left of it—explained his rough-and-ready plan. Hausser, who wore a black patch over one eye socket (he had lost an eye in Russia) and who would be wounded again before the terrible ordeal was over, explained that remnants of his five panzer divisions would attempt to break through the British line at a place called Chambois.

Die Leibstandarte, the premier division of the SS, which bore the Fuhrer's own name, would lead the breakthrough attack. Panzermeyer, whose 12th SS had lost half its strength and twenty-two commanders since the D-day invasion, would attach himself and his survivors to General Eugen Meindl's 3rd Parachute Division. Behind them would come what was left of the 2nd SS "Das Reich" and the 2nd Viennese Panzer Division.

"*Hals und Beinbruch* [Break your neck and leg], Meyer!" Hausser wished the much younger general, and then aligning a machine pistol around his neck, clambered onto a tank on which Hausser would attempt to fight his personal way out. He took one last look at the hollow-eyed, unshaven Meyer, who felt that

Hausser—the "Father of the SS"—thought "our situation was hope-less." It was.

Everything went wrong for them from the start on that terrible 24 August. British fighter-bombers struck the Leibstandarte and Das Reich as they were forming up for the breakout. Soon thereafter, the stalled SS tanks were subjected to a terrible shelling by British and Canadian artillery. All order was lost. SS troopers, veterans all, lost their heads. They fled the holocaust of burning Panthers and Tigers. Even the Leibstandarte broke and dove for cover.

By midnight, Panzermeyer and a mixed handful of survivors had reached the banks of the River Dives. But they had lost contact with the others. The retreat of his old outfit, die Leibstandarte, under the intense fire of the Canadian 25-pounders had almost broken the young general's spirit. Now haggard, hungry, and virtually heartbro-ken, Panzermeyer watched by the light of the flickering cherry-red flames as groups of SS men were cut down as they tried to cross the river. Still Panzermeyer could tell that some Germans had managed to get across the River Dives at the village of St. Lambert. He could hear mixed fire from both friend and foe. Indeed some two hundred Canadians of the 4th Infantry Division under the command of Major Currie, who would win the Victoria Cross this day, were slowly being ground down by the superior German numbers. Twice he had directed Canadian artillery on his own positions to drive the German attackers away. Still Panzermeyer decided that wasn't the way for him and his survivors. They would swim the "damned River Dives."

As silently as they could, the SS edged their way into the river. It was filled with corpses. There were bodies floating face downward on all sides. But in five years of war, the young SS general had seen bodies enough. What worried him were the Canadian Shermans on the high ground on the other side clearly outlined a stark black against the brilliant red every time a shell exploded. Panzermeyer knew that he would have to get to that line of tanks if he and his sur-vivors were going to make it.

Once on the other side, he gathered his men together. In a whis-per, he told them he was prepared to lead only those soldiers, SS or otherwise, who carried weapons. The rest would have to fend for themselves. His hard-nosed statement seemed to encourage the waverers. Those officers and men without rifles started crawling about the darkened field looking for German dead who still clutched their weapons.

Half an hour later they were ready to attack. Up front, Panzermeyer, his chief of staff, Colonel Hubert Meyer, and his loyal orderly "Michel"—a Cossack whom Meyer had "found" in Russia—crawled forward to inspect the Canadian line. As far as Panzermeyer could see, the enemy position was occupied by a couple of infantry companies in a thin line of foxholes. "Surprise attack," he announced after a while, in a whisper. "The Tommies won't expect us to rush them."

Michel looked at the bloody bandage which his master had wrapped around his wounded head. "Bandage no good," he said. "I make ... other, later." Panzermeyer understood his servant's broken German. The bandage would make him a conspicuous target in an attack. So he allowed Michel to remove it and once again the blood started to flow down his forehead.

The two hundred or so attackers crept toward the Canadian positions along the Trun–Chambois road. On either side the Shermans were pounding the rest of the escapers but no one seemed to take any notice of the Panzermeyer group. Perhaps they took them for fellow "Canucks."

Suddenly, out of nowhere, a bren-gun carrier rattled up. "Duck!" Panzermeyer hissed urgently, as his "heart beat furiously." But they had not been spotted—the enemy carrier moved off. The SS general waited no longer. "Now!" he commanded.

The escapers raced forward. In the lead there were Meyer, his servant, and his chief of staff with a bag of stick grenades around his neck. But he hardly needed them. For they had indeed caught the defenders by surprise and the Canadians fell back. But not for long. "Look out!" Colonel Hubert Meyer called in sudden alarm. A Sherman tank had appeared out of nowhere, almost hidden by a hedge thirty meters away.

"Hubert, you take over," Panzermeyer called, weakening visibly now as the blood poured down his left cheek. "I'm beat!" He fell behind as the others raced on to freedom. "Only a hundred meters more, Commander," the loyal Cossack servant urged. "You keep going." He grabbed Panzermeyer's arm to support the SS general, who had killed hundreds of his fellow countrymen over the last bloody years in Russia. Gratefully, one of the most hard-bitten commanders in the Waffen SS, wounded and about at the end of his tether, allowed himself to be dragged to safety by the humble Russian peasant.

September now saw the shattered remnants of the SS who had managed to escape the debacle of Falaise streaming through northern France to the Belgium–Luxembourg border in full retreat. General Harmel of the Second SS Corps stood with his officers, all armed with machine pistols, trying to control the panic while his men fled across the frontiers eastward toward the *Vaterland*.

Harmel was shocked by what he saw. Two divisions of his corps, SS Frundsberg and SS Hohenstaufen, had come out of Falaise reduced to 6,000 men and a handful of tanks. They had lost two-thirds of their effectives. The premier divisions of the Armed SS, die Leibstandarte and Das Reich, were even worse off. The tanks of their panzer regiments could be counted on the fingers of both hands; while the panzer grenadier regiments, normally 3,000-men strong, were reduced to battalion size. The "Hitler Youth Division" was in the worst state of all. When Panzermeyer, ragged, wounded, and exhausted, reported to senior SS Commander "Sepp" Dietrich, a burly Bavarian general who had formed Hitler's bodyguard regiment die Leibstandarte, he exclaimed: "But we all thought you were dead, Kurt!" It was too much for Meyer who burst into tears.

With six hundred men left out of a total of 20,000 on the day of the invasion, Panzermeyer crossed the border into occupied Belgium. Now the problem was not the Allies, hot in pursuit, but the Belgians who had a score to pay and were looking for easy victims among the fleeing Germans. In the deep forests on the eastern side of the great River Meuse there seemed to be Maquis everywhere looking for stray groups of fleeing Germans.

Erich Olboetter, the former commander of Panzermeyer's 2nd Panzergrenadier Battalion, who had served with the latter since 1939, had both his legs taken off at the hip by a partisan mine planted in a country road. He died a few hours later in a ditch filled with dirty rain water. One day afterward another "old hare," as the veterans called themselves, Captain Heinz Schrott, a comrade and battalion commander, was shot in the back by a partisan.

Now the Americans of General Courtney Hodges's First Army

were hot on Panzermeyer's heels. Amazingly he turned and wiped out their bridgehead. But a treacherous German fortress commander fled, leaving the way ahead wide open for the Amis (German slang term for the Americans). They started to advance once more.

On that September night, as Panzermeyer recommenced his flight, the survivors were pulling back to a village named Durnal when they heard the rumble of an enemy tank. Even before the SS could react, a Sherman rounded the bend and with its first shot knocked out a looted jeep driven by a Captain Heinzelmann. Panzermeyer knew the tank could not turn in the tight country road. He made a lightning decision and dove from the jeep and over a wall. He landed on his feet and was running at once as if the devil himself was after him. Ahead loomed the stone outline of an old farmhouse. He started to pelt towards it but almost immediately he realized with a sense of shock that he had run into a trap. There was no back way out of the farm. The house had been built with its rear dug into rock.

Just then another dark shape landed where he was crouched. It was an old comrade, Major Max Bornhoeft. Together they crawled on their bellies to a nearby chicken coop. Hurriedly they squirmed inside. The air was loud with the squawking protests of its stinking, frightened, lousy occupants. The two fugitives ignored the racket, now being drowned out by the rumble of the Shermans as a whole column of them passed the farm being cheered on by the local peasants.

Panzermeyer, impatient as always of delay and knowing they'd be discovered soon, crawled out to check the road. He peered over the top of the wall. There were men dressed in a kind of white overall everywhere—and they were all armed with British Sten guns and Lee Enfield rifles.

Panzermeyer knew immediately who they were—members of the Belgian resistance, the "White Army" ("*Armee blanche*"), armed by the British. And they were obviously on the lookout for German fugitives. He ducked down behind the cover of the wall again, just as it began to rain. Panzermeyer thought that a piece of good luck. He guessed the partisans would be good weather soldiers and that as soon as it started to rain in earnest, they would seek shelter. He informed Max and together the two high-ranking SS veterans, now soaked to the skin, headed for the local churchyard, where they went to ground among the weathered eighteenth-century graves. Max hid behind a pile of discarded wreaths from a recent funeral while Panzermeyer drew his pistol and stood guard.

But they were out of luck. Two gendarmes, their capes streaming with rain, came running into the churchyard, weapons at the ready. Panzermeyer fired immediately and the two policemen in their high, old-fashioned shakos hit the ground. Panzermeyer began to run. Shooting broke out everywhere as there were partisans all around the graveyard. He jumped over a wall and landed on the ground four meters below. It felt as if his legs had been driven into his stomach. In a minute he'd be sick. Before he could do so, he heard a cry of sudden agony behind him and swung around. Max had been hit.

Panzermeyer ran on. He knew he had one bullet left in his Walther. Should he put an end to it all? "Once," he remembered ten years later, "there had been a time in Russia when we had all sworn we should never be taken alive by the enemy. Now I was faced with the moment of truth. What was I to do?" He raised the muzzle of the pistol to his temple, but he couldn't do it. "Each time I was tempted … to pull the trigger and finish it all, I thought of my family … I just couldn't do it."

Just then there was a shout. A young lad, armed with a carbine that was much too big for him, had spotted the fugitive who had retreated to a barn. A couple of shots rang out. The rotten wood of the door splintered. "Come out!" yelled a partisan, the boy's father. Panzermeyer was desperate. He leveled his pistol at the boy and cried, "I could shoot the boy. But I won't, if you treat me correctly."

Anxiously the man pulled the boy to his side and promised the SS general he would be fairly treated. Panzermeyer let his shoulders slump in defeat. It was the end of the road. His meteoric career as the youngest general in the Armed SS was over. He dropped the pistol. Kurt Meyer, known as "Panzermeyer," commander of the one-time elite 12th SS Panzer Division "Hitler Youth," soon to be sentenced to death by the Canadians as a war criminal,* surrendered to a middle-aged Belgian farmer and his son.

The surrender of Panzermeyer and the panic-stricken flight of

---

* Panzermeyer was sentenced to death for the alleged shooting of Canadian POWs. His sentence was later reduced to twelve years imprisonment. On his release he was feted by his old comrades and became a power in the postwar Armed SS Relief Organization (HIAG).

what was left of Hitler's elite Armed SS divisions toward the Reich seemed to symbolize the end of their will to continue the fight in the West. As one survivor of the Leibstandarte described the great retreat that August/September: "No human account could ever match the misery the men of this division alone suffered. No one who finished this retreat still alive will ever forget this Gethsemane because each village, each road, even each bus, is seared into his brain with memories of terrible hours, insufferable misery, of cowardice, despair and destruction."

The new commander of the beaten army, Field Marshal Walther Model, stated in an order of the day: "We have lost a battle, but I tell you, we will win this war." Now as the rest of the elite Armed SS divisions closed with the frontiers of the Reich, none of the survivors, even the most fanatical, believed Model's message of that terrible Saturday which ended: "At this moment, everything adds up to the necessity to gain the time which the Fuhrer needs to bring into operation new troops and new weapons.... We must gain this time for the Fuhrer."

What new troops, they must have asked themselves. What new weapons? As for time, it was running out for the "1,000 Year Reich" of Adolf Hitler.

On the morning of that wet Saturday, 2 September 1944, General George Patton, the commander of the U.S. Third Army, received an urgent phone call at his headquarters in Chalons in Northern France. His army group commander, General Omar Bradley, wanted to meet him at his headquarters in the old cathedral city of Chartres some 130 miles away. Patton was expected to be there at eleven o'clock that rainy day when their chief, General Dwight "Ike" Eisenhower, would arrive for a conference. Unfortunately, the weather was too bad to fly. So an angry Patton, impatient to get on with his bold drive to the German border, would have to go by automobile and at top speed.

As he and his driver set off Patton's mood was not improved by the fact he was going to be late for his meeting with "Ike," whom he had not seen at his headquarters for three long months—nor by Eisenhower's praise for Bernard Montgomery, his British rival, the previous day. Ike had told the press: "He [Montgomery] is not only a very close and warm friend [but] one of the great soldiers of this or any other war." The fulsome praise of the "little Liney fart," as Patton habitually called his supposed rival, rankled, and Patton's anger at Eisenhower grew even more as he realized just how late he was about to be for this suddenly summoned and, he assumed, very important meeting at Chartres. In the end he was just short of two hours late.

Eisenhower appeared angry as they shook hands. He was. But not because Patton was late but as Eisenhower's secretary-driver, Kay Summersby, noted in her diary for that Saturday, because: "Eisenhower says he is going to give Patton hell because he is stretching the line too far and therefore making supply difficulties."

The "vital" conference commenced. But to his listeners' surprise, Eisenhower treated them to a lecture in military history. He pontificated at length about the German military philosopher Clausewitz, whom all of them had last dealt with at West Point over a quarter of a century before. Patton's anger grew apace. Clausewitz, the nineteenth-century Prussian general, had commanded a force of foot-and-horse soldiers who numbered at the most some 100,000 men. He, Patton, commanded four times that number, equipped with armor, planes, and weapons the Prussian wouldn't even have dreamed of.

Ike did not notice his listeners' boredom and questioning looks. He continued his boring lecture about the future "great battle of Germany" and how Clausewitz would have planned it. Listening with ever-growing impatience, Patton thought that "if we wait here much longer, there will be a great battle for Germany." The Germans would be waiting for them. He decided it was time to play his hand.

In his high-pitched voice, which contrasted so strongly with his erect martial figure and that "war face number one" which he practiced in front of his mirror each day, he rose and said, "We have patrols on the Moselle near Nancy, Ike." This was stretching the facts a little. For Patton's 35th Infantry Division was still miles away from Nancy, the capital of the French eastern province of Lorraine. Then Patton, in his eagerness to obtain military concessions from Ike for his beloved Third Army, stretched the truth even further. He announced proudly, "Patrols of my Third Cavalry have actually entered Metz."

The fact that Patton's men had captured Metz, France's third largest city (which they hadn't, of course), really made the brass sit up. If Patton had Metz, the German frontier was less than a day's march away. (In fact, Patton's Third Army was at Verdun, twenty-five miles away. Indeed, it would take Patton three months to finally capture Metz.) Patton pressed home his advantage. "If you let me retain my regular tonnage [of supplies], we could push on to the German frontier and rupture that goddam Siegfried Line." Only a day before he had boasted to his admiring staff that if he "got the green light, I could go through the Siegfried Line like shit through a goose." Now Patton added, "I am willing to stake my reputation on that, Ike."

Eisenhower was not sure. "Careful, George," he cautioned, "that reputation of yours isn't worth very much." He was referring to the series of unpleasant incidents associated with Patton, dating back to the latter's slapping of a GI suffering from combat fatigue in Sicily in 1943. These incidents had resulted in very bad publicity for the then commander of the U.S. Seventh Army and demands for his dismissal.

Eisenhower said the words with his usual disarming broad smile which had made him the darling of the Western European and American cinema public over the last twelve months. But they hurt Patton. Suddenly he remembered the most recent batch of newspaper clippings from the States, received two days before, that had praised both his Third Army and his leadership of that army in France. From those clippings he had concluded that the press had forgiven him. So, hiding his irritation the best he could, he hitched up his belt (as he told it afterward) and said quietly: "The reputation is pretty good now."

Ike did not comment. The conference continued. Eisenhower, since the day before the overall commander of all ground forces in the West (he had taken over from Montgomery on 1 September, much to the anger of the latter), gave Bradley his approval for a continuation of the general's drive eastward. In particular, Ike allowed Patton the green light to move toward the German frontier. He would be supported on his left flank by Gerow's V Corps of General Hodges's First Army.

However, Eisenhower warned his generals about problems soon to come:

We have advanced so rapidly that further movement in large parts of the front, even against the very weak opposition, is almost impossible. The closer we get to the Siegfried Line, the more we'll be stretched administratively and eventually a period of inaction will be imposed upon us. The potential danger is that while we are temporarily stalled, the enemy will be able to pick up bit and pieces of forces everywhere and organize them swiftly for defending the Siegfried Line or the Rhine. It is obvious from an overall point of view that we must now, as never before, keep the enemy stretched everywhere.

Eisenhower's view was correct, especially in light of his own "broad front strategy," which was that all his armies should close up the front before the last great offensive into Germany commenced. But the plan did not go down well with his generals. Patton and Bradley tried to convince Eisenhower he was wrong. They had much bolder "intentions" (one couldn't really call them "plans" though they did). "We have an excellent plan," Patton in particular persisted, "for a drive through the Nancy–Epinal gap. The Siegfried Line is not manned yet, and the Huns have little if anything in the area to stop us. If you let me go and give me what we need, we can be in Germany at the Rhine in ten days."

Eisenhower remained adamant. Neither Field Marshall Montgomery's plan to drive to the Ruhr and from there to Berlin, nor Patton's to attack through the Siegfried Line and head for the Rhine, the last natural German bulwark, would work. The key to the future battle of Germany was, in Eisenhower's view, supplies. Until the supply situation to the rear was cleared up—the bulk of these were still coming from the Normandy beaches—all his armies would advance till they reached the German frontier in any manner available. Until then there would be no major individual army assaults on the flanks of the West Wall, however bold. That was that.

It was the unforgiving moment. On that wet Saturday afternoon in September so long ago, Eisenhower's decision helped to change history. It meant that three giant army groups, Bradley's Twelfth, Devers's Sixth, and Montgomery's British Twenty-first would lumber ponderously toward the German frontier. Not one of them would be powerful enough alone to break through the German West Wall.

Both Montgomery and Patton would attempt to outflank the German fortifications. Both would fail.

Ever afterward Patton, in particular, and under Patton's influence his boss Bradley, would blame Montgomery for this. They maintained Eisenhower had favored Montgomery that September; Ike had given the Englishman an unfair share of the available supplies. In consequence, they were rationed, especially of petrol, essential for the kind of swift-moving armored advance that Patton favored.

For his part, Montgomery would feel the American top brass were at fault for his own failure at Arnhem–Operation Market-Garden, the bold land-and-airborne operation which would fail lamentably, though Montgomery naturally insisted it was a "ninety percent success," whatever that meant, as well as his proposed forty-division-strong thrust to the Ruhr and on to Berlin. He felt Eisenhower, in particular, was responsible for not giving him the twenty-odd U.S. divisions he had needed from Patton or Hodges for the drive to the "heart and head" of Hitler's Reich, as Montgomery put it.

On that wet, gloomy Saturday when Eisenhower flew back to his new headquarters at the French port of Granville, he had made a decision that would determine the course of the rest of the war in northwestern Europe. He, in common with probably all the other Allied generals, thought he had plenty of time. The Germans were virtually finished after the destruction of the Wehrmacht in France a few days before. The enemy would fall apart sooner or later; had not Hitler's generals attempted to assassinate the Fuhrer in July? That was a sure sign of the way they were thinking. Once Hitler was out of the way, they were released from their oath to him and they could sue for peace, at least in the West.

Although Patton and Bradley were angry at Ike's decision to mark time, they were still planning to go ahead with their plans for an attack, just as Montgomery was with his celebrated "Market-Garden" operation. As Patton said afterward, "I was convinced then [that Saturday] that there were no Germans ahead of us except those who were actually fighting. In other words they had no depth." Ten days after that conference at Chartres, Generals Patton and Hodges reported to Bradley that both their armies still had sufficient gasoline and ammunition to carry them to the Rhine. Later they would tell a different tale. But that was later.

Yet however much Patton, in particular, would blame Montgomery for the failure of his own attack, it was Eisenhower himself who made the original fatal decision that Saturday. The official U.S. Department of Defense history states on the fuel situation of that September: "British Red Lion convoys exceeded their target. Almost half of this consisted of supplies for the two U.S. airborne divisions participating in the Holland operation, a statistic often ignored by the partisans who so heatedly criticized this diversion of U.S. resources. Furthermore, the operation (i.e. Market-Garden) took place after the pursuit had definitely been halted and both the First and Third U.S. Armies had come up against the prepared defenses of the West Wall."

Of course, none of them knew it at the time. Victory was in the air. Whatever the outcome of their various plans, all of them felt that the Germans were beaten. Back home the papers were talking of bringing the "boys home for Christmas." But that Saturday afternoon, as it continued to pour, a decision had been made, the outcome of which they could not visualize in their wildest dreams. It would result in a third of all the casualties to be suffered in the eleven-month long European campaign. The war would drag on for another nine months. It would take six of those alone to break through the Siegfried Line.

Division after division would be thrown into the attack. Thousands upon thousands of young Allied soldiers would be killed and wounded trying to penetrate Hitler's West Wall. That day, though unwittingly, Eisenhower, the supreme commander and future president of the United States, had established the greatest killing zone in the history of American warfare.

Perhaps that wet Saturday afternoon, the top brass (and Montgomery busy on his ambitious Market-Garden plan, too) would not have been so sanguine about the future if they had known what was going on over on the German side of the front—virtually under their noses. Although at the time it would have seemed small fry to them, if they *had* known about it—"Operation Brutus" would later be clearly seen as a definite signal that the enemy was not going to surrender so easily and so swiftly as Allied intelligence thought the they would. Indeed half a century later, it is obvious that this top secret operation, carried out in the midst of apparent total defeat, was indicative that the Germans were not only about to fight on, but were preparing to strike back.

Operation Brutus commenced about three in the afternoon when a group of German officers, both Wehrmacht and SS, appeared suddenly at the remote turreted Chateau du Boise St. Jean in the deepest Ardennes not far from the border village of Poteau. Their arrival at his chateau in the middle of the Ardennes forests shocked the middle-aged Count Charles de Limburg Stirum, the aristocratic owner of the eighteenth-century castle. He had thought he had seen the last of the Germans after four and a half years of occupation. He had other reasons too for his alarm when the Germans politely requested billets for some 250 men and their equipment of an artillery unit with the army number "Battery 444."*

But with true noblesse oblige, the aristocrat said he had no objection to the new arrivals using his castle for their mess and his outbuildings, all well protected from aerial observation by the forest, for the artillerymen and their weapons. Glasses were brought. Toasts were exchanged. The Belgian hosts and their unwanted German guests made small talk and then dispatch riders, all heavily armed, were sent to bring up the rest of "Battery 444" under cover of darkness and bad weather. Thereafter the remote blacked-out castle, which would be a scorched ruin before the year was out, settled down for the night. Outside the rain continued to pour down.

Despite the heavy rainfall, however, there were scores of watchful eyes hidden on the grounds, all fixed on the Germans, with runners, mostly boys, being dispatched at regular intervals to report to headquarters on what the enemy was doing. For the officers who had selected this remote site for the nefarious activities to come had unwittingly picked not only the center of the Belgian Maquis, but also the operational area of Major Eddy Blondeel's Belgian SAS, one of the most efficient and ruthless squadrons of the British Special Air Service.

Eddy Blondeel, charming, slightly eccentric, and an excellent linguist, had left his native Belgium to study medicine at Chicago's Northwestern University before the war. In 1940 he had volunteered

---

* Later the surprised Count would find out the number was just a cover for an outfit armed with a much more sinister form of weapon than the traditional German 88mm cannon.

to go to Britain to join the exile Belgian Army being formed there. In 1942 he and his whole company, now all trained parachutists, volunteered once again, this time for Britain's Special Air Service.

It had taken two further years for Blondeel to get into action. But in June 1944 he had jumped into France and then jumped again as the Allied armies drove deeper and deeper into Europe. It was said that each time he was scheduled to jump he was up at dawn before his men, polishing up his Russian verbs for the anticipated link-up with the Russians one day. But that was not to be just yet. Major Blondeel jumped on the night of 28 August 1944 into the *Foret des Ardennes*, despite his advance party signaling that the Ardennes was full of retreating SS men, which was very true indeed.

Now the sudden arrival of these mysterious German artillerymen without cannons had upset Blondeel's and the Maquis's plans. For they were expecting further SAS troops, who would be accompanying a major supply drop. This latter would arm the hundreds, perhaps thousands, of Belgian resisters wandering the forests without arms, waiting to have a crack at the fleeing Germans. For the SAS brigade, currently spread over three countries, hoped to be instrumental with the aid of the locals in holding up the Germans before they ever reached the Reich and their West Wall. If the SAS–Maquis teams could do that, then conventional Allied troops might well be able to take the Siegfried Line fortifications on the run and without a fight. For Eddy Blondeel and other SAS commanders, British, French, and Belgian, it was a great risk but one worth taking. But what about the Germans? Why were they here? Did they know something? A lot of questions, a worried Major Blondeel must have thought, but few answers.

That night, with the rain still coming down in torrents, the Belgian SAS commander could hardly have realized just how serious the situation was in the Ardennes. For it was totally confused and involved elements of three armies: his own unit of the British Army and their Belgian allies; the Germans, naturally; and the Americans.

The Belgians found themselves on the linguistic border and, since the German occupation of their country in 1940, the national one between their country and the Reich. On the right-hand side of the road which led from Poteau to the Chateau de Bois St. Jean, the natives spoke French; on the left-hand side, German. Moreover, the latter were now German citizens, with some 27,000 of their menfolk serving in the German Army. In 1940 German victors had restored the old pre-Versailles Treaty (1919) border with Belgium, taking back a large chunk of German-speaking Belgium, the so-called "East Cantons," in which most of the battle of the Bulge would be fought.

Therefore the strange German officers who had arrived so surprisingly at the chateau this afternoon probably still thought they were in Germany, despite the fact that most of the locals seemed to speak Walloon French. In any event, the German officers of "Battery 444" knew that to their immediate rear the population seemed to be solidly German, with most of their men fighting in the ranks of the Wehrmacht for the same cause as they were.

But that was not all. Blondeel had felt he was safe in this little enclave in the Ardennes, where he was trying to rally and arm the local Maquis and expecting the further SAS drops of troopers and weapons at any moment. The SAS major had felt even safer knowing from his initial briefing of four days before that he could expect the arrival of American troops to his left and right flanks at any time. General Gerow's V Corps of the U.S. First Army was pushing through the Ardennes, heading for St.Vith on his right and Malmedy on his left. And Blondeel reasoned an American corps of some three divisions would protect him from any interference from the Germans.

Now another very alarming factor had been added to this tangled and confused situation. Worrying reports were coming in from the Maquis's spies east of the River Meuse in the general area of the great Belgian industrial city of Liege, where the Wallon anti-German communist party held sway, that one of the Reich's most feared SS divisions was straggling back to Germany between the pincers of Gerow's corps—right through his own area. An explosive situation was developing very rapidly indeed.

The division, the 2nd SS Panzer "Das Reich," had a fearsome reputation. Within days of the D-day landings, the 2nd SS, stationed on the French Mediterranean coast, had set off marching northward to Normandy right through the Occupied country, 15,000 strong, a third of its members Frenchmen by birth. They were Alsatians, who had been incorporated into the Reich like their Belgian German-speaking Frenchmen had been forced to join the Armed SS. But most were volunteers. These "booty Germans," as they were called cynically by their German-born comrades, were indeed more fanatical than they. Their record in Southern France would show that.

As soon as the members of the 2nd SS were away from the coast and marching along the valley roads through the mountains that led to the new front on the Normandy coast, they had started to be hounded mile after mile by the Maquis, often led and armed by members of the British SOE (Special Operations Executive), the American OSS, and the SAS, doing the same job as Major Blondeel was now supposed to do in the Ardennes. For Eisenhower had commanded that the 2nd SS Panzer Division "Das Reich" should never reach Normandy. German armor was the greatest threat facing his newly landed infantry. At all costs the Germans and their renegade running dogs had to be stopped.

And they were. But the cost was high, very high indeed. That two-week march of the division's 15,000 men and 209 tanks and self-propelled guns which covered 450 miles has gone down in history. Their march had been supposed to take at the most three days. But General Heinz Lammerding, the divisional commander, had been held up and frustrated at every turn. His men were kidnapped, sniped, captured, and shot at in seemingly every tinpot little French hamlet and village; and the French *franc tireurs* were seemingly getting away with it. After all they were civilians, dressed in the same blue overalls as the average French laborer and small-time farmer. Once they had carried out their attacks, they could melt into the background, looking no different from anyone else. The time came when Lammerding ordained revenge. The reprisals commenced.

The first major massacre had taken place at the small town of Tulle. Another and more terrible one occurred at Oradour-sur-Glane, where the SS torched the whole village and shot the villagers, men, women, and children. As one who lost his son, Andre, a M. Hyvernaud recalled after the war:

> I went to hunt for my children and I actually found one of the boys. He was my youngest. He lay on his side and was half-charred ... he still had one of his wooden shoes on. His other leg was completely out of joint and was twisted behind his back. His throat was half

cut through ... I went on searching for my other son ... but I did not find my older boy. Behind the altar [in the church which had been fired too], crammed close together, lay at least twenty small children who had tried to find shelter there ... they had all been suffocated by smoke or burned to death. I also saw prams with dead infants in them. Some were burned, others were riddled with bullets. Then I went home. That evening we dug a grave for Andre in our little yard.*

But it wasn't only the French citizens who suffered for the attacks of the Allied-led partisans. The partisan leaders did too. SOE agents captured by the Germans, even if they were women, were executed in concentration camps. SAS captives were shot out of hand, although they were in uniform and recognizable in combat as Allied soldiers.

Now though, the 2nd SS Panzers, decimated as they were after the debacle in Normandy and possessing only a handful of armored vehicles, were moving into and through the Ardennes, avoiding engagements with Gerow's V Corps wherever possible, trying to slip through the two wings of his advance and reach their homeland before it was too late. This time, their move was worse than that back in June. Then they had still been a disciplined formation and most of the atrocities they committed were carried out under orders and at the command of their senior officers. Now, however, they were a rabble, their motto *"sauve que peut."* Their officers had lost control. They were split into small, self-contained units. Discipline had been thrown overboard. Each group was intent solely on surviving until they reached the supposed safety of the West Wall—and they would go to any lengths to do so.

Exhausted as they were from the long retreat from the Normandy killing ground, they took the back roads. En route they made up for the loss of their armor by seizing civilian vehicles—hay wagons, motorbikes, milk delivery vans, Parisian buses being pulled by Belgian butchers' dray horses—anything on wheels that would move. In front of these vehicles, especially the few remaining officers' staff cars, they had fixed wide brooms to prevent flat tires from the pieces of scrap metal and nails which the underground threw in their path when they weren't looking. They lived off what they could loot from the villages they passed through. When they could not find

---

* The village of Oradour has been left exactly as it was in June 1944. The rusting automobiles, children's prams, toys, etc., and the ruined buildings are now a permanent memorial to man's inhumanity to man.

chickens, rabbits and the like, they helped themselves to the overripe pears and apples on the wayside trees. As a result their trail was marked by the light yellow of ordure—the "thin shits," as they called it.

And when they were unable to loot anything from the Belgians, then they robbed their own kind, in particular, the Wehrmacht store houses around Liege, which were scheduled for rapid demolition as soon as Gerow's Americans hove into sight.

That night Major Blondeel, worried as he was by the German officers close at hand in the chateau and unconfirmed reports coming in from the Maquis to his rear that the 2nd SS appeared to be setting up a major headquarters at Sart just outside the township of Spa (soon to become the headquarters of General Hodges's First Army), received yet another strange report. This time it was confirmed. For it came from one of his own men, and a very brave one indeed.

Unlike the rest of Blondeel's SAS men, who were among friends and their comrades of the local Maquis, this trooper had dropped right on the German frontier near the village of Grufflingen. The German-speaking village was located to the east of the main road, Route Nationale 62, leading from St. Vith to Luxembourg—in other words in the heart of German-occupied territory where the locals speak that language and where he could expect no help.

Now this lone SAS soldier, hiding out near the hill village with potentially every man's hand against him, running the risk of being shot immediately if captured, reported he had spotted some huge German transporters, the like of which he had never seen before. Their loads, great long things, were heavily camouflaged so that he couldn't make them out and the strange convoy that was staying the night in the village was currently being guarded by some 250 Cossack renegades serving under German officers in the Wehrmacht. One thing, however, the lone SAS agent had been able to ascertain, risking his life to do so. It was the number of the unit to which these huge vehicles and their curious loads belonged—"Battery 444."

Thus it was that Blondeel made a guess about the connection between the unexpected arrival of the Wehrmacht and SS officers at the Chateau du Bois St. Jean in the middle of Maquis country, and the strange convoy settling in for the night, some twenty-odd kilometers away as the crow flies. It wasn't difficult. The German unit now at Grufflingen was the same outfit that the German officers expected the Count to accommodate at his remote castle. But what in heaven's name would a German artillery battalion (if that was what it was) be doing advancing westward, when the shattered Wehrmacht was in full retreat—even the elite Armed SS?

2

Forgotten Firsts

Late on the night of 5 September 1944, the converted RAF Stirling bomber set off from the future long-term U.S. Air Force base at Fairford, England. The weather had improved since Saturday and it had finally ceased raining. But the small group of SAS inside the big aircraft had other concerns than the state of the weather. For despite the fact they all had British cover names and ID, they were, in fact, members of the Belgian SAS squadron and most of them were returning to their homeland after an absence of years. They viewed the prospect with understandable excitement and happiness. At the same time, they knew too, that if they were captured and their real identity discovered, the Germans would shoot them out of hand. For now the panicked Germans were shooting all parachutists, whatever their identity, on the spot and without trial.

Still they occupied themselves with the usual routine tasks, as the Stirling ploughed steadily eastward, crossing the Belgian coast, skirting the still-occupied capital of Brussels, following the secret ground beams and signals that brave Belgian civilians had been manning ever since 1940. They checked parachutes, radio sets, and the fifteen large bundles of supplies they would be dropping for the Maquis under Major Blondeel's command. Once the Maquis's DZ in the forest, to the south of the country road leading from the German frontier town of Monschau to Belgian Malmedy, had been proven reliable, the 1st SS Brigade headquarters would send in ever more supplies and men. The escape of the German Army to its homeland had to be stopped at all costs.

Sometime after midnight, the red light started to glow in the cockpit. It was followed almost at once by the green one. They were approaching the DZ. Hurriedly the SAS stick prepared for the drop. Out went the fifteen great packages, one after another as quickly as possible though towards the end of the drop there was a slight delay. Soon the Belgian SAS, commanded by Captain John van der Heyden, would realize to their dismay that, slight as it was, that delay was putting all their lives at risk.

Now it was the turn of the stick. One by one they jumped with practiced ease. After all, some of them had been training for this moment for nearly two years. As their camouflaged parachutes opened with a sharp crack and their dizzy descent was braked, they thought that in a matter of minutes they would be on the soil of Belgium once more. Unfortunately, they were sadly mistaken.

One by one the paras hit the deck. They had come down in what appeared to be a ploughed field on a height, for they could feel that the wind was cold for September. But that was about all they could discern. They might have been the last men alive on the earth. Now Captain van der Heyden collected his little stick and was just about to order them to spread out and ascertain exactly where they were, for even in the darkness, the lonely height did not seem like the DZ as it had been shown to him back at SAS Brigade headquarters, when he was startled by a strange, high-speed whistling noise. Moments later it was followed by the clatter of tracks. Then it was gone, leaving behind a loud echoing silence which was broken by Sergeant Emonts-Pohl, who announced calmly, "*We zijn in Duitsland.*"

The news shocked the others. Van der Heyden, one day to become a lieutenant-general in the Belgian Army, asked, "How do you know that, sergeant?"

Hastily, the NCO explained that German locomotives made a different sound when they whistled than did the Belgian trains. This one had whistled in the German fashion. In his opinion, they had just heard the Vennbahn, which ran roughly between Cologne and Bonn with branch lines going off to Malmedy and St. Vith in their native Belgium. Emonts-Pohl's seeming expertise almost convinced the rest. But Captain van der Heyden wanted to be quite sure. He ordered them to make a definite assessment of their location. So they began moving cautiously along the bank of a small river that later was discovered to be the Schwalm, which ran three miles to the south of Monschau.

Under the command of Sergeant Flasschoen a three-man patrol of the SAS followed the course of the tiny river until they came upon a small hotel-inn. Cautiously, their hands gripping their Sten guns tightly, they approached closer. Sergeant Flasschoen spotted a small, white flag draped to the right of the place's entrance. For a while he thought it was the customary flag advertising that the inn sold a certain ice cream. With a shock he discovered he was wrong. It was a flag giving the name of the inn-hotel: *Gasthaus zur Muhle*. And it was in German! The SAS stick had dropped into the Reich and thus they were the first Allied servicemen to enter that country, beating the leading Americans of Gerow's V Corps by six days.

On receiving Sergeant Flasschoen's alarming report, van der Heyden made an instant decision. He told his men they were getting out of there at once, for they could hear noise in the far distance and the faint baying of hounds. That could mean only one thing. German patrols were already out looking for them. Van der Heyden ordered a retreat to the west in the general direction of Belgium, where they knew the Maquis of the failed reception committee would already be looking for them.

The ten men of the SAS stick needed no urging. They set off at the double and crossed the Schwalm, wading thigh-deep in the icy water. They came to a main road, leading north to Monschau and from thence up into the Hurtgen Forest.

Then, suddenly and surprisingly, they found themselves in a tangle of rusty barbed wire strung between bunkers and pillboxes, all long abandoned. They had unwittingly penetrated the vaunted Siegfried Line on which, in what now seemed another age, the Tommies wanted to hang "our washing, mother dear." But they had no time to savor their singlehanded triumph. The baying of the German dogs was getting closer and closer.

Corporal Mas, who had become separated from the rest, was the first to be discovered by their pursuers. He did not give the enemy time to react. He fired first. The German went down with a groan and the equally surprised SAS man was up and running, as if the devil himself were on his heels. He joined the rest later. They found their "escape boxes" where they had dropped, and although they dared not smoke the British Woodbine cigarettes these contained— the enemy would have been able to detect their delectable fragrance a kilometer away—the famished, unshaven troopers in their maroon berets feasted on the rationed boiled sweets "like a bunch of greedy schoolkids," one of them recalled later.

On the height now to their immediate front was the village of Kaltherberge: a huddle of half-timbered houses, surrounded by the high, thick hedges typical of the area. It looked as if it lived up to its name (Cold Harbor). Though nothing moved there, it was German and they had to be careful now that the general alarm had been raised in this remote border area.

They started to circle the place cautiously, knowing that the old German–Belgian border pre-1940 was only a matter of meters away. Night had now fallen. But they could hear the faint snap and crackle of a small arms battle to the southwest. It was clear that the enemy was somewhere in front of them—and they were right. Some of Major Blondeel's command were attacking the fugitives of the 2nd SS Panzer Division. They had now reached the famous prewar racetrack of Spa–Francochamps. Soon the Maquis would launch a daring raid at the SS headquarters itself, located at nearby Sart.

Van der Heyden knew nothing of this. All he knew, as his weary hungry men plodded down the dead-straight road through the forest which led from the border to Malmedy, was that it was clear there were active enemies to their front. He knew, too, that this particular road had been very unlucky for the Belgian Army back in May 1940. Then a company of the local Chasseurs had been almost wiped out there by Germans allegedly led by the future "Desert Fox," Field Marshal Erwin Rommel himself. Here and there on the roadside there were gravestones for those unfortunate light infantrymen who died in vain. Now the Germans were advancing once again, albeit in the other direction.

All the same he did not want the same fate to overtake his own lightly armed small band. Thus they pressed on. The next day they engaged in a firefight with the SS, ambushed a couple of their trucks, and although they suffered two casualties to add to the two SAS men who had gone down with malaria, they had killed an SS major from the 2nd's divisional headquarters. But on the third day of their odyssey they struck luck. They came across a lonely farm where the farmer and his wife weren't afraid to take in the weary, filthy men with their straggly beards. Indeed the lady of the house served them coffee (albeit ersatz) in her best silver in her spotless "salon." There they took a few hours out of war to deal with their casualties (40 percent) and rest up before attacking once more.

They did so in three groups. Again they bumped into the SS, and from prisoners learned that the 2nd SS divisional staff were pulling out of their Sart headquarters at seventeen hundred hours that particular afternoon. This was important news that had to be sent back immediately. But their English-built radios were not working. Then by chance one of the three SAS groups bumped into an advance reconnaissance party of Gerow's U.S. V Corps.

Excitedly the Belgians told their news to the Americans in their fractured English. The Yanks, probably taking them for yet another bunch of "hopped up frogs" they had been meeting ever since they had landed in France, listened in bored silence. Then they turned their vehicles and returned the way they had come to Francochamps. As one of the survivors of the unknown operation, which might well have led to great victory if the U.S. High Command had ever known that the SAS had discovered the Siegfried Line was empty, wrote in his report: "He, the head of this American advance guard, received our information, with '*un supreme dedain.*'"

In the end the first Americans of Gerow's V Corps would still arrive to find the West Wall not manned. Yet within hours of their doing so, the 2nd SS and other German infantrymen would be doubling into the bunkers and pillboxes, sighting their weapons and preparing for the fight which would last six long bitter months.

On that 5 September 1944, when the little SAS unit was the first to enter wartime Germany, Blondeel and his Maquis helpers made yet another surprising discovery—one that again should have encouraged Eisenhower to immediately speed up his advance toward the German frontier.

A general of the SS had suddenly made a brief appearance in their area; and later they would reason he had a definite connection with "Battery 444" currently located in Grufflingen and in the

Chateau du Bois St. Jean. But what, they asked themselves, did his sudden appearance signify?

One immediate result of the arrival of the tall, young SS general occurred at Grufflingen and the Chateau du Bois St. Jean, when the vehicles of the mysterious "Battery 444" moved out. As far as the Maquis could ascertain, they were heading for the general direction of the railheads of Beho and Gouvy just southeast of the important Belgian border town of St. Vith. As for the SS general, whom the Maquis had still not identified, they had traced his progress from the frontier to the largest French-speaking town of Houffalize where he spent the night of 5/6 September.

Houffalize was a very dangerous choice for any general of the hated SS. It had a strong force of Maquis, recruited locally and hiding out in the wooded, rugged heights around the town. Moreover, Blondeel, at least, knew that it was a prime objective for one of General Gerow's infantry regiments.

Colonel "Buck" Lanham's 22nd Infantry Regiment of the battle-experienced 4th "Ivy League" Infantry Division, that had landed on Utah Beach on D-day, was heading straight for the place. Houffalize was going to be the regiment's final objective before it and the division to which it belonged crossed into Germany proper. There the 4th would undoubtedly barrel through Hitler's Siegfried Line just as they had done now through Belgium.*

Houffalize then was very definitely no place where SS generals who valued their safety ventured. In this first week of September 1944, this remote part of Eastern Belgium should have been strictly out of bounds for the unknown SS commander.

The 44-year-old, tall, slim SS general, who wore his cap at a rakish angle above a tough, set face, looked as if he might be a long-time "front swine," who had fought on every front since war had been declared back in 1939. In fact he was a strictly desk-bound warrior who had probably never heard a shot fired in anger throughout the war. He was *Gruppenfuhrer und General der SS, Dipl. Ing.*, Hans Kammler, the university title indicating that he was an engineer by profession, who had joined the SS because its uniform was smarter than that of the larger Nazi Party organization, the SA. Now Kammler was, on SS Reichfuhrer Heinrich Himmler's orders, in charge of a vital secret weapon campaign that Hitler believed would

---

*In the end, the valiant 4th Infantry Division would still be fighting in roughly the same area five months later.

change the face of war, bring Britain down to its knees, and perhaps force the victorious Western Allies to offer Germany a better peace than that harsh, uncompromising one of "unconditional surrender."

It was a campaign that the British and their senior U.S. allies had been long expecting, ever since the V-1 "flying bomb" attacks on Britain had commenced the previous June. But time and time again the Allies had overrun the sites earmarked for the campaign before it could commence. Only days before, Field Marshal Montgomery had been asked by Winston Churchill if he could capture some of those sites in Holland in time. The little British commander had replied in the affirmative. "Operation Market-Garden" might not capture all the German launch sites but it certainly would cut off the Germans, about to start their deadly new form of warfare, from their supplies and weapons. Accordingly one day before the enemy fired the first shots the planned evacuation of London was secretly halted. That same evening, Mr. Duncan Sandys, Churchill's son-in-law, announced to a hurriedly summoned press conference that the new aerial attack on the British capital was over before it had actually begun. "Except for possibly a few last shots, the Battle of London is over." The hastily scribbling journalists probably thought the sharp-featured minister was referring to the "flying bomb" campaign. They were wrong. Sandys was talking about something far more sinister— a weapon against which there was no possible ground or air protection. The "Second Battle of London" had not yet commenced.

By 7 September the mysterious Germans and their chief, SS General Kammler, had vanished from the immediate Poteau area. Major Blondeel and his Maquis dismissed them from their minds. Whether the Americans took the threat posed by the 2nd SS Panzers seriously or not, *they* did. Now they were engaged in a desperate running fight with the retreating Germans. In essence it was a bold attempt to prevent what was left of the Reich from manning the northern end of their West Wall roughly between Monschau and Dasburg.

In the meantime, Kammler's "444th" had firmly established themselves in a thick wooded area between the tiny Ardennes hamlets of Tierre-Rical and Sterpigny along the minor road that led from Gouvy in that direction. It had taken a long time and circuitous journey to get to this remote place from their starting point at Blizna in

Occupied Poland. But now at last, on the orders of Kammler, who was already moving on to his second secret location in Holland, they were prepared to start this new kind of warfare, which would persist to our very own time. With practiced ease, the technicians prepared their liquid oxygen mixtures. The gunners occupied themselves with their huge 19-ton weapons which carried warheads of one ton of high explosive. All seemed controlled confusion as finally the Germans started to strip off the camouflaged canvas covers from the huge transporters, first reported by the brave SAS spy in Grufflingen, revealing the terrible new weapon that on this 8 September 1944 was still known solely by its code name—"A-4." Soon, after years of planning, experimentation, disaster, tragedy, and terrible Allied aerial attacks on the German trial grounds, the A-4 would go into action for the first time.

But even in this remote place there were witnesses other than the Germans to what happened next. One was Theophile Claus, located at the Ferme d'Halconreux some 800 yards away from the A-4 site. At that moment, three Germans, who had managed to dodge away from work, were eating a meal in his farm kitchen when, as Claus recorded later, "there was a Dantesque groaning and moaning, followed by a terrific orange jet of flame."

As the three Germans threw themselves to the kitchen floor in sudden panic—perhaps thinking the A-4 had exploded prematurely—Claus looked out of the tiny window to see what "looked like a comet rapidly disappearing into the heavens ... It was a spectacle that remained in my memory till now and till my grave."

The lone Belgian observer did right to remember. For he had been an eyewitness to the start of a new kind of warfare—that in space. He had just seen the first combat firing of the A-4—more famously known as the "V-2"—the forerunner of the many thousands of missiles, large and small, which would be launched in the next half a century.

That first one, traveling at over 2,000 miles per hour, struck in a Parisian suburb killing five civilians including a child. The second launch from Holland slammed into London's Chiswick at 6:43 P.M. It killed three people and seriously injured seventeen more—including the author's grandmother. London's first-ever supersonic double-crack was heard all over the British capital. Mr. Duncan Sandys, who the day before had predicted the end of the "Battle of London," heard it too. Ruefully he exclaimed to no one in particular, "That's a rocket!" It was the first of one thousand A-4s to come that would kill 2,700 Britons and injure 6,000 more to add to the total of 80,000 British deaths in the years of the blitzes. By November four of these terrible weapons from the stratosphere were striking London each day.

The A-4 campaign against London was no immediate concern of Eisenhower though it would be once the Germans switched some of their V-2 rockets to aim at his new, most important supply port at Antwerp in Belgium. But even in that first week of September this attack from outer space should have been a warning to Eisenhower.

It should have indicated to him that the Germans were not going to surrender tamely, as the pundits and his intelligence men advised him, and that his new strategy of the "broad front" could very well fail. While all his armies ponderously approached the German frontier and he attempted to restrain the advances of Patton on the right flank and, to a certain extent, Montgomery on the left, the Germans were being given time to prepare. Time was of the essence but Eisenhower and his advisers did not seem to realize that.

Perhaps blinded by the civilian euphoria instigated by the press, they too felt that time was on their side. But one thing they should have realized when they learned the full details of what had happened in the Ardennes that first week of September 1944 was this: ordinary Germans, right up to the rank of a desk-bound engineer masquerading as an SS general, were prepared to risk their lives to stop the Allied advance.

On the morning of 11 September 1944, the great writer Ernest Hemingway and his entourage came to the cliffs above Houffalize. They were a strange wild bunch—Americans, Brazilians, French, and a lone Briton, Peter Lawless—but then Hemingway had a habit of collecting such folk around him. The town was set deep in the valley of the River Curthe. It was the center of a small road network but a bit of a bottleneck. Before the year was out, due to the fact it was the center of that network, it would be almost completely destroyed. Now, however, although it had been visited from the air by the boys of "Bomber" Harris's RAF Bomber Command, it was relatively intact. And although the enemy had apparently vanished over the nearby frontier with Germany, the "liberators" had not yet made an appearance, save for this little band staring down at the town square, drinking while they watched.

But as they poised there, a kind of liberator did finally make their appearance: they were the Maquis, dressed in the white overalls of *"de Witte Armee,"* or *"L'Armee Blanche"* according to which of Belgium's two official languages you use. But they were not alone. As the Maquis appeared, creeping forward somewhat apprehensively, firing broke out. A small party of the 2nd SS had remained behind to contest possession of the little township. Thus it was that Hemingway, already half drunk, was treated to the spectacle of the last fight between the 2nd SS and the locals on Belgian soil.

That night, as Hemingway celebrated and Colonel "Buck" Lanham, commander of the infantry regiment of the U.S. 4th Infantry Division, briefed his officers at Beho (through which Kammler's artillerymen had so recently passed), up and down the banks of the Our and Sauer, American patrols started to cross the two linked border rivers. First to cross into Germany, as they thought at least, was a small squad of the 5th Armored Division. It slipped across the River Sauer at a small bridge that had been blown between Luxembourg and the Reich, to find the Siegfried Line bunkers on the other side totally empty and devoid of armament.

That night, First Army headquarters issued a statement, couched in the dry, unemotional prose of the U.S. Army, reading: "At 1805 hrs on 11th September, a patrol led by S/Sgt Warner W. Holzinger crossed into Germany near the village of Stolzemburg, a few miles northeast of Vianden, Luxembourg."

Not to be outdone by its running mate, Gerow's other infantry division, the 28th, sent a reinforced company across, too, slipping in between the Luxembourg village of Weiswampach and the German one in the valley below the Sevenig. The jubilant infantrymen brought back with them some worthless German paper marks, a farmer's black cap, and some German earth in looted wine bottles. These were to prove that they had actually been on the sacred soil of the "1,000 Year Reich." Perhaps today, these bottles still hold pride of place on the mantelpiece of some suburban front parlor—that is, if their possessors lived to send them home.

That night a strong reconnaissance patrol from the 4th Infantry Division's 22nd Infantry was organized to do the same. First Lieutenant Robert Manning, the regiment's scout and raider leader, was selected by Colonel Lanham to lead the patrol across the other linking border river, the Our. The patrol consisted of the scouts and raiders, plus two self-propelled tank destroyers armed with massive 90mm cannons and five jeeps.

Manning's mission was to obtain information about the enemy and the Siegfried Line on the heights above the River Our; and perhaps most importantly collect a jar full of Kraut dirt which would be forwarded to no less a person than President Roosevelt, some of whose ancestors had come from this very area. As always the 4th Infantry Division kept a keen eye for self-publicity. After all their own "personal war correspondent" was Ernest Hemingway.

After an eight-mile journey from the Houffalize area, they descended the steep country track to the railway bridge across the Our from the German village of Hemmeres. The town was a straggle of a dozen or so stone houses, leading up the hill, past a small chapel, toward the V Corps's main objective, the road and rail junction at Prum.

The bridge had been blown so the patrol was left with wading across the muddy brown waters of the Our. But the self-propelled guns were not prepared to risk crossing the shallow river, some ten yards broad, although it could have been easily waded at that time of the year. So the two officers of the patrol, Manning and Lieutenant Shugart, flipped a coin to see who would lead a foot patrol across. Shugart won and at half past nine that night crossed into a strangely silent Hemmeres.

Although both of Gerow's other divisions, the 5th and 28th, and (unknown for years) the Belgian SAS, had beaten the "Ivy League" Division into Germany, Captain Stevenson, the 4th's publicity officer, was quicker off the mark in reporting the great news to the press. Under the headline, "Crackers of the Hindenburg Line, First to Break Siegfried Line," the *Stars and Stripes* journalist reported: "The US 4th Infantry Division, first outfit to crack the Hindenburg Line at Meuse-Argonne in the last war and first to enter Paris in this one, also was first to penetrate Germany though the Siegfried Line in force, it was disclosed yesterday."

Now things moved fast. Further patrols from the regiment's 1st and 2nd Battalions were alerted to cross the River Our. At twenty-nine minutes after eight on the following morning, Tuesday, 12 September, Battery C of the division's 44th Field Artillery Battalion fired its first light shells into Germany. Again Captain Stevenson, the division's PR man, claimed that these were the first "shells to strike Germany proper." They were not. The "Big Red One," the U.S. 1st Infantry Division, had already had that honor, firing into Germany in the Aachen region. Still it was that kind of war now—the first to be fought in front of the eyes of the media correspondents.

At quarter to nine, the whole regiment was ordered to move to the high ground just west of the German border, ready to venture into the Reich. Colonel Lanham briefed his officers at Beho. Then they were off into the unknown and the long months of bitter fighting that lay ahead for these still eager, confident young men.

The German military had commenced blowing the bridges over the Sauer and Our thirty-six hours before. In some villages they had waited until the very last minute before they did, allowing the last German survivors of the debacle in France to cross from Luxembourg and Belgium into the supposed safety of the Reich. In others, frightened senior officers whose first priority was to save their own skins ordered the bridges blown with soldiers left on the enemy side of the river border. In the village of Bollingen on the Sauer, an aged general who gave such an order was nearly lynched by the local folk, especially as a great boulder from the central tier of the ancient bridge smashed into the houses of the main boulevard along the riverfront.

Naturally there were many of the lice-ridden, unshaven "*stubble-hoppers,*" as the German infantry called themselves, who would have preferred capture by the Americans rather than being forced to fight again once they had crossed into Germany. There were deserters and stragglers everywhere. In Trier alone, the nearest large city, there were forty thousand of them, the equivalent of three divisions, a confused mass of tankers who had lost their tanks, artillerymen without guns, and infantry who more than likely had thrown away their weapons. But as they heard the muffled explosions of bridge after bridge being blown, those on the enemy side of the border who were prepared to fight hurried to get across the river line before it was too late.

Near Sevenig at what the Germans called the *"Dreilandereck"* ("three country corner"), Michel Weber was taking a short break from helping his few neighbors who were still sticking it out with their harvest in the threatened area. As he puffed at his *Schagpfeife,* enjoying his home-grown tobacco, he heard the noise of someone on the Luxembourg side of the border. With his weak old eyes he tried to make out the three figures approaching. Were they Germans or Americans?

Then he spotted the tattered field gray of the first. He was a German and a captain. Behind him came two private soldiers, both as ragged and dusty as their officer. The captain saw Weber sitting on his bench in the golden sunshine of the *"Altweibersommer"* ("Old Woman's Summer," i.e., Indian Summer) and snapped angrily, *"Was, Sie sind noch hier?"* ("What, you're still here?")

Before Weber could answer, the officer said, "Save yourself, man. After us, it's the enemy."

While the old man with his pipe stared at the three of them in wonder, they were off climbing into the pine forest of the slope opposite, leaving Weber to ponder their words, his ears already taking in the rumble of the enemy artillery. A little later he called the aged bell-ringer, whose job it was to wander through the village ringing his hand bell to alert the locals, to whom he now announced: *"Bekanntmachung ... Bekanntmachung ... Schnell, die Amis sind da!"* ("An announcement ... quick, the Americans are here!")

But if the civilians were surprised by the rapid appearance of the Americans crossing the border from Belgium and Luxembourg, the men who would defend the area that September were caught off guard, too. Not by the Americans. They knew well they were coming. After all they had been retreating before them since 24 August. No, what surprised them was the state of that Great Wall of Germany of which Hitler had boasted back in 1938, "I am the greatest builder of all times."

Those first defenders of the West Wall against Gerow's V Corps could hardly believe their eyes. The survivors of the First SS Corps, the men of Das Reich and die Leibstandarte who had just conducted a fighting retreat of nearly five hundred miles, were bitterly disappointed by what they found at the border. As Obersturmfuhrer Rink of the 1st SS, whose battle group had successfully driven off the Maquis at Houffalize, expressed it: "Damnit! Where were the bunkers? Silence over the fields and nothing else." Then he spotted a firing slit. There was something there. But as he recorded bitterly, "We'd expected a lot more. Still we got cracking. Two squads off the halftracks, left and right, dig in the mortar. Camouflage. Hurry up with the anti-tank guns. Hand over the commander with the most service and then off like the wind to Bitburg or Prum. Surely there had to be someone there who knew what the hell was going on?"

But young Rink, with his typical arrogant style of command that made the SS hated by the rest of the Wehrmacht, was out of luck. In Bitburg, the nearest big road and railhead, he was handed the keys to the bunkers now under his orders. But there were no plans, no knowledge of where their equipment was after having been removed in 1940. "Nothing. I tried to find out as much as possible," Rink explained later. "It wasn't much." The bunkers had had all their gear removed after the victory in the West four years before, then they were locked and virtually abandoned. "All I had was the keys and that was that. I didn't even know if there were still the original pre-war minefields surrounding the individual positions." When Rink returned to his command he found there weren't. Not only had the local farmers stolen the barbed wire, but they had used the rear of the bunkers to store their winter feed for the cattle and even built on chicken coops.

On the same day, 24 August 1944, that the SS had begun their break-out in France, Hitler signed an order called "*Befehl uber den Ausbau der deutschen Westellung.*" This might be translated as: "Order for the Enlargement of the German Western Fortifications." Apparently innocuous, the order was calculated not to cause panic among the civilian population. In reality, it meant the opening up of the Sieg-fried Line which had seen six month's wartime service during the "phony war" of 1939/40; whereupon it had been closed, neglected and virtually forgotten.

Now the West Wall was to be opened up once more, new fortifi-cations built, and trench lines dug, plus new gun pits for the larger cannons and machine guns of 1944 vintage. It was going to be a giant undertaking, with the pressure on, and German "volunteer" labor recruited to the tune of a million—Hitler Youth, local workers, female and male, plus slave labor and even trusted POWs. It would be a tremendous rush job, with the Allies advancing eastward rapidly each new day. So command of the new construction was given to local *kreisleiter* (county leaders) and *gauleiter* (district leaders) of the Nazi Party. In due course most of these would flee once the Americans made their first appearance on that endangered frontier.

At the same time as these efforts were made to open up the Siegfried Line before the enemy could reach it, the German military authorities in the interior instituted draconian new measures, aimed at making up the great losses suffered by the Wehrmacht in France. Effective from 1 September 1944, all theaters, music halls, and cabarets were closed. All publishers, save those publishing medical textbooks and Hitler's own *Mein Kampf,* were shut down. The universities (save the schools of medicine, where doctors for the army were being turned out after three years of study) followed, as did many high schools. After all, boys and girls were eligible for some sort of military service at the age of 16; both sexes often being sent to man the flak guns to relieve older personnel for active frontline service.

The Armed Services also were not exempt from this rigorous *levee en masse.* Pilot training came to an abrupt halt. In the German Navy all remaining capital ships were mothballed and their crews transferred to the infantry. Even U-boat men who were without boats suffered the same fate. Some authorities maintain that that month navy personnel were reduced by as much as 30 percent, with all fit men and new recruits transferred to the army after four weeks' basic infantry training.

The German military authorities went ever further in their search for "bodies." "*General Menschenklau,*" as the mythical figure who stole these "bodies" was named, didn't even stop at military hospital and convalescent units. "General Body Stealer" organized the various sick individuals into battalions that could be more easily dispatched to the front. Men with severe stomach problems were combined into "white bread battalions." They were fed the more palatable white bread instead of the tough black bread of the Wehrmacht. "Ear and Nose" battalions followed. In these outfits orders were often given in sign language. Woe betide any guard commander who did not make his presence known well in advance, especially at night. He ran the risk of being shot by his own men if he did not.

Naturally military prisons were combed for recruits. By 1944, the Wehrmacht had shot the equivalent of a whole division of men for military offenses. Now it was decided to let the enemy do it for the High Command. Hundreds, perhaps thousands, of military criminals were recruited into *Strafbattalions* for the front. If these unfortunate men, who were poorly armed and given the most dangerous objectives, died in action, at least they had died "for Folk, Fatherland and Fuhrer," as the motto of the time had it, instead of uselessly against the wall of the great Wehrmacht military prison at Torgau.

As one young German soldier wrote to his fiancee in that desperate first week of September (the letter was picked up from his dead body later): "Today I was transferred to the 42nd Machine-Gun Fortress Battalion as a messenger, destination West Wall. The battalion is composed of Home Guard, soldiers and half cripples. I found many among them who were obviously off mentally. Some had their arms amputated, others were short of one leg. A sad sight." A sad sight indeed, but they were warm bodies and the German High Command obviously thought they would be able to hold the frontier line until the new fortifications were completed and the young, fit, new recruits from the army, navy, and "reserved labor" of the German war industry were sufficiently trained.

Gerd von Rundstedt had not been involved in the July 1944 plot of the generals against Hitler; therefore, unlike most of the survivors of that abortive assassination, he was not attempting to keep a low profile. He could talk openly to the Fuhrer without fear that he might be clapped into jail if he overstepped the mark. More importantly, cynic as he may have been, he was a patriot of the old school, who knew what he could expect of the ordinary German soldier, and when the situation required it, would demand from the *landser* that he should do his patriotic duty even to the death.

He was fortunate too in his immediate subordinate. Von Rundstedt might well call him "*der Bubi-Marschell*" ("the Boy Marshal"); yet the former knew that Field Marshal Walther Model, now in his early fifties, was just the kind of officer this desperate situation in the West required. He was no Rommel, his one-time subordinate in France at the time of the invasion, but Model was ruthless, aggressive, and possessed a tremendous drive—all three vital qualities in the current situation.

Model, commander of Army Group B under von Rundstedt since 1 September 1944, looked like the Hollywood B movie stereotype of a Prussian officer: arrogant, cap set at a jaunty angle with a monocle he didn't need screwed into his left eye. But he was not descended from a long line of Prussian aristocratic warriors. Rather he was the scion of three generations of music teachers, all strictly Lutheran, unwarlike, and firmly middle-class. Indeed the community into which the burly, bustling, middle-sized officer was born was far from those far-flung Eastern Prussia estates of Germany's Junker generals (*"Monokelfritzen"* ["Monocle Fritzes"], as Hitler called them contemptuously), who treated their farm workers like serfs and who were sent in their preteens to the cadet schools which turned them into wooden soldiers (*"Kadavergehorsamkeit,"* as they called themselves), who obeyed orders with "the conscience of the corpse."

Despite his pious, middle-class background, Model nevertheless displayed all the virtues and habits of that Prussian caste. Unlike most of the U.S. generals against whom he was going to fight for the rest of his career until he committed suicide in April 1945, Model had seen a lot of war. In World War I, he was wounded four times. On one occasion a bullet had passed straight through his body. The surgeons pronounced him a "medical wonder," for the bullet had not touched one single vital organ. Within days Model had made life hell for his doctors, demanding to be released for active service at once.

And Model was just as ruthless as those aristocratic officers from Prussia. Most of his staff officers hated him on account of his violent temper, intolerance, and overbearing manner. Once when he departed on one of his infrequent home leaves, his chief of staff signaled the gleeful staff: *"SCHWEINFURT!"* It was, of course, the name of a southern German city. But it also meant "the swine has gone."

On another occasion in 1942 when the German Ninth Army had reached breaking point on the Russian Front, Model arrived unexpectedly at the army headquarters. He was dressed with a fur-collar coat that reached his ankles and wore old-fashioned earmuffs. He flung his battered cap on the nearest chair. Ignoring the salutes of the surprised staff officers, he strode to the wall map.

"Rather a mess," he declared after a few moments' study through his monocle. Then he proceeded to bark out a series of orders. The officers stared at each other in amazement. Where in three devils' name was Model going to find the men to carry out these bold plans? Finally, Oberst Blaurock, the 9th's chief of staff, ventured, "And what, Herr General, have you brought us for this operation?" Model surveyed Blaurock with a quizzical look through his eyeglass. "Why, myself," he answered, as if it was the most obvious thing in the world.

The answer was typical of Model's arrogant, overbearing vanity, which made him disliked by his staff officers. But if he was unpopular with his high-ranking staff, he was liked by the ordinary stubble-hoppers of the infantry. He spent eight hours each day at the front with his combat soldiers, sometimes taking over command of battalions, even companies, when the situation became "ticklish," as Model called it. Time and again between 1940 and 1944, he saved one front after another by his aggressive manner of leading from the front and not being frightened of putting his own life on the line. In essence, he was a soldier's soldier.

Although Hitler, once a private soldier himself, generally detested his Prussian senior officers who led his armies, he though highly of Model. He called him "my fire brigade"—sent to wherever a conflagration broke out, he usually putting out the blaze. He promoted the cocky little field marshal over the heads of older and more senior officers—hence von Rundstedt's cynical nickname for Model as "the Boy Marshal." But Model had one defect. He did not possess what the Germans called "Zivilcourage." He did not talk back to the Fuhrer, even when he thought Hitler's orders were wrong.

But for the time being that did not matter. In September 1944, Model agreed with his Fuhrer. He believed that if Germany were to be saved, or at least gain a more favorable peace with the Western Allies, the latter would have to pay dearly for every meter of German ground that they won. Both felt that in a pure infantry battle as the coming one would be, the Americans, in particular, did not have the staying power. If the Americans could not use their superior artillery and air force, the infantry would not keep on attacking alone.

Model concluded that under the circumstances the West Wall would hold with the available resources until the situation turned in Germany's favor. Both the "Young Marshal" and the "Old Marshal" (von Rundstedt) agreed that the Americans wanted a quick, easy victory. If they were made to pay a high and bloody "butcher's bill," however, their attitude might well change drastically on the Western Front.

But on the same day that the 2nd SS Panzer Division began to man the Siegfried Line and whatever additional resources which could be hurried up to the obsolescent fortifications, the GIs of the U.S. 4th Infantry, who would launch the first U.S. attack on that line, were still confident that they could achieve a swift victory. That night Colonel "Buck" Lanham of the 22nd Infantry and his staff celebrated their first night on German soil at a dinner with Ernest Hemingway. Colonel Lanham, somewhat of an amateur poet, wrote later of that happy relaxed first dinner on German soil: "The food was excellent, the wine plentiful, the comradeship close and warm. All of us were heady with the taste of victory as we with wine. It was a night to put aside the thought of the great West Wall, against which we would throw ourselves within the next forty-eight hours."

Nearly a thousand miles away, at Hitler's headquarters, an obscure major of the German general staff was puzzled that same night by a strange assignment that had been passed his way by cunning, pale-faced Colonel-General Alfred Jodl, the brains behind Hitler's top planners. The major was Percy Schramm, a former academic from the University of Gottingen. Normally it was his task to keep the daily war diary of the High Command (the OKW) in order, ensuring that it was as accurate as possible. Now he had been given the job of traveling to the army headquarters at Berlin's Bendler-strasse to have a detailed look at some plans, dating back to a campaign four years earlier which had been practically forgotten in the intervening years.

They were *"Fall Gelb"* ("Case Yellow"), the master plan drawn up in 1939/40 for the great attack on the Low Countries and the

Anglo–French armies in France and Belgium. In particular the ex-professor of history had been ordered to sort out those plans detailing the German right hook through the Ardennes, from the German fortifications that ran through the German Eifel region.

He wondered why.

3

Wunder am Westwall

On that same evening that Lanham was celebrating on German soil, Colonel Thomas Ford, G-2 of the U.S. V Corps to which the 4th Infantry Division belonged, was equally optimistic. Once General Courtney Hodges, First Army commander, gave the green light, Gerow's V would attack the Siegfried Line.

"There is no doubt," Ford briefed Gerow's staff, "that the enemy will defend the Siegfried Line with all the forces that he can gather." Here Ford allowed himself a smile and concluded with: "that which the enemy" would be able to gather was "very much to be questioned."

In a way, Colonel Ford was right. SS General Keppler, commander of the SS Corps scheduled to defend the West Wall roughly between Moschau and Dasburg, was indeed so short of effectives that he could form only two divisions from his original four to oppose any attack by the three-division-strong U.S. V Corps.

But like most SS commanders, Keppler was very energetic—and high-handed. He pretended to see no difficulties. He overruled the objections of Wehrmacht officers when they tried to keep their own troops from the grasp of the SS. He set up roadblocks. Stragglers were stopped at pistol point and told they had the choice of joining the SS or else. They joined. The rear areas at Trier, Wittlich, Bitburg, Kyllburg, etc., were combed for "bodies." New units arriving at these railheads were whipped away before they could be billeted by the army and carried to the front line in the SS's remaining half-tracks. The SS knew no pardon, entertained no excuses, accepted no apologies; and because they represented Reichsfuhrer SS Heinrich Himmler's police state, feared by even the highest-ranking Wehrmacht generals, Keppler's officers got away with it.

Thus while Gerow's officers celebrated, talked, and planned, the Siegfried Line, empty on that first day that the Allies crossed into Germany, started to fill out rapidly. The quality of the troops didn't really matter. For as one disgruntled infantryman who fought there snarled to a *Yank* magazine reporter afterward: "I don't care if the guy behind the gun is a syphilitic prick who is a hundred years old— he's still sitting behind eight feet of concrete and he's still got enough fingers to press triggers and shoot bullets!"

On the morning of Thursday, 14 September 1944, the U.S. Army made its first attack on the Siegfried Line. The attacking force was "Buck" Lanham's 22nd Regiment of the 4th Infantry Division, supported by tank destroyers. It would attack in a column of battalions. Lanham's 3rd Battalion would lead and assemble at the one-horse village of Buchet, northeast of a known fortified position at the hamlet of Brandscheid, located on a small hill dominating the area. There the 3rd was to take Brandscheid, consisting of half a dozen farms and houses located around the rather large church in the center. Once that was done, the 1st Battalion was to jump off from Bleialf, the largest village and lead mining center of the area, and roll up the first Siegfried Line positions on the ridge line behind Brandscheid. Colonel Lanham's 2nd Battalion would remain in reserve for employment against any German counterattack, though intelligence thought that was a remote possibility in view of the current state of the Wehrmacht. Lanham with Hemingway would watch the attack from a farmhouse on the outskirts of Buchet.

The regiment would attack the pillboxes from behind. Lieutenant George Wilson, one of the few veterans of the 22nd Regiment to survive the war and the first man of that regiment to spot the Siegfried Line, wrote afterward: "The vulnerable part of the pillbox was to the rear. The (German) crossfire support did not reach there and all they had was some barbed wire and whatever rifles and machine guns could be transferred to the rear trenches ... The trick was to get behind the pillbox quickly." What the tough veteran and his fellow soldiers of the "Ivy League" division did not take into account at the time was the quality of the German opposition.

On the face of it, the eight hundred men who were to stall the first U.S. attack into Germany were not very formidable. "Battle Group Kuehne" was led by an SS major of that name and, as the German tag has it, "*nomen es omen*" ("the name is an omen"). For "*kuehn*" in German means "bold"; and Major Kuehne was a very bold commander indeed.

He had thrown together his battle group from recruits and invalids of the German 105th Training Battalion, located at the Adolf Hitler Kaserne in nearby Wittlick not far from the River Moselle. For two nights they had traveled through the great Eifel forests in the halftracks of the 2nd SS Panzer and then been deposited in small packets in the West-Wall between the positions of the 2nd SS's Regiment Deutschland to the north and south of the general area of Brandscheid. Then they waited, 800 men and invalids facing the attack of a 3,000-man strong U.S. infantry regiment.

At eleven o'clock that Thursday morning Lanham's 22nd Regiment's attack started to take shape. So far everything had been going well. On the 22nd's flank the sister regiment, the 12th Infantry, was running into some difficulties with SS Regiment Deutschland, or what was left of it. But the 22nd was advancing according to plan. By one that afternoon the 22nd was within range of Kuehne's positions. Up in the van, the Shermans, churning up the mud of the plowed fields and pastures ahead of the infantry, began to come under fire. The first tank was hit. It rumbled to a stop, trailing one track behind it like a severed limb. A little later another Sherman was struck. Almost immediately its petrol engine caught fire and it went up in flames. No wonder its crews called the very vulnerable Shermans "the Ronson lighter." The 22nd's attack began to bog down.

As Hemingway described it (though we have good reason to believe he was not really there): "They [the infantry] started coming back down across the field, dragging a few wounded and a few limping. You know how they look coming back. Then the tanks started coming back and the TD's coming back and the men coming back plenty. They couldn't stay in that bare field and the ones who weren't hit started yelling for the medicos for those who were hit and you know that excites everybody." It was clear to Lanham, now watching the attack across the fields from the farmhouse in Buchet, that his men were running out of steam.

Captain Howard Blazzard of the 3rd Battalion, who was observing the battle with Lanham, cried, "Sir, I can get out there and kick those bastards in the tail and take that place!"

Angry now, Lanham retorted, "You're an S-2 [operations officer] in a staff function and you stay where you are." The two of them remained at their observation post for another quarter of an hour. More wounded—and others who had had enough—drifted back. Blazzard told himself, "We're gonna lose this battle."

Then, according to Hemingway, Lanham said suddenly, "Let's get up there. This thing has got to move. Two chickenspits [though he didn't say 'chickenspits'] aren't going to break down this attack." With Lanham carrying a drawn .45, the two of them, crouched low, ran to a kind of terrace on the ridge where some of the 22nd were lying down, taking cover. Angrily Lanham bellowed at them above the racket, "Let's go and get these Krauts ... Let's kill the chickenspitters ... Let's get up over this hill now and get this place taken!" He fired a couple of shots in the direction of the German defenses. Then he encouraged his reluctant heroes with the words, "Come on. Nobody's going to stop here now!"

Thus Lanham got the advance moving once more. But already it was too late. Soon darkness was falling and Lanham knew that to continue would be too dangerous in the confused fighting—it would not be the first time that one battalion had fired upon another. He ordered his men to dig in for the night. On the morrow, he told himself, he would change direction and attack Brandscheid to his right. Little did he know that soon the hamlet on the hill would become known as the "Verdun of the Eifel," changing hands eight times and that it would take another four months before it was finally captured by the U.S. Army. But by then Colonel Lanham's regiment would have been totally consumed by the greedy god of war.

The next day, as soon as Lanham's men attacked once more, they were hit by a spirited counterattack by Battle Group Kuehne. Colonel Dowdy, commanding the 22nd's 1st Battalion, was killed and his Company A was forced to retreat. The company returned with only two officers and sixty-six men left. That meant they had suffered 50 percent casualties.

Under the command of a new CO, a Major Lattimer, the 22nd's

1st Battalion resumed its attack. But as the official U.S. War Department History noted, "Enemy shelling so unnerved several officers including the commander of the attached tank platoon that they had to be evacuated for combat exhaustion. About 0830, as Company A moved to the line of departure, another severe shelling so upset the company commander that he, too, had to be evacuated."

Lanham ordered his 1st Battalion to withdraw. In the meantime the 4th Division assistant commander, Brigadier-General George Taylor, drove to V Corps headquarters to report on the situation in the Eifel. Taylor told General Gerow that the 22nd Regiment had suffered severe casualties. Not only that, but the whole of the 4th Division ran the risk of being attacked on both flanks, where the 2nd SS's Regiment Deutschland was still holding its positions. Finally Taylor requested that the 4th Division's attack should be halted.

Gerow, who had personal problems (he had just been summoned to Washington to a congressional inquiry and his French wife was suspected of being linked to a collaboration scandal with the Germans during the recent occupation of her country), did not take much convincing. As we shall see, his other two divisions were in trouble also. That Saturday night, he ordered Taylor to tell his boss, General "Tubby" Barton, commander of the 4th Infantry Division, to call off his attack on the following morning.

In three days of combat the U.S. 4th Division had torn an initial gap of about six miles in the West Wall. It had, however, captured no ground or road systems of any strategic importance which could be used for that celebrated dash for the Rhine (save for some inter-village country tracks). At the cost of eight hundred casualties, the 4th had inflicted only a dent in the German positions which in this part of the Eifel were hardening by the hour. Kuehne, meanwhile, lost 680 of his men. Accordingly, with the approval of his corps commander, General Barton stopped his attack. Instead he would go over to the face-saving role of aggressive defense; and that was what the 4th Infantry Division would do for the next two weeks until it was relieved by the 2nd U.S. Infantry Division on 4 October 1944.

On Saturday, 16 September, General der Flieger Werner Kreipe represented his Luftwaffe boss, Hermann Goering, otherwise known as "Fat Hermann" (behind his massive back, naturally) at Hitler's daily conference at his Rastenburg headquarters. It was customary that the only record of these *"Fuhrer-Konferenzen"* was the official and probably censored one made by Hitler's secretarial staff.

Kreipe, however, a former pilot with something of an independent nature, had been risking imprisonment, perhaps even his head to the traditional German executioner armed with an axe, by ignoring that ban. Day after day for a long time he made secret notes of what transpired in his own personal diary. Thus we know what happened at the "Wolf's Lair" (which one regular visitor described as "half monastery and half concentration camp") that Saturday afternoon.

In his diary, Kreipe explained how Jodl had opened the conference with a comparison of the friend-foe strengths on the Western Front. Then the pale-faced staff officer, who had seen little combat in his long military career, reviewed Germany's shortages in tanks, heavy weapons, artillery, and shells. Then suddenly to everyone's surprise, Hitler, who had appeared lethargic and uninterested, broke into this formal expose.

As an excited Kreipe later noted in his diary in a kind of staccato shorthand: *"Fuhrerentschluss ... Gegenangriff aus Ardennen ... Xiel Antwerpen ... Nahtstelle zwischen Englandern und Amerikanern aufreissen ... neuse Dunkirchen...."* ("Fuhrer Decision ... Counterattack out of the Ardennes ... Target Antwerp ... Cut the joint between the English and Americans ... a new Dunkirk!")

This was the first written documentation of what would be later named "the Rundstedt Offensive." It was Churchill who gave it its historic name, "The Battle of the Bulge," through his parliamentary reference to the "bulge," usually associated with tubby gents like himself. In principle, Churchill intensely disliked flippant names for great attacks, but by then it was too late to do anything about. So America's greatest battle of the twentieth century was saddled with a title that is usually connoted with weight loss.

That Saturday night, Gerd von Rundstedt knew nothing of the offensive being planned under his name, which would, in the end, involve millions of men, both friend and foe. Instead, at his headquarters just off the autobahn, on the other side of the Rhine opposite Koblenz, the 69-year-old, incredibly wrinkled, commander in chief in the West, was worried about an attack in the Eifel by a handful of U.S. infantry accompanied by a squadron of Sherman tanks.

For surprisingly enough, while Gerow's two infantry divisions, the 4th and 28th Infantry, had been unlucky in their first attacks on the Siegfried Line, it was the V Corps's armored division, the 5th, which had made a clean breakthrough.

This secondary attack by an armored formation, supported by one regiment "borrowed" from the 28th Division, which had already suffered 1,500 casualties elsewhere, had been launched across the Sauer near the village of Wallendorf. There, with resistance minimal, the defenders had been caught by surprise. As usual, the Germans had reacted quickly. They had thrown in a company of Mark IV tanks from General Fritz Bayerlein's Panzerlehr division. For once, however, the Sherman gunners had beaten the Germans to the draw. One by one the jubilant "Victory Division" tankers knocked the Germans out. As one of the Yanks exclaimed happily afterward, "It was just like an old style turkey shoot." As the rest of Bayerlein's Mark IVs fled, the Shermans scuttled forward heading for a feature known ominously as "Deadman's Creek." By nightfall they were six miles inside the German territory with the Siegfried Line behind them.

Now von Rundstedt called General von Knobelsdorf, the army commander responsible for the area of the breakthrough. For at Rundstedt's headquarters, a near panic had broken out. By chance, Gerow's V Corps had attacked at the "joint" between two German army groups, Model's Army Group B and to the south of Model, General Blaskowitz's Army Group G. In essence the defense of these remote valleys in the Eifel was being conducted by two group commanders, whose headquarters were 150 miles apart. And the "old hare" Rundstedt knew that such a defense was a recipe for disaster.

Von Rundstedt rasped: "How is it possible that the Americans could break through the Wall [West Wall] like that?" The commander of the German First Army, a capable soldier, yet totally surprised by this call from the grand old man of the German High Command, stuttered: "They crossed the Sauer in tanks and used flame throwers to block the pillbox stilts and smoked the defenders. They [meaning the defenders] weren't very experienced."

Von Rundstedt was not one bit interested in the army commander's excuse or the inexperience of the defenders. He snapped, "But

only eight U.S. tanks have been reported." If von Rundstedt expected some kind of reassuring answer from von Knobelsdorf, he was disappointed. Thoughtlessly, von Knobelsdorf told his army commander, "Others [tanks] have crossed since."

Von Rundstedt's answer is not recorded, but von Knobelsdorf
moved on soon thereafter, if that signified anything. But now von
Rundstedt was really worried. If the Americans managed to break
out of their bridgehead over the River Sauer, all hell would be let
loose.

In the weakly defended area, it did not seem to von Rundstedt that
the Americans would have much difficulty in reaching Bitburg, the
largest town in that part of the Eifel. Bitburg not only possessed a
splendid brewery (which might encourage any fighting hairy-chested
GI to do his utmost to capture it) but also a road network and a nearby rail center. This rail network and the roads leading northeast might
well put the Americans on the road to Germany's last natural bulwark,
the Rhine, in next to no time. And that would spell disaster.*

Von Rundstedt reacted immediately. Swiftly he changed the
army boundaries so that only one army group commander would be
in charge of halting the breakthrough. Then he personally decided
to conduct the battle of the bridgehead. Thus it was that a humble
U.S. divisional commander, General Lunsford Oliver, CO of the 5th
Armored Division, was now to be confronted in battle by no less a
person than Germany's most renowned field marshal in World War
II. Von Rundstedt prepared to throw in a massive counterattack of
at least six divisions against the unsuspecting head of the "Victory
Division." As he had done so often before, the German officer, who
had led the attack through the Eifel back in 1940 and four years
later had commanded all the German troops in the West on that
June day when the Allies had landed on the beaches of Normandy,
was going to pull out all the stops. The time had come, as the field
marshal declared to his worried staff, "*den Knuppel aus dem Sack
zu holen*" ("to pull the club out of the sack"). It seemed the as yet
unsuspecting General Oliver didn't have a chance in hell.

So far General Oliver, the 5th Armored Division, and the accompanying infantry from the 28th Infantry Division had been surprising-

---

* When Patton captured Bitburg in late February 1945, his 4th Armored Division
set off from the town and reached the Rhine in the first week of March in just under
fifty hours.

ly lucky. After their crossing of the Sauer they found themselves faced by *"Alarmbataillon Trier"* supported by *"Alarmbatterie Trier."* Both were ad hoc formations, hurriedly thrown together from the 40,000 deserters, stragglers, shirkers, and the like, who found themselves in the ancient Roman city of Trier on the River Moselle. Both commanders were useless and in the case of the infantry, it was discovered later by U.S. intelligence that the men of the Alarmbataillon came from thirty different formations; not exactly an elite unit to stop an up-to-strength, experienced U.S. armored division.

Still, while von Rundstedt and his staff frantically organized their counterattack, these formations did attempt to stop the Americans. They had no alternative. Those of their officers who still believed in Fuhrer, Fatherland, and Folk, would have shot them out of hand if they had laid down their weapons prematurely.

Surprisingly, one such officer in Alarmbataillon Trier was Company Commander Captain Karl Kornowski, who also happened to be a Catholic priest in civilian life. He was rushed with his mixed bunch to a village on the perimeter of the American breakthrough. There he met a fellow priest, still a civilian, who advised Kornowski to "take off your field gray uniform and put on your priest's robe"; in other words to desert and wait for the Americans to come.

Kornowski would have none of it. He fobbed off the civilian priest, who gave him some cake and a bottle of home-brewed schnapps, saying, "It's too early for that," and off he went to battle with the Americans.

The former Catholic priest and his men had some difficulty in finding them, though they could hear the ominous roll of gunfire in the distance. He came across a major—"a real tit," as he described the latter. The man was hiding in a foxhole and started bellowing out orders from his safe position as soon as he saw the ragged little band. Kornowski, a frontline veteran of Russia, asked where he was supposed to attack. The major was unable to answer, for as the ex-priest said later in decidedly non-churchlike language, "he was too busy crapping his pants to show us." So off they went again into the unknown until finally they landed in that ominously named "Dead Man's Creek." There they found the war. Under

Kornowski's leadership they succeeded in recapturing eight West-Wall bunkers before they were ambushed and captured by the Americans.

The ex-priest was taken for interrogation (of a sort) to Wallendorf on the River Sauer where his meager possessions were looted. First, naturally, went his precious bottle of local firewater. "But first," as Kornowski remembered long afterward, "I had to taste it [the schnapps] to prove it wasn't poisoned. Then it went the round of the victors' throats. But they did give me back my tobacco pouch, rosary and picture of the Virgin Mary. Nice of them."

But while these rather useless ad hoc formations started to attempt to stop the Americans's drive to Bitburg (and failed to do so), von Rundstedt pulled out all the stops to stage a major counter-attack in the area. As his clever chief of staff, General Siegfried Westphal wrote: "Up to the middle of October the enemy could have broken through [the western front] at any point he selected. Then he could have crossed the Rhine and, virtually unhindered, driven east-wards anywhere he wished." But in September the most endangered point in the whole western front was the *"Moselpforte"* ("Moselle Gate") of Trier. Unwittingly, General Oliver of the 5th Armored Division and the 112th Regiment of the 28th Division had selected that gate, and both Westphal and von Rundstedt knew it was imper-ative to securely bolt and lock that "gate" before the Americans stumbled onto the fact that they had found the key that could open it and perhaps end the war in 1944.

Although the divisions available to von Rundstedt were, in most cases, the battered, burned-out formations that had fled from France, low on tanks, transport, and heavy guns, they were being filled out rapidly and they were led by very experienced comman-ders, such as Bayerlein of the Panzerlehr and von Luttwitz of the 2nd Panzer. The pressing need for defensive and later offensive personnel in the hills of Eifel with its poor road network was infantry. They were the ones who would hold the ground and later recapture lost ground. As for air cover, the Eifel was beginning to live up to the nickname the GIs would soon give it—the "Awful Eifel." Rain, fog, and early morning mists were moving in. The weather gave the Germans the air cover they needed and prevented the Americans from using their greatest advantage of the campaign in the West so far—their air power. In this third week of September 1944, this was strictly an infantry battle—man against man.

Thus von Rundstedt stopped the point of the American attack. That done, he attempted to prevent any further enemy penetrations on the left and right flanks of the bridgehead, especially the one to the left. For he feared the Americans there might link up with their comrades of the 28th and 4th Infantry Divisions to form a line along the old Roman highway between Bitburg and Prum. One by one he threw in new formations, however battered they might be—Panzer Brigade 108, parts of the 2nd Panzer, the 36th and 19th People's Grenadier Divisions, Bayerlein's Panzerlehr, the demonstration formation of the German Army, and finally what was left of the 5th Parachute Division.

Now the U.S. 5th Armored Division was coming badly unstuck. Later General Oliver would report his losses as 792 men for the whole of September, of which there were 148 dead and missing-in-action. As for the 28th Division's 112th Regiment, it reported it had suffered 37 percent casualties for the same period of time. Cruel as it may seem to say, these losses were not too high. After all, if they *had* helped to bring the war to an end in the West that fall, perhaps the lives of another quarter million Allied soldiers might have been saved.

In the light of the great propaganda campaign launched by the "Poison Dwarf,"* Doctor Josef Goebbels, Nazi Minister of Propaganda and Public Enlightenment, alleging American cruelty and torture against German civilians during their occupation of the "Wallendorf Bridgehead," it might be of interest to look at some civilian accounts of the period.

Photos taken at the time, admittedly by the U.S. Army Signal Corps, show GIs helping German civilians to evacuate their belongings from burning buildings at Wallendorf immediately after the crossing of the Sauer. Eyewitness accounts after the war depict the advancing Americans to be tough yet without apparent malice. Hermann Puetz of the village of Nusbaum emerged from the cellar of his house where he had been sheltering from an artillery barrage to find his first *"Americaker"* standing in the road. "He was armed with a machine pistol [grease gun]. Next to him lay another Ami

---

* Nicknamed thus on account of his small stature and vitriolic tongue.

behind a machine gun. I must admit I was scared. But the first one made a peaceful impression on me. He looked drawn and tired. With his hand he gestured he was thirsty. He wanted something to drink. I remembered a bit of my school English and told him there was no water, but I had some milk. He replied he'd like hot milk so I made the milk for him, as more and more soldiers poured through the village and we were glad. We thought the war was over at last."

Not far away at Stockhem, Peter Hankas, a soldier who just happened to be on leave in his native village, watched as German artillery smashed into the place causing a panic-stricken flight of his fellow villagers. Up on the hill above there were, he knew, American guns. Would they now take up the challenge and pound on unharmed civilians? "They didn't. They couldn't have missed if they had opened fire there and then. And they had good reason to. Our own guns had pounded Ami positions without mercy." So the villagers escaped, men, women, and children, and Peter Hankas survived to record the incident, despite Goebbels's depiction of the Americans as "the arsonist-murderers of the Wallendorf-Bridgehead."

On 16 September, or so it was stated afterward, Gerow ordered the evacuation of the Wallendorf salient. According to the U.S. official history, there were several reasons for this strange decision. Gerow was handing over command to his successor while he went to Washington to attend the official inquiry into the Pearl Harbor affair; he was running out of supplies which were now going to the V Corps's two sister corps who were to support Patton's bete noir, Montgomery; and casualties in the 5th Armored and 112th Infantry were mounting. And, as a final justification, the breakthrough at Wallendorf had not been specifically approved by the supreme commander, General Eisenhower.

Of course it hadn't. How could Eisenhower have known it would take place when he had approved further *limited* action by Patton's Third Army and Hodges's First Army, to which Gerow's V Corps belonged, at Chartres on 2 September? But that latter reason for the withdrawal does raise a host of questions, which really are not the remit of this book. One, in particular, however, stands out: Was "Ike" so inflexible and so set in his "broad front strategy" that he would not seize this golden opportunity to break through the

West Wall and head for at least the Rhine? Both his two top-level German opponents, von Rundstedt and his chief of staff, Westphal, have gone on record that the breakthrough at Wallendorf could have spelled final disaster for the German Army in the West.

Indeed, if Eisenhower had been really so inflexible and short-sighted, how was it that he sanctioned, that very same September, First Army's protracted and costly attacks on both Aachen and the Hurtgen Forest? Why, if supplies were so short, allow these attempts at breakthroughs when the Siegfried Line had already been breached significantly at Wallendorf?

Once again questions without answers; questions which have not been answered to this very day, nearly sixty years after the event. But in 1951, the former General Siegfried Westphal wrote: "If the enemy, i.e. Eisenhower, had thrown in more forces he would not only have broken through the German line of defenses, which were in process of being built up in the Eifel, but in the absence of any considerable reserves on the German side, he might have effected the collapse of the whole West Front within a short time."

So events took what can only be regarded as their tragic course in the light of what was to come in the remaining nine months of the campaign in Europe. Gerow handed over command of V Corps to General Edward H. Brooks, stating in his farewell message that the opposition the Germans had mustered against his V Corps had failed to impress him, adding, "It is probable the war with Germany will be over before I am released to return to the V Corps." Tragically, that was not the case.

In the meanwhile, three days after the decision to withdraw had already been made, the Americans began abandoning their positions or were forced to do so. Von Rundstedt's counteroffensive commenced. His divisions pressed in on the salient from both sides. Village after village, bought with American lives, was retaken by the enemy. Here and there, according to German sources, there was near panic.

Hidden once more in his barn, Hermann Puetz, who had liked the first Americans he had ever met and had thought the war was over, now watched the Americans leave. "Already they had pulled down the cooks' tent. A cannon had been towed away and people were running back and forth. I guessed something was up. Now only a big truck was going round and round in the wet meadows. But it was clear the Amis had had enough ... At nine that morning we crawled out of our cellars and drew in deep breaths of clear air."

Naturally Puetz doesn't say they looted what the Americans had left, stating solely that they "ate a good breakfast." Sometime later a lone, camouflaged German soldier came down the road from Frelingen. Behind him "came the personnel carriers, filled with triumphant young panzer grenadiers ... they started to loot the vehicles the Americans had left behind so hastily. That was their rewards." They went on their way following the retreating Americans, "munching Hershey bars, smoking Ami cigarettes like a bunch of happy school kids."

It might have been a happy time for the attacking Germans; it was not for the retreating Americans of Gerow's V Corps. On 23 September, the bad weather cleared and the sun shone. Von Rundstedt ordered up twenty-five fighter-bombers from the Rhenish fields on the west side of the Rhine. As they came zooming at treetop height, cannons and machine guns pounding, Bayerlein of the Panzerlehr threw in his last twenty-odd tanks.

Bayerlein was a master of his métier. He had fought in Russia, against the British Eighth Army in Africa, and against the Allies in Normandy and later in Eastern France. Although he and his tankers were outnumbered by the Shermans of Oliver's 5th by two to one, Bayerlein was a superior tactician.

The Americans started to pull back. To the rear, U.S. TAC (Tactical Air Corps) threw in its fighter-bombers. According to German witnesses, there were up to a hundred machines in the air at one time. They wheeled and twisted, trying to gain the advantage, while below the Americans fought desperately to retain some hold on their bridgehead.

Later that day, American infantry attacked the key German position on the Romersberg. By now fog had started to form. The infantry moved forward like bent, thoughtful khaki ghosts. Just when it seemed they might reach the top of the height, the fog lifted. Immediately the German artillery cracked into action. Their shells bombarded the slopes (you can see traces of the shell holes to this day). The attackers fell back. But bravely they came again and again.

About eight o'clock that terrible September night they managed to capture the summit of the Romersberg.

But it was no use. Von Rundstedt threw in a new division, the 19th Infantry. It advanced along the line of the River Sauer, capturing the American-held bunkers to the rear of the defenders. The new division moved closer to the men on the hilltop. One by one the Germans knocked out fifteen Shermans from behind. The American defenders started to break. According to German sources, that night an American captain threw away his uniform, dressed in looted civilian clothes, and was captured thus, fleeing toward the river.

It was not without satisfaction that the War Diary of Rundstedt's headquarters noted that day: "The main battle line is now firmly in our hands. In hard-fought battles, LXXX Corps had succeeded to throw back the enemy, who had penetrated ten kilometers into the main battle area with 60 tanks. 31 tanks and 10 reconnaissance vehicles were destroyed. In addition, nine enemy planes have been shot down and 52 prisoners taken. The enemy dead numbered 531 ..."

The first U.S. attack on Germany had ended in failure. As J. Nobusch, a German historian who as a schoolboy was present as these first battles took place in the Eifel, has commented: "It is of interest that General Gerow ... ordered the offensive stopped on 16 September; the attack was too costly. On 21 September, the withdrawal from the bridgehead was approved." Professor Nobusch's point is clear: why wait those five days between 16 and 21 September, if the offensive was so costly in human life? Was this an American cover-up?

Nobusch goes on with a certain amount of *schadenfreude*: "American sources give the impression that the Americans were in control throughout the operation; that their V Corps was not stopped by the Germans. We can doubt this version, for although the bridgehead was defended (after 16 September), it was not extended."*

Nobusch's point is again clear. Gerow did not order the withdrawal on account of lack of supplies, high casualties, or even fear of Eisenhower's wrath. Gerow did so because he found the German defenders just too tough for him.

Be that as it may, the die had been cast. In the Eifel–Ardennes region with a narrow strip of German territory around Bleialf, the Americans were back where they had started at the beginning of

* J. Nobusch. *Bis zum Bitteren Ende*. Kreisverwaltung: Bitburg-Prum, 1978.

September. Now the V Corps, and Middleton's VIII Corps, which would soon take over that section of the front, were limited to their main battle line and supply bases in Luxembourg and Belgium. They would continue to patrol the Our–Sauer Line during daylight hours. But at night they would retire to their main line on the thickly wooded heights in those two countries, which overlooked the valleys below. In theory they could have hawked and spat across the twin rivers, where the German forward positions were located. But they didn't.

Slowly the sound and fury of the recent battle began to die away. The cannons ceased their thunder; the machine guns their lethal, high-pitched chatter. The grind-and-groan of tanks vanished. There would be no need of the steel monsters on this particular front now. The American infantry dug, wired, beefed, tried to keep warm and "shot the breeze." One day they might get lucky. They'd draw a three-day pass from the company office and set off for "Gay Paree" and the sexual delights of "Pig Alley" (Place Pigalle) as long as their dough held out. One day ...

Once, back in 1940, a hard-pressed Churchill, whose army had just been run out of Europe at Dunkirk, complained: "From Dover [opposite Calais on the Channel] I can read the time on Calais' town hall clock through my glasses ... but that's all. As far as I am concerned the Continent is a totally foreign and unknown world." Those GIs in that remote border country must have felt the same that fall so long ago. In some cases, the "Krauts" were only a mere hundred yards away on the other side of the river line. But as far as the U.S. infantry manning that line were concerned, the enemy could well have been a thousand miles away.

Now as September gave way to October 1944, someone (we don't know who) created a name for this strange sixty mile section of the long Allied line where nothing happened.

It was the "Ghost Front."

OCTOBER
1944

4

Live and Let Die

After a summer of defeat after defeat, the Germans made the most of their victory on the Our–Sauer River Line. Dr. Goebbels had a field day. Not only did he celebrate this "great victory" over the detested Americans, he used V Corps's capture of German territory as a warning. The cunning little dyed-in-the-wool Nazi maintained that those who believed that the Americans would bring freedom and peace at last were sorely mistaken. His propaganda experts in Berlin used the recapture of the dozen or so German villages to warn the nation what happened when the enemy took over.

According to Goebbels, the temporary U.S. occupation of the Wallendorf bridgehead had been a nightmare for the local Germans. The Americans had behaved like the "barbarians of old." They were all ex-convicts, the scum of the U.S. jails. Together with their Belgian, French, and Luxembourg "running dogs," the "Ami swine" had mounted a "reign of terror" in these newly occupied German territories. They had burned, looted, raped, and murdered.

Under alarmist headlines such as "The Raped Village" and "Women and Children used as Human Shields," the Goebbels-controlled German media depicted just how bestial these "boys from over the Ocean" could be. In one case, "using chocolate as bait," they had supposedly beaten a "mother of four" in the American occupied "hamlet of Kruchten senseless." In vain her fellow peasants had pleaded "on their knees for mercy. To no avail. After beating the woman into unconsciousness, the brutal Amis had set every 'humble house' in the place alight, crying as they torched the peasants' homes, 'This is what we'll do with every German village we capture—burn it to the ground.'"

Goebbels's propaganda efforts were weakened slightly when next to the details of these atrocities appearing in Hitler's own paper, "*der Voelkische Beobachter,*" there was another, smaller piece warning the Germans not to listen to Radio Luxembourg. The prewar commercial radio station which lay ten miles from Wallendorf (and of which we will hear more later) was now in American hands. It had become a typical tool of enemy propaganda. "Naturally," the unknown journalist commented, "anyone listening to this station can expect to be punished most severely."

The small article gave the lie to the Goebbels's allegations of American brutality to the German population. Why, if Goebbels were right, would they want to listen to American propaganda, especially if they risked being sent to a concentration camp if they were caught?

Indeed as the Catholic priest of Bleialf, rotund, middle-aged Father Franz Hartel recorded when the first infantry of the U.S. 4th Division entered the border township in mid-September 1944: "I opened the door, waved a dirty-white handkerchief and called 'Catholic priest' and made peace between them and us. They came in, wanted something to drink, but didn't take one step into the vicarage. Around morning they rang the bell and asked if they could shelter from the cold rain in the scullery." Half an hour later, "after the entry of the enemy troops," the priest recorded sadly in his diary, "we heard in our hiding place in the cellar, the first whistle and howl of a shell. It was a German one that detonated outside. It was either the third or fourth shell which hit the church."

A few days afterward when the American Civil Affairs team collected the villagers for evacuation out of the front line toward the rear in Belgium, the morning air was again torn apart by the screech of the first shell from the enemy lines on the ridge beyond. Systematically German artillery began to bombard their own panic-stricken countrymen and women. Again it seemed there was more truth in the placard which the U.S. Civil Affairs had posted in Bleialf, "*WIR KOMMEN NICHT ALS SIEGER, SONDERN ALS BEFREIER*" ("We don't come as conquerors, but liberators"), than in Goebbels's propaganda.

Slowly, on the German side of the front things started to settle down after the American withdrawal over the Our–Sauer Line. The general border area had been divided into two zones even before the start of World War II. They were the "Red Zone" which ran to a depth of eight miles from the twin rivers; and the "Green Zone" which extended for a further eight miles inland.

The "Red Zone" had already been evacuated twice, once in 1939-40 before the German drive westward and again on the approach of the Americans in September 1944. The "Red Zone" was *officially* empty of civilians, who had supposedly been evacuated by panic-stricken Nazi Party officials in that first terrible week of September. In fact there were still thousands of them living "wild," i.e., illegally, in the shelled, bombed villages of the front line, and, in some cases, even in no-man's land itself.

Many of them had simply disappeared into their barns and cellars when the Party bosses had appeared to evacuate them. Their cattle they had taken to caves and the wooded areas of the heights, feeding them under artillery fire at night. Others had smuggled themselves back to their home villages and hamlets. Some had declared boldly to the front- and rear-line troops that they had been ordered to return to take care of the thousands of animals locked in the pastures and barns of the area.

Now these civilians had restored some sort of gypsy-like existence for themselves, unbothered by the Nazi officials or the military, living by barter and what they could loot from abandoned farms and cottages. As Father Hartel recorded of that time on the front line (on the U.S. side): "We lived on an island. There was no government, no ration cards. We didn't need money because there was nothing to buy with money—and no shops. There were no taxes, no newspapers, no radio and no electricity anyway for a radio. But we didn't live badly. There was enough good food. The only thing we were ever short of was salt." The good priest with the ample belly naturally didn't mention in his diary that he had a well-filled cellar and, if worse came to the worse, there was the communion wine.

On the German side of the line there were not only civilians living illegally on a hand-to-mouth basis, but also soldiers who were returning for one reason or another to the Eifel villages. One such was artilleryman Klaus Ritter, a 22-year-old. He had come back to his native village of Weinsheim near the one-time U.S. 4th Division's objective of Prum on emergency leave. During the abortive American offensive his parents' home had been hit by an "Ami bomb." He had been summoned from Russia to help rebuild the family cottage. That done, "the old hare," as such experienced soldiers were called in German Army slang, felt it was better to stay at the "quiet front than return to the hell of the Russian one." So he had asked for a transfer to a new division, the 18th People's Grenadier Division, which had just arrived in the area, and had been accepted.

Now he and the other crew members of a 105mm cannon, towed by a captured Russian tractor, lived deep in the forest. Their billet was a deep hole they had dug on a hillside covered with logs. They called it their *"Gartenlaube"* ("bower"), beloved of German weekend gardeners in peacetime. The place was plagued with weeds but it was warm and comfortable and was lined with deep pile carpets looted from bombed and abandoned houses.

They didn't go short of food either, although they were short of rations. At first there were ample supplies of abandoned cattle, pigs, and chickens. These were looted, in the same manner that the civilians living "wild" did. Brought back to the woods, the animals were slaughtered by their elderly sergeant who had been a butcher in his native Alsace across the border in France.

It was a rough-and-ready sort of existence. But young Ritter was not complaining after the Eastern Front. He had escaped the slaughters of the killing fields of Russia. Now he was on a quiet front, where virtually nothing happened. The high point was the weekly journey to the next village where the battery headquarters was located. There he picked up the crew's rations, was deloused, and enjoyed the luxury of an hour's hot bath; the rest of the week he indulged simply in a "cat's lick" and more often than not didn't even shave. After all, the sergeant, who was still officially a French citizen, wasn't going to tell off a native-born German for possessing an unsoldier-like appearance.

Otherwise he and the rest of the eight-man crew spent their time playing skat, a German card game, telling tall tales of their wartime experiences, and most importantly, foraging in order to supplement their meager rations. Once the little group of looters, for that was what they were, crept by night almost into the American lines where they found an abandoned house that had been partially wrecked. Their Ami counterparts hadn't dared to venture into no-man's land to loot the place themselves; so they found the cellars still well stocked with summer preserves—and the decaying bodies of two dead girls.

No, it wasn't a bad life Klaus Ritter recalled nearly half a century later. It was "a kind of time out of war. Indeed the only danger was when we passed through our own lines on our way back to 'Luleika,' as we called our hiding place later. You had to be quick off the mark when one of the new kids called out the password. Some damn silly thing like 'pot,' to which you had to answer quick as lightning, 'lid.' If you didn't, you risked coming to a sudden end."

Not that it must have seemed much like a fighting front to the "old hare," Ritter. He had heard that there were raids and long-range reconnaissance penetration groups active a little further south on the old German border with American-controlled Luxembourg. But the terrain was more suited to that kind of thing down there. It was rugged, hilly, and wooded and there were fewer villages where the Americans might have set up permanent strongpoints.

All the same, Ritter, an intelligent man who became a school-master, was plagued with nagging doubts. The SS armored divisions, which had been the mainstay of the Eifel fighting front when he had first arrived back home on his emergency leave, had been withdrawn one by one. Why? Was it because this had become a static front where armor used in the assault wouldn't be needed? If that were the case, why were new infantry divisions, such as his own 18th People's Grenadier Division, replacing the ad hoc infantry formations that had helped to throw back the Americans in September. After all, any old grandpa capable of aiming and firing a rifle would have been able to hold the fortifications of the West Wall.

At night when he lay in his underground bunker, with the rain-drops trickling through the logs above his head and dripping into the empty tin cans, Ritter pondered these questions while around him his comrades snored and smelled of unwashed foot rags, all save the artillery gunner on duty who fed their stove with logs. Every now and again, when he would open the looted stove's door to do so, the bunker would flood momentarily with a blood-red light. Then, Ritter would screw up his eyes and pretend to be deep in sleep, too.

He didn't want to talk. He wanted to think.

Thus the long autumn nights passed, broken only by the changing of the sentry and the steady putt-putt of the new V-2 wonder weapons heading for the great Allied supply base of Antwerp or far-off London. The locals called the unmanned rocket-bomb the "Eifel Terror," for oftentimes it landed not far from where it had been fired in the Eifel, killing Germans, not Belgians or Londoners. Then Ritter would tense and hold his breath, checking if the engine would cut out—the sign of imminent danger. But the gunners were always lucky. They would survive to die at the hands of the enemy.

So Ritter tossed and turned trying to see into the future, but always failing. There was something going on, he knew it in his very bones. After all, he had served on the "hot" Russian front long enough. Why was this particular front in his own birthplace remaining "cold" for so long, with the Americans only hundreds of meters away? But each night the young soldier would find no answer to these overwhelming questions. In the end he would fall asleep, lulled by the October wind and the tiny chirping noises the rats made in the roof of "Luleika," to waken to a new day.

Now on the American front, being taken over by Middleton's VIII U.S. Corps, winter was not far off. The wooded ridges of the sixty-mile front of the Eifel–Ardennes, which portly, bespectacled Troy Middleton commanded from his headquarters in the Belgian township of Bastogne, were constantly wreathed in mist. Frequently a cold drizzle fell. It dripped from the soaked firs with a mournful persistence. Often that was the only sound the GIs heard as they wakened in the morning, save if they strained their ears. Then they could hear the muted gunfire from the north, where the U.S. V Corps now battled purposelessly in the "Death Factory" of the Hurtgen Forest. To the south, Patton's Third Army fought for Metz, the great Lorraine fortress, with equal lack of success. But that was too far away for Middleton's GIs to hear.

Two of his eventually four divisions, the 2nd and 80th Infantry, each took over twenty-five miles of Middleton's sixty-mile-long front. They replaced the 4th and 28th Infantry Divisions which were dispatched to be slaughtered by the hundreds and thousands in the futile battle of the Hurtgen Forest. These were long fronts to be held against soldiers like the Germans. The U.S. military textbooks suggested that each division should occupy no more than five miles of front when engaged with the Germans. So understandably, these new divisions of Middleton's were not eager for offensive warfare. The Ghost Front became, according to the official Department of Defense historian: "At once, the nursery and the old folks' home of the American Army, to which were sent new divisions for 'blooding' and old ones to rest and replenish the gaps in their ranks caused by combat."

That October when Captain Charles MacDonald, who would become the official Department of Defense historian, went up with his company of the 2nd Infantry Division, it didn't seem much like a "nursery." After leaving the last Belgian hamlet of Schoenberg, his truck convoy wound its way up the steep hill toward Bleialf and Germany. They passed "a big white signboard with glaring letters [which] told us that 'You are now entering Germany—an enemy country. Be on alert.'"

They met their guide from the company they were relieving. He told MacDonald to remove his silver captain's bars as they might attract a sniper. Then they moved on. "We crossed a slight knoll," MacDonald wrote just after the war, "and the anti-tank wall of the Siegfried Line came suddenly into view. It looked like a prehistoric monster, coiled around the hillsides, the concrete dragon's teeth were like scales upon the monster's back—or maybe headstones in a kind of crazy cemetery."

Finally they reached their position—a small farmhouse near Buchet. They trooped down into the dirty cellar. It was crowded with unshaven soldiers "in every conceivable position on the floor." These dirty, unshaven troops were commanded by a first lieutenant whose "eyes were bloodshot and a half week's beard covered his face. His voice trembled and he would start at the slightest noise." The new boys were in the line, and it must have been clear to the 22-year-old then that this was no nursery. Men like that were in no position to get on their hind legs and do battle with the enemy.

But eventually Middleton's men came to terms with their environment along the Our–Sauer and in the border forests of the Eifel–Ardennes. They weatherproofed their foxholes, covering them in the German fashion with logs and grass sod. Just like their

German counterparts such as Ritter, they scavenged and looted, making their holes more homey with rugs and, most important, the *kachelofen* (tiled stoves) of the area, which stayed warm for a long time even when the log fire inside went out.

The weather now became more of a hazard than the enemy, who in some cases was just on the other side of the river. According to the official figures, more infantrymen were laid low at this point through disease than the enemy. In the case of Middleton's 83rd Division, which would serve at the front through October and November, it suffered exactly twenty-five dead, killed in action, plus 176 wounded, out of a division 15,000 men strong; 550 men, on the other hand, were laid low by chest complaints and the dreaded trench foot, which would soon reach epidemic proportions among Eisenhower's riflemen. Once, Eisenhower visited the base hospital at Verviers, Belgium, where he was shocked to find hundreds of men lying on cots, with cotton wool soaked in chemicals between their toes in an attempt to cure their trench foot and prevent the onset of gangrene. It was said that if circulation had not returned to the afflicted men's feet within forty-eight hours, they would have to amputate to prevent the gangrene from spreading its black curse to their legs.

As one angry rifleman complained to the BBC reporter who had come up to the area to report for London: "Have you ever slept in a hole?" He answered his own question with, "Of course, you haven't. You've never slept in a hole in the ground which you've dug while somebody tries to kill you, a hole dug as quick as you can. It's an open grave, but graves don't fill with water."

Afterward the BBC man commented for the benefit of his listeners: "At night the infantryman gets boards or sheets of tin or an old door and puts it over his slit trench, then he shovels on top of it as much dirt as he can scrape up nearby. He sleeps with his head under this. Did I say 'sleep'? Let's say collapses." As the BBC correspondent pointed out finally, "The next time you are near some muddy ditch after the rain, look at it. That's where your man lives."

But as the days and weeks passed, conditions improved, as "squad huts" were built right up to the front line and the native ingenuity of GIs from the country helped to improve their conditions, even in the gunpits and foxholes. It had all become very cozy and for most of the infantry the war could have been a million miles away.

Indeed, it seemed that Middleton's divisions in the line couldn't even draw enemy fire when they exposed themselves to the German artillery observers hidden only yards away. In fact, on 20 October, Middleton ordered no less than three river crossings of the Sauer and the Moselle by men of the 83rd U.S. Infantry Division. As Middleton reported later, "[They were to] trick the enemy into firing and revealing his gun position." The result? "The Germans fired, but not much."

Why? Why didn't the Germans react and slaughter such a tempting target—engineers out in the open, immobilized by the water of the Sauer and Moselle; infantry waiting with their rubber boats; high-ranking officers poised on the high ground of the American bank, waiting to observe the three crossings to be carried out in full daylight?

Troy Middleton reasoned it was because "they put second-class troops from their infantry divisions in the line opposite the VIII Corps. They had a pretty good idea that the Americans weren't really planning an offensive any time soon." In Middleton's opinion, it was therefore a matter of live and let die, like some remote section of the trenches in the Old War, in which he had served as a battalion commander, and where the local commanders had agreed, "I won't shoot if you won't."

After all, Middleton stated afterward: "The four divisions in the VIII Corps through October and most of November thoroughly familiarized themselves with the terrain they were defending. They organized defenses to absorb a heavy punch without letting the enemy all the way through. They prepared withdrawal and counter-attack plans."

But that was a defeated Middleton's rationalization after that fatal Saturday, 16 December 1944, when the balloon finally went up.

But there were Americans on that front of much lower rank than Major General Troy Middleton who sensed that the Ghost Front was not as deserted and tranquil as the VIII Corps's commander maintained. Combat Engineer S/Sgt Henry Giles, older than the average GI at that time, wrote in his diary at that period: "Some of the wildest things can happen [in his sector]. A work detail had to go out and repair a culvert. They didn't know the password or had forgotten or something went snafu. Anyway some kid got excited and thought they were Krauts and started shooting off his rifle." The result was a massive artillery barrage, similar to the one that had just fallen on Captain MacDonald's 2nd Division. That had resulted in the 2nd's commander, General Walter Robertson, ordering his troops to blow up some of the Siegfried Line bunkers, captured the month before by the 4th Infantry. The Germans had used them to infiltrate into the 2nd Division's lines.

But how had these "second-rate" German infantry known about the 2nd's positions around Bleialf and the heights of the *Schwarzer Mann*" ("Black Man") beyond? Either they had spies among the remaining German population or their patrols had previously penetrated the 2nd's line without the defenders knowing about it. These were second-rate troops?

An instance of what the average GI knew of this supposed "Ghost Front" where nothing happened was encountered by Captain Robert Merriam of the Ninth Army's historical section and one of the future best historians of the battle of the Bulge. He was riding with a driver along what the GIs called "Skyline Drive," the main highway between Luxembourg City, Bradley's headquarters, and his own headquarters in Holland not far from Luxembourg's township of Wiltz, when he decided to find out from the chauffeur where exactly the Germans were located. For he knew they were somewhere on the other side of the River Sauer which ran through the valley far below.

The GI didn't hesitate. "With a flourish," he said, "See that ridge line over there, sir, just across the valley?"

Merriam nodded.

"That's it," the GI said.

"What?" the officer queried. He thought the German positions would be visible in the West Wall, "bristling with guns behind every bush." But there was nothing to be seen on the ridge such as lines of spiked-helmeted Prussian grenadiers marching in rigid formations.

The GI at the wheel told him that that was the "Kraut" position all right. He added, "Have to be careful at night. Krauts like to sneak over patrols, just to make a social call. Ambushed a jeep by daylight the other day and got us a battalion commander. He didn't even have a chance to report in. But the only shelling we get is when a Jerry goes to the latrine. Seems they have a machine gun and a mortar there and each one fires a burst." With a smile on his face at the look on Merriam's face, he concluded, "Hope they don't get diarrhea."

The GIs of the Ghost Front who made contact with their German counterparts were not gung-ho adventurers eager for some desperate glory and medals. Nor were they solitary heroes like Audie Murphy, the boyish-looking NCO of the U.S. 3rd Division, who reputedly killed more enemy soldiers than any other single American soldier in the U.S. Army in World War II. In the main, these young U.S. soldiers were confused and lost and blundered into the Germans, equally confused and lost, by chance. Each side surprised the other so that by the time they recognized they were enemies, they had had no time to open fire and had to find some other way of dealing with this totally unexpected situation. (There were, however, some specially trained German-speaking GIs who volunteered to go behind the Germans lines and lie up there for as long as two weeks to report on German troop movements. These brave young men were seemingly to be found mostly in the U.S. Ninth Army area to the north of the Eifel–Ardennes.)

Forward Observer Albert Summerer of a German People's Grenadier Division stationed in the area of Vianden on the River Our was an 18-year-old who had just been transferred from the navy to the Wehrmacht by the levee en masse decrees of early September 1944. He made his first contact with the Americans in the last week of that October.

As a forward observer he had been excused by his *feldwebel* from normal infantry duty on the river line opposite the Luxembourg town of Vianden, dominated by its ruined castle that had once belonged to the Dutch de Lannoy family, ancestors of President Franklin Delano Roosevelt. Instead he was given a series of errands for his platoon, picking up mail and rations and, once a day, water from a cistern some two kilometers away from their bunker. As carrying the water was a slow business, this was usually carried out in the late evening when it began to grow dark.

At first the intelligent young ex-sailor, who had been transferred to the army after his mine-sweeper had been sunk by a British flying boat in the North Sea, thought he had been given a "cushy number"

until he had a run in with nearly seventy "*Bagdolio*." This was the
name given to Italian soldiers of Marshal Bagdolio, who had
remained loyal to the deposed Italian Duce, Mussolini, and had
thrown in their lot with the Germans in spite of the fact that their
native country was now fighting on the side of the Allies against
Hitler. The Italian renegades were a rough, lazy lot. They couldn't be
bothered to fetch the water ration themselves so they robbed passing
Germans, especially if they outnumbered them, and took everything
else the soldier might possess of value.

Thereafter, Summerer decided he would find his own source of
water for his comrades, one that was well away from that popular
but dangerous cistern. He found it at the nearby River Our.
Admittedly the Americans were just on the other side of the river, but
it was generally supposed in Summerer's battery that the Americans
packed "their bags and went home" to the nearby villages when
darkness fell. Thus the young German forward observer reasoned he
would be relatively safe fetching his water from the Our. Besides, the
journey was half that of the distance to the cistern.

Thus it was that Summerer discovered his three Amis. Naturally
the three young GIs were startled to be suddenly confronted by a
German, armed with an automatic rifle but burdened by water cans.
Indeed they were so startled that neither side fired as they confronted each other near a ruined bridge not far from a German machine-
gun bunker which had since been abandoned.*

Somehow the four men came into conversation in a rough and
ready mixture of school English (Summerer's part) and Luxembourg
German dialect, which one of the GIs had picked up during his stay
in that country. Thus it was that the supposed deadly enemies met
for several nights thereafter, swapping cigarettes and Summerer's
schnapps ration—he didn't drink. (After smoking the rich perfumed
American "Virginia" tobacco, the German always fanned his breath
to drive away the odor in case the *feldwebel* noticed the smell and
asked him "where the hell" he had obtained Ami cigarettes.)

Long afterward, Summerer recalled how they had squatted in the
darkness at the side of the ruined customs house chatting about
"God and the world." He knew about German defenses in the area
but the Americans seemed totally without curiosity. "They never
once asked leading questions. They didn't even want souvenir badges

---

* The little border machine gun post is still there, guarding the rebuilt bridge, looking every bit as menacing as it must have done in 1944.

from my uniform and the like as they did later when I became a pris-
oner-of-war after the Rundstedt Offensive [battle of the Bulge]."

Those unknown GIs's attitude seemed to be typical of the whole
VIII Corps on the Eifel–Ardennes front, and indeed that of General
Bradley's Army Group Headquarters in the Luxembourg capital, a
mere forty miles or so from where this strange little group of friend
and foe met nightly. Then one night the three young GIs did not
return and vanished from Summerer's life—"sadly," as he confessed
half a century later, as he wondered if they had survived the war.

The man who should have directed all and every means of obtaining
information on what the Germans were doing on the other side of
the Ghost Front, even down to the squad level of Summerer's three
American friends, was General Edwin Sibert, head of Bradley's
Twelfth Army Group Intelligence.

Sibert, a West Pointer who came from an old army family and
would become instrumental after the war in helping to found the
CIA, did not want to be regarded as a "Nervous Nelly," as most
intelligence officers were by the other members of staffs. The latter
invariably thought that intelligence officers were constantly seeing
dangers where there were none and inhibiting their plans for active
combat by making incorrect estimates of the enemy's strength, based
mainly on a fertile if gloomy imagination.

General Sibert, for his part, was an optimist and always confident. He shared his boss' belief that the Germans had shot their bolt
and that it was only a matter of time before the enemy collapsed of
their own volition. He felt the Ghost Front was secure, even though
Middleton's VIII Corps was so thinly spread out. In his opinion, the
enemy's line was held by third-rate troops, ad hoc formations, boys
still wet behind the ears, even cripples and sick men. Indeed, General
Kenneth Strong, Eisenhower's Scottish chief of intelligence, had to
warn Sibert not to be over optimistic.

It never seemed to occur to Sibert or his boss, Omar Bradley, that
these were, on the whole, the same kind of German soldiers who had
defeated Gerow's first attack into the Reich the previous month. Nor
that similarly composed German formations were holding—and
sometimes beating—first-class American troops in the Hurtgen
Forest and in the dying battle for the old German imperial city of

Aachen, where the experienced and efficient U.S. 1st and 30th Infantry Divisions, plus the 3rd Armored had taken seven weeks to defeat 6,000 German infantry. Indeed the First Army was suffering such great casualties that the fighting would almost die away there completely in November, and most of the First Army area would become another "Ghost Front" like that part of the line held by Middleton's VIII Corps. Later, the top brass would excuse the "lack of offensive action" by again using the old business of lack of supplies: the same one that had been used when Gerow had failed to take his objectives. In fact, the U.S. Army had simply run out of men—and steam!

In retrospect, it almost seems that the staff were whistling in the wind. Like Charles Dickens's Mr. Micawber, they were waiting for something to turn up and provide them somehow with the victory that they had been anticipating weekly, even daily, since the Wehrmacht had fallen apart in France the previous summer. Bradley and his staff officers perhaps reflected the mood current at Eisenhower's huge Supreme Command Headquarters at Versailles. But that did not provide ample excuse for their own failure to carry out the routine duties of those commanding an army in the field.

For too long the top brass had relied on ULTRA for information on German intentions. How easy it had been to read Hitler's and his High Command's instructions to their field commanders as swiftly (perhaps even sooner) than they themselves could. But now ULTRA, the top secret, war-winning decoding operation, was being run down by the Allies. The Germans were no longer using their (unknown to them) compromised ENIGMA coding machine as much. Instead they were employing secure internal land lines, scrambler phones, dispatch riders, officer couriers, and the like.

The field commander on the American side of the Ghost Front knew this, of course. Eisenhower had his own private "cosmic" secret "Black ULTRA," but that was reserved, in general, for the supreme commander of the Allied forces. Besides it revealed only top-secret German intentions and plans. So why didn't Bradley, Sibert, and, above all, Middleton, responsible for the defense of the Ghost Front, use the main means of obtaining information on the battlefront, the method they had been taught at West Point as had generations of cadets before them—patrols and the taking of prisoners.

If one reads the "After Action" and "Daily Reports" of those units which served in the Eifel–Ardennes area before the storm broke loose, one will find they are filled with details of routine activities—the number of sick, the few battle casualties, the German (or more usually, foreign-born) deserters, etc. But rarely is there mention of a prisoner captured on a patrol or even of a patrol itself.

In their hotel billets along the lower reaches of the River Sauer between Wallendorf–Pont and Echternach where the Eifel River flows towards the River Moselle, the American forward infantry could stare across at the German-held heights and the second largest fortification of the whole long Siegfried Line, the outposts of the seven-story deep *"Katzenkopf"* ("Cat's Head"). Yet those GIs, seemingly occupied in keeping themselves warm and bucking for a pass, might have been staring at the moon for all they knew what was going on there.

At the little river township of Bollendorf, for instance, halfway between Echternach and Wallendorf, the German grenadiers of the 31st People's Grenadier Division had a battalion headquarters right on the waterfront, perhaps some one hundred yards from the nearest Americans in the two hotels on the Luxembourg bank. But for the whole three-month period before the balloon went up and the battle of the Bulge commenced, there is no record of the Americans ever trying to cross the Sauer on a raid. The first Americans the remaining villagers in Bollendorf would ever see would be the ever-swelling stream of dazed and wounded GIs from the 4th Infantry Division taken prisoner on 17 and 18 December. Scores of them ... and then hundreds. Young men who would be paying the bloody butcher's bill on the Siegfried Line for the second time in a mere three months.

Understandably, General Bradley would have an uneasy conscience after disaster struck his command in December 1944. He failed probably due to his own carelessness and obstinacy in not believing that the Germans might rally and take the offensive in the West once more. As he wrote in his account of the war, *Soldier Story*, published in 1948: "Although the prospect of victory that autumn had faded, the exuberance of the September pursuit lingered on in our armies. It was still inconceivable to many that the enemy could have rallied sufficient resistance from his torn armies to stand off the strength we had amassed in our Allied Armies on the Western Front." We can take it that Bradley was one of those "many" who believed that the enemy was beaten; that it was all over but for the shouting.

While Hitler was finalizing his plan for what was to come, an event occurred that gives a glimpse of the mindset of the Allied leaders that they were very willing to believe Hitler's army was falling apart instead of gathering for battle. General Hodges, commander of the U.S. First Army, was electrified by some startling news received at his intelligence headquarters in the Belgian resort town of Spa. Indeed, Hodges's G-2 had been so excited by this wonderful piece of news that he had the audacity to disturb Hodges in his personal caravan. It came in the form of a broadcast that First Army's radio intercept unit had plucked from the airways. And it was in clear: a sure indication that all hell must have broken loose on the other side of the border with Germany, just as it had done on 20 July 1944, when the German generals had thought they had succeeded in assassinating the Fuhrer and wanted all the world to know.

Immediately Bradley was informed of what was afoot. Apparently, according to Hodges's staff, an SS colonel had delivered to Field Marshal von Rundstedt, who was located in Cologne, an order from the German High Command in Berlin to launch an immediate counteroffensive in the West. The aged field marshal had refused. He told the SS colonel that if he carried out the order, his troops in the West would be annihilated. They had no hope of successfully attacking Eisenhower's armies.

The SS colonel had insisted the order be carried out. It was the urgent wish of no less than the Fuhrer that it be executed forthwith. A firefight had broken out between von Rundstedt's staff and the SS colonel's bodyguard. The colonel had been shot and von Rundstedt, who had told the July plotters that he was too old to take part in the assassination attempt on the Fuhrer's life, had finally decided to throw in his lot with the anti-Nazi faction.

Then, the report went on, von Rundstedt had ordered all Wehrmacht units to rally to him and to forget their oath of loyalty to the Fuhrer. They were to disarm all Waffen SS units that refused to rally to his cause and shoot all senior SS commanders out of hand and without trial. Thereupon, he proclaimed himself military governor of Cologne, which was only fifty miles from the American-occupied part of Germany and a good place to begin negotiating with the Allies. And in a public broadcast to the German people he had urged them to rally to his side. He promised them that as soon as they did so, he would conclude an honorable peace with the Western Allies and bring an immediate end to the terrible Allied bombing of their cities.

In retrospect, it can be seen that this account of what turned out to be a false hope and a great piece of "black propaganda" did reflect on a large scale the 12th Army Group commander's own wishful thinking that October, accounting for the strange lack of activity on the Ghost Front. After all, Americans of all types did pride themselves on their "get up and go" attitude and U.S. Army dogma was knocked into every West Point graduate that the army never went on the defensive; the U.S. fighting man always and in every case attacked.

Here, however, Bradley chose to believe that the German Army would fall apart of its own accord. The German generals alone would ensure that Hitler was deposed. Then the successful German military plotters would sue for an immediate peace with the West, just as their unfortunate predecessors of the failed July assassination plot had intended to do. Under these circumstances, therefore, why should the U.S. Army suffer any further casualties by attacking at the Reich's weakest point—the Ghost Front?

This definitely must have been General Bradley's train of thought that last week of October 1944 when this remarkable and exciting piece of information was relayed to him from Hodges's headquarters at the Belgian town of Spa. He must have thought the war in the West was almost over and the boys would be going home before Christmas after all, as the press had predicted.

The rude awakening came a day later. As Bradley himself confessed ruefully: "The bubble broke when G-2 rechecked its monitoring detachment. The report had originated not from Cologne." It had ironically enough originated in a small secret radio which he, General Bradley, had been instrumental in setting up. Indeed he had often boasted to "visiting firemen" that he was the only general in the whole of the U.S. Army who "had his own radio station."

The report of the von Rundstedt revolution had come not from the enemy side of the Ghost Front but from a hilltop site, some ten miles from his own headquarters in the Hotel Alfa in Luxembourg City.

5

Office So Hush-Hush

Back in that first exciting week of September 1944, when the 5th Armored Division set off to win the race to be the first division of Gerow's V Corps to cross into Germany, the "Victory Division" paused briefly to liberate the Luxembourg capital on 10 September. One day later the troopers drove up the hilly road that led to the German border at Echternach to capture a small villa and later a radio station set on a hill at the Luxembourg township of Junglinster. From there they could see the German hills which hid the Siegfried Line.

But at that moment the coming battle to capture Hitler's West Wall was far from their minds. General Bradley himself had ordered the priority occupation of this twenties-style commercial radio station, set in a field of high transmission masts, which for some reason the retreating Germans had not destroyed. Later it was discovered they had hoped to retake the place which had played an important role in the secret war in the shadows during their four-year occupation of the little principality. Hastily the Americans nailed up a board outside the deserted radio station. It read in the military shorthand of the time: "PWD-SHAEF—NO ADMITTANCE." To the average GI passing on his way to the coming battle, it meant nothing save "no admittance," which meant no looting or souvenir hunting. But to General Bradley and later Washington, it meant a lot. For what was to be set up on that little prewar commercial station with the powerful transmitter, which had broadcast to England, France, and Germany before the war, would be the first of its kind on continental Europe.

Almost immediately the station was placed under the command of a U.S. colonel who was then replaced on 23 October by Colonel Samuel Rosenbaum, a prewar lawyer from Philadelphia. But Colonel Rosenbaum was really only an able front and administrator. The real power behind the throne was a dark-haired, hook-nosed German-Jewish writer, who had fought in this same area as a sergeant-volunteer in the French Army back in 1940 and had now returned as a first lieutenant (later) captain in the U.S. forces.

His name was Hans Habe, who had been trained by the U.S. Army first in intelligence and then in a new form of warfare—psychological. A form which the Americans had borrowed from the British "black" broadcasting stations, which had long been trying to suborn the average German soldier with propaganda made up of a clever mixture of truth and lies.

With him Habe brought a mixed bag of German and central European Jewish refugees of various political convictions, including communism, but who all spoke fluent German. Most were writers or connected with the arts, and under Habe's guidance they set about misleading their German Army listeners some ten miles away and even further afield with "white" propaganda during the daylight hours. At night, however, when the old commercial transmitter was officially closed down, their "black" propaganda experts took over.

These experts went to work after midnight from a heavily guarded villa in Luxembourg City's Rue Brasseur. For they were not going to run the risk of being attacked and captured in the lonely and poorly guarded hilltop station at Junglinster. Instead their broadcasts, which went on until dawn, were patched in from a sealed, blacked-out van outside the secret headquarters and were given the code-name "Secret Broadcasting Station 1212."* This strangely named station broadcast a mixture of truth, lies, and half-lies. It was one of these broadcasts which had so excited Hodges's G-2 with its account of von Rundstedt's supposed bid for power in Cologne.

Station "Radio Annie," as it was known to its German listeners who risked imprisonment or even death if they were caught listening to it, also had another and more important function than just broad-

---

* It may well be that the British, too, were involved in this secret operation, although it came under General Bradley's direct control. For the British SIS (Secret Service) gave numbers to their target countries and Nazi Germany was "12." Their German counterparts used to toast in their cups (for they knew the code) "*Twelveland uber Alles.*"

casting propaganda. Under the command of American Major Patrick Dolan, it also worked for the "Office of Strategic Services." The OSS, or "Office So Hush-Hush" as it was sometimes maliciously called, was America's first real secret service and a forerunner of today's CIA.

In this capacity, Dolan's German-speaking broadcasters feigned to be members of a secret German resistance movement, mostly made up of high-ranking Wehrmacht officers who were working within the Reich. In other words, they weren't renegades, being paid by the Americans to do their dirty work of subversion for them from some comfortable and safe billet in a U.S. camp. On the contrary, these were supposedly brave men, working within Germany, who were risking both *"Kopf und Kragen"* (literally "collar and head," i.e., risking their necks) in an attempt to overthrow the Hitler regime.

But the fake resisters hoped for more from their black propaganda broadcasts. They hoped to achieve the long-term aim of the most powerful OSS representative in Europe, the Switzerland-based Allen Dulles, future head of the CIA and brother of U.S. Secretary of State for Foreign Affairs John Foster Dulles.

Allen Dulles had more concrete plans for the future of Germany than did the boss of the OSS, General Donovan, and his commander, President Roosevelt. Donovan wanted Germany's defeat and that was about it. Roosevelt wanted "unconditional surrender" from the Germans and was a supporter of the "Morgenthau Plan," proposed by his friend and secretary of state for agriculture. This plan stated that a defeated Germany should be reduced to an agricultural country as it had been back in the eighteenth century. For his part, Allen Dulles, who had done a great deal of business in Germany before the war (his sister was probably a Nazi and his brother, Foster, had been on the prewar board of IG Farben, the great German chemical conglomerate, which produced among other things "Zyklon B," used in the concentration camp gas chambers), wanted a prosperous, relatively independent postwar Germany.

Naturally he wanted this postwar state to be rid of Nazis. Yet he advocated it should be ruled by the same right-wing class who had supported Hitler for personal and professional reasons; the kind of people he had already done business with and with whom he could do business again in the future. In short, Dulles envisaged a postwar

German Republic that was not broken and beaten as the circle around Roosevelt believed should be the case.

But in order to achieve this aim, he would need a body of people in that country—generals, aristocrats, senior government officials, businessmen, even politicians—who could take over Germany when the inevitable collapse came. He had already built up such a circle of anti-Nazi resisters from Switzerland in 1943-44. But the failure of the July assassination on the Fuhrer had destroyed that circle. Now he tried again using, in part, "Radio Annie."

Eisenhower, he knew, would not dare deal directly with the Germans from Paris. His headquarters there was too transparent, and "Ike," who already knew that he would go into politics, could not risk being involved in such negotiations after Roosevelt had lectured the Joint Chiefs of Staff on the subject, concluding with "I am not willing at this time to say that we do not intend to destroy the German nation ... I think that the simplest way of approaching this whole matter is to stick to what I have said—that the Allies have no intention of destroying the German people ... [but rather are] determined to administer a total defeat on Germany as a whole." In other words, official policy toward Germany was simply beat the Germans and don't plan any cooperation with, or future for, the German people.

This placed Eisenhower in a quandary. He did not like Morgenthau or his "Morgenthau Plan." Neither did he take to Roosevelt's policy of unconditional surrender. He knew both doctrines meant that a Germany without hope for a future would fight to the bitter end. What had the Germans to lose?

As a result his directives to his intelligence staff assigned no priority to deep penetration of the front, especially that in the Eifel–Ardennes area, the Ghost Front. Indeed General Hodges banned the agents of the Office of Strategic Services from the area of his army (not that they took much notice of that ban, as we shall see). Eisenhower ordered that any secret intelligence missions run into the Reich should take no risks or enter into no long-term gambles, "save in exceptional circumstances with the express permission of this headquarters." As one of Allen Dulles's crestfallen assistants summed up Eisenhower's directives: "The Western Allies did not propose using German militarists to defeat German militarism."

But that was Eisenhower's *official* policy, issued to cover himself and make sure that his political future would never be tainted by any hint of having done a wartime deal with Hitler's Nazis.

Unofficially, it seems, he was prepared to make some kind of deal with the Germans, in particular, their generals, which might help him get through the Siegfried Line and to the Rhine. This would break the winter stalemate on Germany's border where casualties in riflemen were running so high in the fighting divisions that General George Catlett Marshall, his boss and mentor, once he had seen the appalling situation in Europe during his October tour of the front, immediately authorized the dispatch of nine infantry regiments overseas, in advance of the divisions to which they belonged.

But how could these contacts, if any, be established away from the prying eyes of his great headquarters at the Trianon Palace in Versailles? There were spies of all types and nationalities there—Britishers like Lt. Colonel Anthony Blunt, who was working for the Russians; Lt. Colonel Bernie Bernstein, working for Secretary Morgenthau and through him for Roosevelt; perhaps even Kay Summersby herself, as Patton suspected. (General Gavin, commander of the U.S. 82nd Airborne once told the author he thought there was an even higher level Russian spy at Ike's headquarters revealing operational plans to Moscow. General Strong, when asked about this, told me that this was impossible.) How could Eisenhower from Versailles attempt a separate deal with the Germans, already forbidden by Roosevelt, which would not arouse the suspicions of the Russians, perhaps causing a split between the Allies? It would have been impossible.

So another and more secret location had to be found for any possible contacts with the Germans. What better place was there than Luxembourg and Bradley's headquarters with the radio station attached? After all, for an army group commander, in charge of the fate of nearly a million American soldiers, Bradley did exhibit a strangely possessive streak with regard to this supposedly minor propaganda broadcasting station. What concern of his, one would have thought, was this station, run by a handful of foreign Jews, attempting to weaken the morale of a bunch of German privates? After all, they might listen to American propaganda, ribald tales of the sexual activities of their superiors, and Glenn Miller talking to them in broken German and playing them his German-edited recordings of "In the Mood" and "Little Brown Jug," but that did not make them desert and fight less when the Americans attacked their West Wall yet again.

But as a means of attracting enemy contacts in remote Junglinster, away from the gossip, the spying, and backbiting of SHAEF's huge, bustling headquarters, it was ideal for Eisenhower's purpose. And by mid-October 1944, it seemed to be working.

Shortly after Bradley was informed that it was his own propaganda station that had broadcast the sensational story of the SS colonel and Field Marshal von Rundstedt, Captain Habe received a surprising telephone call from a Sergeant Eaton. Naturally, in the circles in which Habe moved, most of the foreign-born GIs didn't use their real names. Eaton was a nom de guerre. In reality the sergeant came from Nuremburg but had moved to the United States as a child. Now Eaton informed Habe he was "in a lot of difficulties, Captain."

Habe queried as to what kind of difficulties, and to his surprise Eaton replied, "With a major general, sir." Captain Habe, who knew that Eaton was always having run-ins with his superiors, though so far it had only been those up to the rank of colonel, queried, "Who ... which?"

He was shocked when Eaton replied simply, "He's a German major general, sir. I brought him in and he wants to talk to you specifically."

Habe was in a quandary. He knew that the whole black propaganda operation was secret, yet his journalistic curiosity was aroused by Eaton's words. So he ordered, "Bring him in as soon as you can—and keep your mouth shut!"

It was just growing light the next morning when Eaton turned up his radio propaganda van with its loudspeakers in the courtyard of the house in the Rue Brasseur, where Habe and Major Dolan, head of the OSS operation, waited for this mysterious German major general.

Dressed now as an American officer, complete with captain's bars (probably to impress his prisoner), Eaton brought in the major general. "General von P," as Habe described him much later, "was a grey-haired, impressive looking figure, with charming manners."

Eaton had captured him (if that was the right description for what had happened) in the woods near Verdun. Now the German general told Habe and Dolan, "The war is over. The continuation of this war is a crime against the German people."

General von P, who had previously been fortress commandant at Metz where Patton was now fighting desperately to take the Lorraine city, stated that he was so sick of the regime that he was prepared to "address the German people over the Luxembourg broadcasting station." How he knew about the Junglinster operation was never explained.

Thus it was that Habe added a German general to his staff who broadcast regularly every evening at eight o'clock in a program beamed at his former comrades and subordinates just across the border.

But there abruptly came a change in the German general's fortunes. Habe was told by his superior, Colonel Powell, that General von P had been captured in the Third Army's area of operations and that he needed to be returned there : "Before General Patton gets on to this, we've got to smuggle your general back into the Third Army area."

That must have sounded like a very silly order. Why should Patton, fully engaged with two corps, concern himself with the whereabouts of a renegade, turncoat elderly German general? But colonels are colonels and captains are captains. Thus it was that Sergeant Eaton commandeered an ambulance and together with Habe took General von P for an "outing." Half an hour or so later, they crossed the border into French Lorraine and halted near a wood leading up to the heights of Verdun. There they suggested General von P might like to "stretch his legs."

The general was not disinclined and the two plotters saw him safely on a woodland path. Before the German officer could realize what was happening, they were back in the box-like ambulance and rocketing back to Luxembourg the way they had come, leaving the general a free man—for a while. Next day, Habe and Eaton heard through the intelligence grapevine that General von P had been "captured" by Patton's men. As Habe commented, tongue in cheek, many years later, "To the best of my knowledge that this was the first time that a warder ever ran away from his prisoner, especially one who held the exalted rank of major general."

What happened to General von P later remains a mystery. Indeed, even his original "capture" by Sergeant Eaton, if that was what it really was, is a mystery, too. But then that last week of October 1944 is filled with mysteries, which have remained unsolved to this very day.

In particular was the mystery of the intelligence war in the shadows being conducted along that remote frontier between Luxembourg and Germany. Today, one of the questions still remaining unanswered is who was the most successful player in this strange game of treachery, betrayal, deception and—possibly—murder.

It has long been generally supposed that the Germans were no good at deception and what the British used to call "the great game." Indeed, if we accept the British version of the secret war between 1939 and 1945, they were the winners hands down. Their "Double Cross Committee" fooled the Germans right to the very end that their spies in the UK were working for the Reich, while, without exception, they were double agents, all "turned" by the clever, calculating upper-class British spymasters. Later came ULTRA. Again, the British and later their American allies never once let the Germans suspect that their top codes had been compromised. It was the same with Anglo-American commanded resistance movements in Occupied Europe. When the Germans had been defeated and their turn came to set up their own resistance movement in postwar defeated Germany, they failed to do so. In short, the Germans were a thickheaded race with no subtlety or talent for deception.

But as they say, the proof of the pudding is in the eating. In this case, the Germans prepared an excellent pudding prior to the great secret counterattack in the Eifel–Ardennes and when it came apparently it caught the Allies by complete surprise. So cannot we conclude that in this particular instance, the Germans won the battle of deception? They won it, not because the Allied code-reading operation, ULTRA, had failed. Nor on account of the euphoric mood of the senior Allied commanders that autumn, who believed the war was virtually won and at any moment the German Army in the West would collapse; therefore, there was no need for other measures to fool them about Allied intentions. The Germans won the war in the shadows at this point because they actively planned and worked to win it.

Lt. Colonel Hermann Giskes, middle-aged, sardonic, and somewhat foxy-faced, as befitted a member of his profession, had volunteered for the reformed and enlarged German Army in 1937. Instead of returning to the artillery in which he had served in World War I, he took the advice of a friend who maintained Giskes would be "shot to pieces" if he ever went to war with an anti-tank gun battery. Instead he joined Admiral Wilhelm Canaris's "*Abwehr*," the German Secret Service, about which he knew nothing.

But in the bad years between the wars, he had been a traveling salesman, was quick at assessing people of all types and classes, and could think on his feet. In his new job in counterintelligence he learned quickly and would end World War II as Germany's most successful agent, with nearly one hundred captured enemy agents plus numerous German traitors to his credit.*

In a mere two years after the outbreak of World War II, Giskes passed from amateur to professional status, bringing off his most successful coup in 1942 when he started "Operation North Pole," which resulted in the capture and partial turning of fifty Dutch agents in the employ of the British SIS. He even fooled Anthony Blunt, the double agent who, while working for British Intelligence, also worked for the Russians and was one of the spymasters responsible for sending the Dutch parachute agents to their doom or the dishonor of having to work for the Germans. Some said too that Giskes masterminded the operation which forecast and betrayed the great paradrop at Arnhem, which ended in a terrible defeat.

By the summer of 1944, Giskes had survived the various disasters which had attacked Germany and in particular his own organization, *Abwehr*. Implicated in the plot to assassinate Hitler, his chief, Admiral Canaris, known behind his back as "Father Christmas" because of his benign manner and shock of white hair, had been arrested and would be strangled slowly to death by the SS guards at the Flossenburg Concentration Camp. Before that happened, his secret service was absorbed into the SS's own spy organization, the

---

* Ironically enough, his success made him an ideal recruit for the postwar "Gehlen Organization," set up by Allen Dulles and General Sibert and which worked primarily for the fledgling CIA. (General Gehlen, head of Russian intelligence in the Wehrmacht, went over with all his staff to the Americans in 1945.)

Sicherheitsdienst (SD), under the command of young, cunning ex-lawyer General Walter Schellenberg. Again Giskes came out of the debacle, which saw the arrest of many of his Abwehr colleagues, smelling of roses.

So it was that Giskes escaped from the chaos of the defeated Wehrmacht in the West, successfully fleeing through the Allied lines and arriving safely in the Reich. But again, the great spy catcher played it clever. Instead of heading for Berlin or Hamburg out of which he had worked originally, he asked for a posting to the remote Eifel area and the relatively quiet (after September) front there. Obviously it was Giskes's aim to keep away from the centers of power— "In such places you get noticed, you know." And as a long-time member of a compromised organization, many of whose surviving officers were making a run for it to safe neutral countries to sell their secrets to the Allies, Giskes did not want to be noticed.

He was granted his wish and was posted to the command of a small secret outfit called *"Frontaufklarungskommando 307,"* with his headquarters in a small town just outside the Rehnish city of Bonn. This "Front Reconnaissance Commando 307" was a "cushy number," and one that did keep Giskes in relative obscurity.

Naturally he had dealings in this job with the civil authorities, police, SD, Nazi Party, Gestapo, etc.; but, in essence, Giskes report-ed directly to the German Army in the form of Field Marshal Model's Army Group B headquarters which was in the process of moving from Krefeld to a remote hunting lodge some ten miles out-side the picturesque tourist town of Munster-Eifel, close to the Ghost Front.

Giskes's tasks were pretty much routine. He had to keep an eye on the many thousand foreign workers (in particular, the Belgians, Luxembourgers, Dutch, etc.) working on extending the West Wall fortifications. For this purpose Giskes recruited, as he had done before in Belgium, France, and Holland, natives of those countries who were prepared to betray their fellow countrymen—at a price.*

Giskes's tasks also entailed the arrest of deserters and what were called in German *"frontlaufer"* (literally, "front runners"), i.e., men

---

*This kind of mass betrayal may come as a surprise to many readers, but it must be remembered that as late as autumn 1944, there were several score Jews, for instance, working in Berlin for the Gestapo, whose task it was to spot their fellow Jews and betray them to their murderers.

and women, sometimes even children, who crossed and recrossed the front between friend and foe for their own nefarious purposes.

In short, that autumn before he was handed his last great double-game of the war, one that would surpass "Operation North Pole" of 1942-44 when he captured so many Allied agents in Holland, Giskes was very much concerned with the many foreigners of all types, races, and political creeds, who worked and lived in the area of what the Americans called the "Ghost Front."

It was work to which he was accustomed and it occasioned the old spy catcher few difficulties. However, there was one Allied organization working in his general area which was threatening to cause him a nasty headache if he didn't nip it in the bud.

To this day, it is not known (at least to this author) who authorized the establishment of this secret Franco-American unit in the outskirts of the Luxembourg city of Ettelbruck, some thirty-odd kilometers to the north of Luxembourg City, and ensured that it remained secret from not only First Army intelligence but perhaps also General Sibert at Omar Bradley's headquarters. We can only guess that it was no less a person than General Bradley, the Army Group commander himself. For the outfit in question was, according to the common rules of military protocol, operating illegally. In essence, an intelligence unit which belonged to Patton's Third Army command was working underground with the Luxembourg Maquis in the area of General Hodges's First Army. Generals, as is well-known, are exceedingly jealous of their rights and prerogatives. They have been known to blow their tops when they sense any infringement of these basic "rights." Hodges, as mild-mannered and colorless as he was, would have been no exception. But Hodges was never allowed to find out.

The unit was established in late autumn in a former mental home (probably a good place for any intelligence outfit) on the outskirts of Ettelbruck by Colonel Bilbane, an officer and future general of the French Army. Under his command he had Lieutenant Jacques Ramet and Capitaine Henri Le Gueranic. All wore U.S. uniforms quite illegally and were without ID and dogtags. In essence, U.S. military police could have arrested them as spies or imposters on sight. All the same, these three French officers stationed in the local *Verrucktenanstalt* came under the direct command of Patton's chief of intelligence, bespectacled, middle-aged Colonel Oscar Koch.

With them, the French had the usual staff of a small unit, drivers, guards, etc., all Americans, plus a small special group who kept to themselves. They were forgers, the whole lot of them. It was their task to fake German passes, leave orders, photos, etc., and as one U.S. officer who was attached to the outfit later wrote: "Make special permissions and the like by means of half a potato." (A juicy potato is sliced in half. The half is then pressed on, say, a German stamp and with a bit of care that stamp could then be transferred to another document.)

Finally, as that same officer, Captain Charles De Mars Barnes of Koch's G-2, wrote, there was a civilian, Victor Abens, who also worked out of the insane asylum. He was this secret outfit's liaison man with the local Luxembourger Militia (*Miliz*). As Barnes noted, "He (Abens) said he wouldn't take orders from us—they were an independent organization—but he and his comrades worked hard on our behalf without pay or recognition. And after the Battle of the Bulge, they never received any kind of official thanks for their contribution."

As Captain Barnes noted in his own privately printed account of the illegal Third Army outfit, it had three tasks: "To work with the local resistance and through it question Luxembourg deserters from the German Army and refugees from over the border. Second, to slip agents over the front line into Germany; and third, to carry out special operations on behalf of the staff."

One might ask what was Patton's staff doing carrying out spy missions in the area of another army command? An answer might be found in that amazing, apparently on the post, decision by Patton on 19 December, three days after the battle of the Bulge had commenced, to turn his whole army around and advance into the Bulge. Even Eisenhower thought Patton had gone mad at last. How could he prepare to send three divisions northward toward the besieged town of Bastogne at such short notice? The simple answer was, Patton could not—he had already ordered his staff on 12 December to prepare for the move, four days before the German attack and seven before his astonishing announcement to Eisenhower at the great crisis conference at Verdun, which changed the course of the battle.

Was it the secret source chaneled to Patton's headquarters from the Ettelbruck insane asylum base which provided "Ole Blood an'

Guts" with his prior knowledge of the German intentions on the Ghost Front? If it was, why didn't the world—and Patton was certainly no shrinking violet when it came to personal publicity—learn about it?

Colonel Hermann Giskes, at his headquarters outside Bonn, was naturally not concerned with such great matters. He wished to sit out the war in peace and in due course, like all good Germans, enjoy a fat pension.* But he knew he had to put an end to the activities of the Luxembourg Miliz working under Patton's orders in such an indirect fashion. Thus again, the reluctant spymaster was brought into contact with foreigners on the Ghost Front, who later would figure so prominently in his great covert operation, *"Untermahen Heinrich."*

The basic problem centered on the small tourist town of Vianden on the Luxembourg–German border. The town in the valley was dominated by the ruined eleventh-century de Lannoy castle, which was occupied by a half company of American infantry. The town below was in no-man's land, where the Luxembourg Miliz and their U.S. allies roamed freely through the narrow, cobbled streets during the daylight hours. At night, however, things changed drastically. Then the GIs withdrew to the safety of the ancient castle while below the Germans crept in like gray sinister predatory wolves looking for pickings.

In those periods when this strange kind of no-man's land was relatively quiet, Captain Charles de Mars Barnes's agents would assemble on the castle walls high above the valley and survey through their glasses the German lines on the opposite ridge beyond the water. Aided by the Miliz, they would select the best route for their forthcoming operations and then, when the time was ripe, disappear. More often than not they never came back. For if the enemy patrols didn't apprehend them, Giskes's people would.

On other occasions, when both sides decided they would make trouble for one reason or another, there would be regular company-sized firefights, even ambushes and all-out battles in the narrow cobbled streets. For the Luxembourg militia, mostly deserters from the German Army (as German citizens since 1940, Luxembourgers were

---

*Giskes was to be disappointed. The British had long memories. And they remembered Holland. Giskes was arrested and according to his statement to the author, "suffered unpleasant and disgraceful treatment" at the hands of his British captors. But he talked, just as they wanted him to.

drafted like the normal German male), if captured they faced immediate execution for desertion "in the face of the enemy." As a result,
rather than surrender, they fought to the bitter end. The Germans did
likewise. The result was a series of merciless skirmishes at company
and platoon level in which quarter was neither given nor expected.

We can suppose that Giskes was not particularly concerned
whether the Luxembourg deserters died or not. But he was very
interested in obtaining all the information he could from them. He
wanted to know two things from whatever prisoners he managed to
save: their contacts on the German side of the front and the U.S.
intelligence setup at both Ettelbruck and Junglinster. For there had
been a surprising development as October gave way to November
1944. He, Giskes, a humble half-colonel, had been invited to eat
with no less a person than Field Marshal Walther Model; and Giskes
was in no doubt about why. Model did not want conventional intelligence; he could leave that to his staff-trained officers at headquarters. The "Boy Marshal" wanted something else, which Giskes alone
could provide—covert intelligence of the most dangerous kind.

6

The Spymaster and the Commando

Field Marshal Model was working against the clock. So far, von Rundstedt had not been told about the coming offensive in the West, though he must have guessed what was going on behind his back. But Model had been in the circle of officers personally briefed by Hitler. The Fuhrer had also set deadlines for the attack. At the end of October he had told his pale, cunning chief of operations, General Alfred Jodl, "I'd rather not wait any later than mid-November. We must attack when the weather is bad. That will create more of a surprise and at the same time hamper enemy aviation."

"It will hamper ours as well," Jodl objected mildly. General Jodl was never one for crossing swords on issues, even vital ones, with the Fuhrer. "Since ours is the weaker, it is to our advantage to have neither one come into play," Hitler had responded. A few days later, after reading the latest army weather forecasts based on data from a secret German weather station in the Arctic Circle,* he decreed that the great offensive should commence on November 15.

All this was relayed to Model, who was working at top speed in his remote headquarters, drinking heavily, and making his staff officers' lives a living hell. He objected that he could not be ready till the forecasted dismal weather period in December. He had other strategic objections, too, but was waiting for von Rundstedt's support before he placed them before the Fuhrer.

---

* Although the British, Canadian, American, and even Russian forces actively sought these German weather stations, they never discovered them and, indeed, the key one, relaying the forecasts for the Ardennes offensive, only surrendered some four months after Germany's defeat.

In the meantime he made his daily eight-hour rounds of the front, sometimes disguised as a nondescript colonel. He often went into the frontline positions in order to observe the American positions facing his troops.

Model had his doubts about the coming offensive. Fire-eater that he was—and at the end, the only German field marshal to commit suicide rather than surrender—he thought the Fuhrer was biting off more than he could chew. But his personal assessment of the Allied capacity for resistance, especially in the Eifel–Ardennes sector, was realistic, even optimistic. As he reported to Hitler:

> The enemy does not have a continuous main line of resistance. He carries on a defensive battle of strongpoints about four to five kilometers in depth. In most forward line areas, relatively strong security elements are placed in well-developed positions. These security elements yield systematically in case of strong attacks and retreat to strongpoints behind them. The strongpoints are organized chessboard fashion, with flanking effect, well adapted to terrain sectors, localities, woodpatches and crossroads. At the strongpoints which are well defended even when surrounded, well-camouflaged tanks, tank destroyers and heavy weapons, especially anti-tank and mortars form the backbone. Stronger reserves are in position several kilometers behind the zone of strongpoints in centrally located points, such as villages or forest patches near main highways. They are full motorized and are committed to combat groups of two or three infantry companies with eight to ten tanks. They go into action about six hours after an attack starts.

This was an excellent analysis of the American defensive tactics, especially in Middleton's Ghost Front, and it shows just how well the Germans had been able to penetrate VIII Corps's lines. Unlike Middleton and Bradley, who seemed to know surprisingly little of what was going on in the rear areas of German Army Group B, Model's reconnaissance groups and patrols had done a tremendous job behind the U.S. lines since late September.

In a matter of six short weeks, while working all-out to build up a large attack force from a shattered Wehrmacht, the Germans had penetrated deep behind the American positions. They had obviously pinpointed U.S. strongpoints, but also the Americans's rearline workshops, POL supply dumps, tank repair sites, and even the all-important top secret landline that linked Hodges's, Bradley's and Eisenhower's headquarters. On 16 December 1944, when the offensive commenced, the wire conduit would be one of the first objectives of the German vanguard. They would cut and break all telephone communications between SHAEF at Versailles and Bradley's Luxembourg City headquarters. This would be a major factor in the later division of command between Bradley in the south and Montgomery in the north, a separation that would have a profound effect on the Anglo-American alliance and the future strategy of the war in Europe.

These long-range German patrols and reconnaissance also showed Model that the American front was held only to a depth of five or six miles. Behind it, right up to the Germans's major obstacle, the River Meuse, the Americans had only a handful of combat units. The front was, in other words, an eggshell, which, if tapped hard enough, would break open to reveal the weak liquid mass beneath.

Naturally this information must have been greeted with joy by Model's hard-pressed staff. But it had an obverse side. The combat formations that were available to the north under the command of Montgomery and General William H. Simpson, the commander of the newly arrived U.S. Ninth Army, and General Patton's Third Army to the south would be available for a counterattack. If the Americans knew the German intentions, they could employ these combat formations (and in early November most of Eisenhower's armored divisions were behind the lines, not engaged in combat) at the most critical point of breakthrough. It was therefore imperative, Model knew, to fool Allied intelligence about his strategic goals.

By now Model knew that the Allies must have spotted his two panzer armies, the Fifth and the Sixth SS, arriving in the general area of Cologne from their refitting areas farther north. He reasoned that Allied intelligence would jump to the obvious conclusion: these armored formations would be used for a German counterattack on both sides of the Cologne–Aachen autobahn southward, once the Anglo-Americans had launched their anticipated attack to the River Rhine along the same axis. If he could convince Allied intelligence this was his intention it would allow him to employ his armor on the

Ghost Front with impunity. After all, the Americans had a mere two armored combat commands of the green U.S. 9th Armored Division to stop his massed panzers along the whole length of Middleton's VIII Corps front.

But would the Allies fall for it? Would they leave their military dispositions as they were? For it was vital that they concentrate their forces in the north and keep them there as long as possible, even after the counteroffensive had commenced. Model remembered how the Allies had tricked the Fuhrer into believing they would invade the Pas de Calais area for some time after they had landed on D-day in Normandy. The German 15th Army around the Calais, including two of the powerful SS divisions, had been wasted when they might have turned the tide in the first days of the invasion when the Allies had little of their armor ashore.

Up to now, his own intelligence service had successfully fooled the Americans about the German build-up on the Ghost Front. Now he needed another intelligence deception which would maintain that status quo. For it was vital that Eisenhower not reinforce Middleton in advance, especially with armor. He knew that Eisenhower would send tank divisions to the point of the German breakthrough once the balloon went up. But until he did, every hour gained would be of value. With a bit of luck, his panzers would be across the River Meuse and heading for their main objective, the key supply port of Antwerp, before the Americans could react.

Colonel Giskes's hour of destiny had come.

Hermann Giskes drove down the side roads of the Eifel between the forested hills wondering why he had really been summoned to the Army Group headquarters. A dozen different possibilities ran through his mind. But as he recalled much later, "It was the same when I was posted from France and Holland to start 'Operation North Pole' [the great double-cross operation against the British in 1942–44], a kind of journey into the unknown. One thing was certain: I had never been ordered to attend a commander-in-chief before."

Another thing was certain, too. Since he had last passed this way during his flight from Brussels back in August, the landscape had changed dramatically. The forest and forest tracks were full of troops and camouflaged dumps of ammunition, cannons, petrol, tanks, and equipment. It reminded him somewhat of the great German March offensive of 1918, the *"Kaiserschlacht"* ("Emperor's Battle") in which he had taken part as a young officer.

The railheads, such as Gerolstein, through which he passed were very busy too, even though it was daylight and there was the ever-present danger of aerial attack from low-flying Allied fighter-bombers, the hated Jabos. Here and there transport staffs were using smokescreens, though Giskes thought this was self-defeating. Smoke might well attract air attacks.

Finally Giskes reached Model's headquarters and was received in the wooden hunting lodge in the middle of the forest clearing, which served as his main building some ten kilometers away from the partially walled tourist town of Munster-Eifel. Together with another colonel of intelligence, Giskes was received by Model himself. The field marshal strode in, cleaning his monocle which was fogged from the November cold outside, and barked at the colonels who were both standing rigidly to attention like recruits in front of the much-feared C-in-C. "Can you think of any plan which would fool the Western Allies as to the strategic intentions of my Army Command?" Without pause the aggressive Model, who had somewhat bulging eyes, as if he might be suffering from a thyroid condition (an affliction of an estimated one-fifth of the German population), added "And by the way, it must involve Allied nationals so that it would be entirely convincing."

Now Giskes realized why he had been summoned. For most of his career, working against the British SIS since 1918, he had used foreign agents and turncoats. Model presumably had been told he was the expert in this. It was flattering but at the same time disconcerting. As he told the author many years later, "Why should any foreign national who was right in the head work for Germany now that the country was about to lose the war?"

Giskes knew that there were millions of foreigners in factories, work gangs, and military formations (one-third of the Waffen SS, for instance, was foreign-born) still in German employ. But they were mainly inside Germany. The only foreigners still working for the Third Reich outside her borders—and, in the main, they did it for money—were employed by Colonel Otto Skorzeny's Jagdkommando.

Most of those were "sleepers" whom the scarfaced head of the German special forces had purposely left behind in the Low Countries and France as the Wehrmacht had fled.

Giskes, however, was by no means a fool. He was not going to tell a German field marshal, especially one with an explosive temper like Model, that a mission of this nature was impossible. Instead he asked for four hours to consider the matter. In his customary brisk manner, Model agreed and handed Giskes over to his chief of staff, General Hans Krebs. The latter had little time to waste on this obscure, low-ranking spy catcher. In his turn he introduced Giskes to Model's chief of intelligence who gave Giskes an excellent lunch—Model did not object to the best—and then left him alone to consider the matter at hand.

According to Giskes, while he considered the problem he found his gaze wandering. Outside it was a typical Eifel November day—grey and foggy, with the mist curling silently through the dripping firs. Somewhere there was the muted sound of artillery. Giskes presumed it was coming from the Hurtgen Forest where once again the "Death Factory" was processing its victims. For what seemed a long time he was undecided. What was he going to tell Model's staff? After all, he had come totally unprepared and although no one had told him, he had now guessed that there was some sort of an offensive in the offing and his plan was going to be part of the overall intelligence deception.

At precisely three o'clock he was summoned to the chief of intelligence's little office once more. Model had left for the front and the pressure on the staff had slightly relaxed. All the same he could see that there was something afoot. Telephones rang all the time, teleprinters clattered, staff officers, elegant but flustered, swept to and fro with folders under their arms, dispatch riders roared away. Yes, Giskes told himself, there was something going on. "*Hier was der Teufel los*" ("Here the Devil was loose"), as he explained it many years later.

Now Giskes made a request. He told the intelligence colonel that he realized Army Group B was going to be involved in some sort of attack; could he see a rough outline of Model's plan? The staff officer was shocked. Everything was being calculated on a "need to know" basis. Even Field Marshal von Rundstedt did not know what was afoot. All he was prepared to tell Giskes, whom he had not met before and was thus an unknown quantity, was that the field marshal was planning something. He, Giskes, would have to take his word for it that this operation was "well beyond the basic planning stage," and that it would shake the "Anglo-American bandits out of their complacency." That was that.

Feeling more uncertain than before, Giskes accepted the condition. "*Jawohl Herr Oberst,*" he snapped with more conviction than he felt. "I shall get to work on it immediately."

The other officer nodded his approval and prepared to dismiss the fox-faced spy catcher. Giskes hesitated momentarily and then added with a careful smile, "But what if my fake cover plan for the enemy ... hits upon the real plan? By mistake, naturally."

Model's chief of intelligence was not amused.

While a worried Giskes cancelled all his other duties in the Eifel to work on the all-important deception plan for Model, Hitler, who was still at his headquarters, took a hand in the business himself. Normally he had little time for intelligence and those who purveyed it, especially if they were concerned with clandestine intelligence. Often he would refuse to shake hands in the German fashion with such people. Now in view of the vital importance of this last counterattack in the West, Hitler was determined to have a say in how intelligence should protect his plan from Allied detection.

In the last week of October, he commanded General Eckhard Christian, chief of operations, to accept one of three copies of one of those customarily long-winded German operations orders, which was entitled "*Die Geheimhaltungsbestimmungen*" ("Rules of Maintaining Secrecy"). The other two went to General Hans Krebs of Model's staff and General Siegfried Westphal, who held the equivalent post of chief of staff at von Rundstedt's headquarters. It read:

> "For us the first two rules are the most important. They read:
> (1) The German High Command is expecting a strong enemy attack against the line Cologne-Bonn ... (2) In order to strike at such a breakthrough ... two strong counter-attack groups will be assembled northwest of Cologne with the other in the Eifel ... Accordingly, in carrying through this deception, it will be necessary

to conceal the massing of strength that will inevitably result in the
Eifel while making out that there are more troops than are actually present in the area northwest of Cologne."

In essence, this cover deception plan maintained that the
Germans would only attack from the Cologne area once the Allies
had started their expected drive for the Rhenish city. It reflected
Model's and later von Rundstedt's thinking for the real attack. For
both favored the "small solution"—a drive from Holland and
Germany with two pincer arms linking up on the Meuse and cutting
off 25 percent of Eisenhower's divisions, American, British, and
Canadian, which were located in that area. As is well-known, Hitler
wanted the "big solution"—the drive to the Belgian coast, which
would split the Anglo-American armies in two.

Giskes naturally knew nothing of Hitler's directive. Such high-
level policy was beyond his ken, just as Model's was. But the middle-
aged spy catcher was a smart man, whose successful career in espionage had been based on his quick wits. Back in 1942, for instance,
at the start of "Operation North Pole," no one in the Abwehr had
really considered turning captured agents and using them in the so-
called "radio game," i.e., relaying doctored information to spymasters in their own countries.

At that time, it had been customary for spy catchers to deliver up
captured spies at once for the kudos they would gain in Abwehr
headquarters in Berlin's Tirpitzufer. Naturally, they thought, promotion and medals depended upon results. Giskes had thought differ-
ently. His captured agents had been hidden in a former seminary in
Holland until they finally agreed to work for the Germans. The
result was that Giskes did not gain immediate promotion for his
efforts; that would come later when he really began to achieve
results.

Now as he looked at the situation in the Eifel, he saw that it centered on the loss of Germany's great imperial city of Aachen, once
the home of no less a person than Charlemagne, a symbolic figure
for the Germans. Hitler, he reasoned (just as American intelligence
officers with a knowledge of German history did), could not afford
to leave Aachen in U.S. hands. Surely he would counterattack, try to
restore the Siegfried Line there, and recapture the old city, perhaps

by Christmas. A "Christmas present" of that kind for the Fuhrer would be a shot in the arm for the German people. Dr. Goebbels would have a propaganda field day.

So the days shortened and—unknown to Giskes—the date of the great surprise offensive came closer and closer. He started to base his deception plan on a German attack on Aachen, once the German armored formations were ready. With the exception of a few minor details, it was the same cover plan that Hitler himself had proposed to fool the Western Allies.

But again, unknown to Giskes, there was an unexpected hiccup which, if the Allies interpreted it correctly, might mean the cancellation of the whole imaginative project. It was a circular sent by ENIGMA (although Hitler had forbidden the use of this means of communication) to divisional and army commands. It read: "VERY SECRET. To Divisional and Army Commands only. Officers and men who speak English are wanted for a special mission. The Fuhrer has ordered the formation of a special unit of approximately two-battalion strength for use on the Western front in special operations and reconnaissance. Volunteers who are selected will report to Dienst-stelle Skorzeny at Friedenthal." It was signed, "Keitel."

Naturally after Bletchley Park had picked up the intercept and translated the German into English the decoders were quite excited. The message was passed on to the related intelligence agencies and was duly read by the relevant chiefs of intelligence on the Continent.

The Keitel circular was naturally a very hot property. In essence, it should have set the alarm bells ringing—it certainly did in the German camp, as we shall see. For it contained three clear indications that the Germans were not going to do what the Allies suspected they might and what Hitler wanted the Allies to believe: counterattack from the Cologne area once the Allies had started their march to the Rhine. First, the circular was signed not by some obscure staff officer but by Hitler's most senior soldier and advisor, Field Marshal Wilhelm Keitel. Second, why would a German army operating inside Germany, when the time came for the Wehrmacht to counterattack, need "men who speak English" for a "special mission?" What kind of special mission could anyone envisage for English-speaking volunteers within the Reich itself?

But the clincher and third clue to German intentions was in the

name and place to which these volunteers would finally report—
"Dienst-Stelle (Place of duty) Skorzeny," located in Friedenthal near
Berlin. Even though a low-ranking Allied intelligence officer might
not know the significance of Friedenthal, which ironically enough
can be translated as "Peace Valley," he would know the man's name.
How could he not know it? For it was a name that had hit the headlines the year before with the ugly mug of the owner of that name
flashed across the world's newsreel screens—why even Churchill had
mentioned Skorzeny in the House of Commons in 1943. And with
good reason. In 1943, his own life had been personally threatened by
that same *Obersturmbannfuhrer*: Otto Skorzeny of the Jagdkommando, Friedenthal.

Otto Skorzeny, a huge man of six foot three with the bulk to go with
it, had a face disfigured by dueling scars from his student days in
Vienna. In German student fraternities, *Schlagende Verbindungen*,*
later forbidden by Hitler, it was the duelist's aim to achieve a facial
scar (*Schmiss*) that would mark him as an "*Akademiker*" and a
brave man to boot. These dueling scars were also an entree into business circles through "old boys" of the same student dueling societies.
With his valor secured early, Skorzeny then went on to make his
name as Germany's leading commando with his daring rescue of the
Italian dictator Mussolini in 1943.

After Mussolini had been deposed, arrested, and spirited away
by his own people to a mountain top in the Italian Gran Sasso, Hitler
had given Skorzeny the task of finding his friend and fellow dictator.
Skorzeny had not only found Mussolini, he had horned his way into
the rescue operation by para-commander, General Kurt Student. To
the latter's chagrin and rage, Skorzeny flew away with the Duce in
the light rescue plane. ("The man was—and is—a terrible upstart.
For the rest of the war I refused to speak to him, save on duty!"
Student, still angry, told the author many years later.) Overnight,
Skorzeny became world famous.

Thereafter in 1943-44, Skorzeny was engaged in several such

---

*A virtually untranslatable term, roughly meaning "striking association," in which
padded and half-masked student opponents from different clubs whacked and
slashed at each other until one of the duelists was cut on the face. This cut (*Schmiss*)
would be doused with a thick black paste that widened it so that in the end a well-
developed scar appeared to mark the duelist as an academic and member of a
"*Schlagende Verbindungen*."

operations. He was probably the mastermind behind "Operation Long Jump," the plot to assassinate Churchill, Stalin, and Roosevelt at their conference in Tehran. It was partially foiled by the local head of security, one General Schwarzkopf, the father of the more famous "Stormin' Norman" of Gulf War fame.

Undeterred by the failure of Operation Long Jump, Skorzeny went on to attempt to assassinate the Yugoslavian resistance leader Marshal Tito. Again he used SS paras for the attempt and barely missed succeeding. But his next daring operation *was* a success.

Code-named "Operation Mickey Mouse," it entailed keeping Germany's ally in the war on Hitler's side by kidnapping the favorite son of the Hungarian dictator, Admiral Horthy. This time Skorzeny, with a handful of SS commandos, pulled it off, snatching the playboy son from under the nose of his father by rolling him up in a carpet and smuggling him out of Budapest. In the end the daring ploy paid dividends and the Hungarians stayed in Germany's camp until the bitter end.

It was an indirect result of that successful Operation Mickey Mouse that Skorzeny was informed by his fellow Austrian, Hitler, of what he intended in the West. After reporting to the Fuhrer on the afternoon of 21 October, and making the latter laugh with the details of the carpet kidnap, Skorzeny was a little surprised when Hitler said, "Stay a while."

Hitler was not one to waste time on his visitors. Some waited for hours, even days, to speak to him. Naturally, Skorzeny accepted the offer with alacrity. Seated side by side on the sofa, Hitler patted the scarfaced giant on the knee and said, "I am now going to give you the most important task of your life." He paused and then added, "In November, Germany will start a great offensive. It may decide her fate."

Skorzeny refrained from expressing surprise. Fanatic, committed, and daring as he was, he felt that Germany was about to lose the uneven struggle. Now the Fuhrer was saying that the Wehrmacht was about to go on the offensive. He waited agog.

Carried away by a kind of enthusiasm which Hitler's court had not seen for months, Hitler explained how the victorious Allies expected to find "a stinking corpse in Germany." Admittedly they had won the "battle of the invasion" only because the Anglo-

Americans had had absolute air superiority. Now however, all that would change.

He, Hitler, had picked a time for his bold counterstroke when the weather would be on his side; it would be "Fuhrer Weather," in this case overcast and bad for flying. In addition, Hitler added, "We will employ two thousand of our new jet fighters that we have kept in reserve for this offensive." He then rambled on about his strategic and political intentions, ending with the words, "I have told you so much so that you will realize that everything has been considered very carefully and has been well worked over...."

Skorzeny must have been in a daze at that moment. Had the Fuhrer gone mad? The army seemed to him to be functioning on a shoestring. As for Germany's cities and key war industries, they were being systematically destroyed day after day by the "Anglo-American terror flyers."

Still he had enough confidence in Hitler's celebrated foresight and ability to pull things out of a hat at the very last moment to keep on listening as he explained the reason for this briefing. "Now you and your units, my dear, Skorzeny," he went on, his Austrian accent getting thicker by the second, "will play a very important role in this offensive. As an advance guard you will capture one or more bridges across the River Meuse between Liege and Namur. You will carry out this operation in British and American uniforms. The enemy has already used this trick," Hitler added bitterly. "Only a couple of days ago, I received the news that Americans dressed in German uniforms during the fighting in Aachen." According to Hitler this use by the Americans of German uniforms had taken place in the last few days of the battle for the old imperial city.*

He let Skorzeny absorb the information for a few moments and the latter tried to recollect the various locations in Belgium and the River Meuse to which the Fuhrer had referred. Then Hitler said, "I know you'll do your best." Then he added that familiar cover plan of which we have already heard. "But now to the most important thing. Absolute secrecy. Only a few people know of the plan. In order to conceal your preparations from your own troops tell them we are expecting a full-scale enemy attack in the area of Cologne and

---

* I have tried to find out more details. There were rangers in the general area, waiting for an assignment in the battle of the Hurtgen Forest, but they deny using German uniforms anywhere.

Bonn. Your preparations are intended to be part of the resistance to that attack."

Skorzeny indicated he understood, but objected, "But time is short, mein Fuhrer, and I have other tasks."

Hitler agreed, but did not offer any assistance to Skorzeny except to tell the commando leader he was sending him a deputy. And that was that, save that when Hitler escorted him to the door to see him out, he warned, "One thing, Skorzeny, I don't want you to cross the front line personally. You must not run the risk of being captured."*

Some ten days later, Skorzeny was shocked beyond all measure when he learned of the Keitel circular. "I thought our operation was betrayed even before it had commenced," he wrote after the war. "I dictated a flaming protest immediately to the Fuhrer's headquarters, and telephoned through my decision to cancel the mission." But Skorzeny's protests to Hitler and Jodl were blocked. He was told he had to go through channels and the channels consisted of Hitler's new brother-in-law, SS General Hermann Fegelein, a vain, womanizing ex-divisional commander who was shot at the end of the war on Hitler's orders as a suspected spy for the British. Fegelein answered Skorzeny by return that it was all very unfortunate. "But I had to abide by the original plan." He, Skorzeny, would have to take his chances just like everyone else connected with the great secret offensive. With that, the commando leader had to be satisfied. Besides he had to get on with other equally top secret assignments, including the use of V-2 weapons against New York (launched from a U-boat) and the first employment of the brand new German underground organization, der Wehrwolf, behind the American lines in the Eifel.

But the great scare occasioned by Keitel's circular blew over, as far as the Germans were concerned, without any repercussions from the Allied side. As we have seen, the British had passed over the information they had gained from the circular to intelligence, in particular to General Bradley's Twelfth Army Group headquarters, run by General Sibert. Amazingly enough no one seemed to take it seri-

---

* Perhaps one should note at this point that the only witness to this conversation who survived the war was Skorzeny himself and as they say in law: "One witness is no witness." Why mention this relatively trivial detail in the light of what he, Skorzeny, had just heard of this tremendous new attack in the West? It is a point bearing in mind when we come to examine Skorzeny's important role in the great deception and what followed.

ously. According to General Bradley, who was questioned about the matter later, the information never reached his headquarters.

To the anxious Germans watching Middleton's Ghost Front for any sign that the Americans had become aware that there was something strange going on—a change of troop dispositions, reinforcements, transfer of armor to the Ardennes–Eifel—it seemed that the Americans had gone to sleep. It appeared to German intelligence that Middleton's VIII Corps was virtually inviting them to attack, for his experienced divisions, the 2nd and 87th Infantry, moved and were replaced by green ones and, in due course, the shattered ones such as the 4th and 28th Infantry from their spell in the Hurtgen "Death Factory."

Three weeks before the commencement of the great secret counteroffensive, the First Army ordered Middleton to put the 23rd Special Troops to work to imitate the buildup of a new division coming into the VIII Corps's line. This was to be the 75th Division arriving, as green as grass from England. The "Special Troops" openly wore 75th Division patches and marked their vehicles and newly erected "command posts" with it. At night they used sound effects of vehicular traffic to indicate convoys of troops coming up front. A whole fictitious radio and wireless telephone center was set up and carried some calls in clear. But as Middleton himself admitted, "For a while the Germans were confused, if not deceived. They placed question marks on their intelligence maps, but removed these after a few days."

As General Hasso von Manteuffel of the German Fifth Panzer Army told his interrogators after the war, "We knew it was a deception within 24 hours." He didn't say how. But he could have mentioned the informants that the Germans had in the border area, whose native dialect was German as was many of their antecedents.

In short, the Germans had gotten the measure of the Americans on Middleton's long front. This gave them confidence—even to disobey Hitler's order of 8 November that stated there would be no further patrolling on the other side of the Our–Sauer River Line. Hitler did not want prisoners taken by the Americans giving the game away, though the low-ranking soldiers taking part in such patrols would hardly be likely to know the "big picture." As we shall see, Skorzeny, in particular, would disobey Hitler's decree time and time again.

But if some of the Fuhrer's officers intimately concerned with the great deception and the secret war in the shadows to and fro across the frontier of the Reich were supremely confident now, Colonel Giskes was not. He was still worried that his fake cover plan might well be the true one. The thought haunted him throughout this period that he, a humble lieutenant colonel, might be the one who was deliberately going to betray the real plan to the Allies. What a catastrophe that would be for Germany; and for him personally.

Giskes had commenced with the problem raised by Field Marshal Model at that brief meeting at his headquarters: How to get Allied civilians to work for Hitler's Germany when the country was obviously facing defeat? Giskes had learned from his past experiences using paid agents—in the final analysis they betrayed you. If they accepted money for their services once, they might well do it again with somone else. So they had to be people who genuinely thought they were working in the interests of their own country when they were working for the Reich on the face of it. It was an old ploy for the veteran spymaster. With this plan in mind, he approached an engineer of his acquaintance, who was currently running one of the frontier labor camps building up and strengthening the West Wall. He told the latter, most of whose workers were Belgians and Luxembourgers, that he wanted him to allow some of his workers to escape.

Naturally the loyal engineer was horrified. He protested it would cost him "his head" if he were discovered. Giskes assured him that he was working in the interests of the Fatherland and told the engineer his "plan."

The engineer had come originally from Saxony. In the great industrial cities of the man's native province, communism had been rife before Hitler had come to power in 1933 (that year six million Germans had voted the communist ticket). Now, Giskes gave the engineer a cover story which fitted in with his past. He was a former communist who had joined one of the new communist cells which were beginning to spring up once more in Germany's cities with encouragement from Russian agents and the Free German Army or Seydlitz Army.* To help his old comrades and naturally the Red

---

*Formed from German officers, mainly captured at Stalingrad, and now working—and fighting—for the Russians. One of the most prominent of the German generals involved was General Friedrich von Seydlitz. Hence the name.

Army which was fighting in the great Allied coalition against Germany, he was now going to pass on information to the Americans on the other side of the Our–Sauer Line.

Naturally the information would contain the details of the counterfeit "Giskes Plan" of the coming German counteroffensive in the Rhineland. The engineer, under Giskes's direction, would select "patriots" among his subordinates who would escape from the daily outside work gangs. These brave Belgians and Luxembourgers would carry with them on their escape the counterfeit information to hand over to the first American officer they came across.

At first this "Operation Heinrich," as it was called and probably named after Giskes's new top boss, Heinrich Himmler, Reichsfuhrer der SS, didn't seem to work, especially in Belgium. That country appeared to be gripped by a spy mania similar to the one existing in Belgium and France back in 1940 when the artist Cocteau mocked people "spied nuns doing up their garters behind every bush."*

The "escapees" were being arrested. In some cases they were shot as spies. Allied commanders seemed to pay no attention to the escapers' reports and a few thought they were a deliberate plant and provocation, which naturally they were. Giskes began to doubt that he would fool the Anglo-Americans this time as he had done in the good years in Holland during "Operation North Pole."

Then he added a new wrinkle to "Operation Heinrich." One of his supposed escapers was supplied with a plan, written in milk (a primitive kind of invisible ink) on odd scraps of paper of the kind available to a poor prisoner. This the escaper secreted in a tobacco pouch deep among the type of coarse Russian shag called "Marhoka," which was their usual ration. The "escaper" was told to hand the pouch and "plan" to the first U.S. officer he encountered once he reached "freedom." He was to tell this officer that if Allied intelligence wanted more of the same, the Junglinster radio station, operated by Captain Habe, should send a message during the 8:15 broadcast to the Wehrmacht. It should read: "And regards to Otto from Saxony." "Otto from Saxony" was naturally the supposed communist agent running the labor camp.

---

*At that time the order was given even to Allied troops to strip suspect women to the waist. This would reveal the red marks of a parachute harness and indicate a German spy. It was probably an order that any red-blooded soldier would have carried out with alacrity, given the chance.

Ten days later the long awaited message from the Habe station came: "And tonight we send regards to Otto from Saxony." Giskes had done it once more. The old spymaster had convinced the Americans, and naturally the representatives of the OSS, America's new secret service, that they were receiving bona fide information. "Operation Heinrich" was working. Now the Giskes message was loud and clear—sure, the Germans would attack; in due course, they would launch "a spoiling assault" from the Cologne–Bonn area." The objective was Aachen; the old imperial city was going to be a Christmas present for the Fuhrer.

Some of the leaders of the German Army in the fall of 1944: (from left
to right) General Kurt "Panzer" Meyer, the commander of the 12th SS
panzer Division "Hitler Youth" who surrendered during the retreat to
Germany in September 1944; General Fritz Witt; SS Commander "Sepp"
Dietrich, founder of Hitler's bodyguard regiment die Liebstandarte; Field
Marshal Gerd von Rundstedt for whom the December offensive was
named.

Generals Omar Bradley [top left], Dwight "Ike" Eisenhower [top right], and George Patton [left] met in Chartres on 2 September 1944 where Eisenhower presented his "broad front" strategy which would create the "Ghost Front" and gave Germany the time for its offensive build-up.

The author visiting the position near Bleialf where the U.S. 4th Division first attempted to infiltrate the Siegfried Line on 16 September 1944.

The town of Bollendorf, located between Echternach and Wallendorf on the River Sauer, was on the German side of the Ghost Front.

Members of the Vianden Maquis who worked with the OSS in the woods and towns of the Ghost Front.

These woods and hills below Vianden castle on the River Sauer made up part of the Ghost Front's no man's land.

Fritz Bayerlein, commander of the Panzerlehr, was one of Germany's top tacticians. He fought in Russia, Africa, at Normandy, and helped hold back the American breech of the West Wall at Wallendorf in September 1944.

Field Marshal Walther Model, commander of the German Army Group B in the fall of 1944, was a ruthless leader hated by his officers but well-liked by the men in the ranks as he often went into the frontline positions to judge conditions himself. Model was one of the few German officers Hitler entrusted with the secret of the planned Rundstedt offensive.

General Troy Middleton, seen above meeting with Allied Supreme Commander Dwight Eisenhower, commanded the U.S. VIII Corps which manned the Ghost Front for almost four months prior to the 16 December 1944 German attack.

Signs such as this one were posted along the German border in the Ghost Front reminding American troops that peril lay beyond the silence of the Allied lines.

Soldiers of the 4th U.S. Infantry Division, some of whom are shown here during the bloody battle of the Hurtgen Forest, were transferred from the Hurtgen to the Ghost Front just a few weeks before the German offensive.

General Edwin Sibert, Omar Bradley's chief of intelligence, held to the idea that the Germans were too weakened after their defeat in September 1944 to do anything but defend their position even though intelligence reports suggested otherwise. Sibert would later be one of the founders of the postwar CIA.

This radio station in Junglinster, Luxembourg, was taken over by Omar Bradley to broadcast propaganda to the German people during the fall of 1944. One of the broadcasts would fool Bradley himself when it was mistakenly intercepted as coming from Germany.

Special German reconnaissance patrols such as this one penetrated behind the VIII Corps's lines prior to and during the German offensive giving vital intelligence reports to Model, Skorzeny, and others of the German command. Many of these patrols used captured American jeeps and uniforms in these forays behind American lines.

The Napoleon Cross in the woods near the crossroads between Poteau and Vielsalm was used as a meeting point for German reconnaissance teams behind the American lines on the Ghost Front.

Otto Skorzeny, leader of the Jagdkommando and the 150th Panzer Brigade, was one of Hitler's favorite intelligence officers. He is thought to have been given the assignment to assassinate General Dwight Eisenhower—an accusation he denied after the war.

The Petit Trianon in Versailles served as Eisenhower's SHAEF headquarters during the fall and winter of 1944-45. This is where it is theorized the attempt on his life was to take place.

Captain Charles Barnes (above center) was part of Patton's covert intelligence group which operated in the area of Ettelbruck behind the lines of General Hodges's U.S. First Army during the days of the Ghost Front. He is pictured here with two other members of the team.

This rare photo shows one of Patton's intelligence officers in the First Army lines passing on important information by way of a tube in a jeep. The champagne bottle is filled with gasoline and would be ignited to destroy the document if detected.

Field Marshall Gerd von Rundstadt's name would be attached to the December offensive even though he was only apprised of Hitler's grand scheme late in the planning.

The German soldiers assigned to the "jeep teams" knew in the end that their mission was most probably a suicide mission, driving American jeeps and wearing American uniforms behind Allied lines would warrant the firing squad if captured. This jeep team met its death in a confrontation with American soldiers during the battle of the Bulge.

NOVEMBER
1944

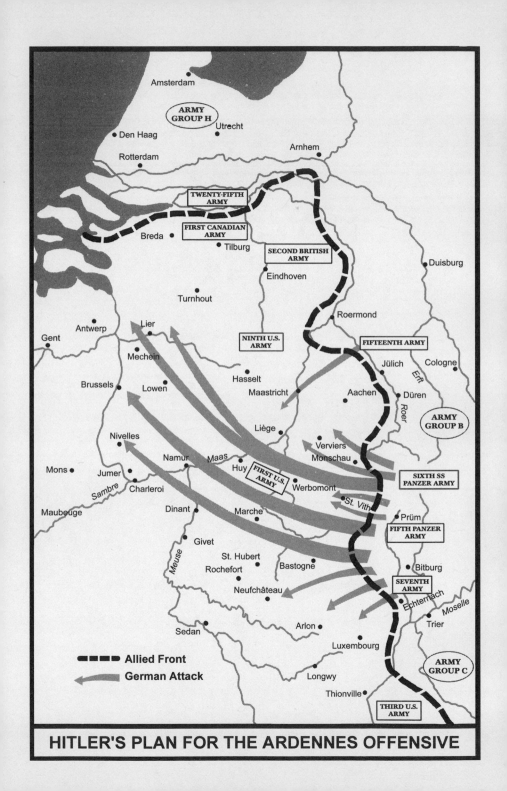

HITLER'S PLAN FOR THE ARDENNES OFFENSIVE

7

The Golf Club and Chess Society

German artilleryman Klaus Ritter, who had asked for a transfer to the 18th *Volksgrenadierdivision* so that he could stay in his native Eifel, began to notice the change in the first week of November. It was beginning to grow cold. There were flurries of snow on the high ground instead of rain and he was glad to exchange the freezing comfort of his underground bunker once a week to go for his hot bath just outside nearby Prum.

It seemed to Ritter on these trips that the men stationed on the Eifel front were changing. The SS had long departed along with those battered armored formations which had fled France back in the summer. The *Alarmeinheiten* ("emergency battalions"), "Ear and Nose" companies, and the second-raters of the "fortress artillery" were vanishing, too. They were being replaced by fit young men of the best ages for the infantry—twenty-one and twenty-two.

These days when Ritter went for his long awaited fifteen-minute bath and a change of underwear, he would encounter some of these newcomers and they would tell him with the openness of their youth that up to a few weeks ago they had been training to fly planes, man submarines, and for other specialities which demanded a longer training than the usual six weeks allotted to the poor old "stubble-hopper," as the infantrymen called themselves with their usual weary cynicism.

Now they had been transformed into stubble-hoppers themselves, as part of the great September levée en masse which had shut down most of the Wehrmacht's training establishments plus high schools, universities, nonessential factories, and the like. Why, the newcomers to the Eifel didn't know. But they did tell Ritter, the veteran "old hare," that their way to the remote front on Germany's southwestern border had been long, difficult, and shrouded in ultimate secrecy, with some of them journeying days, even weeks, to arrive there.

From their infantry training depots in the north and east they had traveled by troop trains till they had reached the Rhine. Their journeys had usually been by night and each train was protected by antiaircraft gunners, who wore goggles and leather masks to protect them from the biting cold as they scanned the night skies for raiders. Time and time again, so they related, their transfers had been postponed and delayed by the RAF and the U.S. 8th Air Force. But in the end they finally crossed the Rhine and reached the Eifel railheads at Gerolstein, Wittlich, Bitburg, Kyllburg, and the like.

There they had been picked up by army trucks or in some cases by convoys of local farmers with their ox-drawn carts and wagons. Packed into these like sardines they had set off down the country roads, often muffled by straw to reduce the noise, with low-flying German fighters helping to do the same. And each road, they had informed Ritter, had been controlled by a "street officer" who "answered with his head" if any fires were lit or forbidden lights were shown which would reveal the presence of these new formations to the Americans on the other side of the Our–Sauer Line. Finally as they reached the limits of the "Green Zone," they had "detrucked" and continued the last leg of their long odyssey on foot. Thereupon, they would disappear into their camouflaged camps in the thick fir woods of the Eifel, being forbidden to light fires even to cook their food which was brought up in hayboxes from central kitchens. Even the hot water used on bath days, to which Ritter looked forward as the greatest pleasure of the week, was heated by a special allowance of smokeless charcoal.

Ritter was puzzled and also a little worried by the appearance of so many of these fresh-faced youngsters on the Eifel front. At the same time they gave him new hope. Perhaps the war wasn't lost for Germany after all? The new boys, or "greenbeaks" as they were called, were very raw and not particularly well-trained, he could see that. Yet they were well-armed with the latest assault rifles and machine pistols, much better than the automatic weapons used by the Americans. Their uniforms and equipment, too, were straight from the factory and depot, unlike his own ragged patched outfit and down-at-heel boots. The "greenbeaks" impressed him as well with their attitude. They were "Hitler's boys" and not defeatists like his fellow "old hares." They projected optimism and confidence. Perhaps, as he recorded years later, "there was hope for Germany after all ... Had we still got a chance?"

At the same time Klaus Ritter also had an uneasy feeling. It grew as the first tank units returned to the Eifel. The feeling of uncertainty increased as the original defensive units in the area began to be sifted and sieved of unreliable elements. The 18th Volksgrenadier-division, as did many German outfits, contained a sizeable number of foreigners. The native-born Germans in these outfits called their foreign comrades—Poles, Russians, ethnic Germans from Romania, and the like—"booty Germans." But it wasn't the "booty Germans" from the East who were removed from the 18th VG. It was those from the West—Belgians, Luxembourgers, and Alsatians from France. These men were classified as belonging to the "*Liste Eins*" ("First List"). Now their kindly ex-butcher battery sergeant from Alsace, who belonged to this category, was quietly posted away to an outfit in the East.

The influx of new blood from the training schools could mean one of two things: either the army was expecting a massive American attack; or the Wehrmacht itself was about to go over to the offensive. It started to become clear to Ritter after his sergeant and the rest of the men he knew who belonged to *Liste Eins* had been posted, that perhaps the latter possibility was the correct one. Why else remove men who might well desert to their relatives just over the border and reveal what they knew to the enemy? As the winter started to tighten its grip on the Eifel heights, which dominated the American positions on the other side of the Our–Sauer Line, Klaus Ritter became a worried man. What in three devils' name was going on in the "Awful Eifel?"

Back in July 1939 with World War II only weeks away, what was mockingly known to the initiated in London as the "Golf Club and

Chess Society" had gone into action. Its head, Commander Alexander Denniston, "the most secretive man I've ever known" according to his son, and Dillwyn Knox, the expert who had helped to crack the famed "*Zimmermann Telegramme*," which had helped to bring the United States into World War I, went to Warsaw, the capital of Poland. With them as a kind of observer went a certain "Colonel Sandwich."

There it was agreed to have one of the new top-secret machines sent to London via the diplomatic bag. Thus on the evening of 16 August 1939, the courier with the precious machine was met personally at Victoria Station, London, by "Colonel Sandwich." He was clad in full formal evening dress and was wearing the ribbon of the Legion d'Honneur. It was, as General Ken Strong, Eisenhower's British chief of intelligence, would remark years later, "Colonel Sandwich's greatest achievement of the whole war." Who was the officer with the ludicrous cover name? None other than Colonel (later General) Stewart Menzies, the future head of the British Secret Intelligence Service.

Now with the aid of the machine that had been smuggled in from Poland, British and French intelligence went to work attempting to break the top secret messages with which Hitler and his Greater German General Staff gave their instructions, among other things, to their field commanders. Menzies, Commander Benniston, and his "Golf Club and Chess Society" known officially as the British "Code and Cipher School" knew they were onto a war-winner. Indeed the whole operation would become the greatest intelligence coup throughout the world in World War II. If they could read Hitler's plans and orders, the Allied commanders could out-think the Fuhrer and, with a bit of luck, then outfight him.

But as the British worked on some means of more rapidly decoding the German ENIGMA messages,* the authorities realized that the whole war-winning secret could be easily blown. It needed to be kept under extremely tight control to prevent this happening; and one of the measures Menzies employed was to restrict the recipients of the decodes to a limited number of well-vetted, high-ranking commanders. For as one ex-member of Menzies's spy operation recalled decades later, "they [the decodes] had the rarity value of the Dead

---

*This would result in the invention of the world's first computer, kept secret, like most things connected with this great intelligence operation, until the 1970s.

Sea Scrolls ... they could not be allowed to fall into the hands of those who might have dirty fingers."

By 1942 the British were allowing certain select American commanders and experts to gain access to the great secret (but being British, the London spymasters didn't tell the "Yanks" everything). Naturally Eisenhower was let into the "ULTRA Secret" as it was code-named. Generals Clark, Patton, Bradley, and Hodges, too, had specially trained U.S. officers at their headquarters who knew the secret and passed on the information received from Britain to their bosses. For example, in the case of Hodges's 200,000-strong First Army, holding the Eifel–Ardennes front in the winter of 1944, only Hodges, Colonel Monk Dickson, his intelligence chief, and his ULTRA adviser, Captain Adolph Rosengarten, knew of the great decoding operation.

By the summer of 1944 the ULTRA decodes had served the Allied commanders well, in particular the American ones. They had clarified the pre-D-day situation on Utah and Omaha beaches; warned Bradley of the "surprise" German armored counterattack at Mortain; and informed Eisenhower that the German Army in France was going to withdraw. But that autumn as the Germans had fallen back to their own frontier, a change began to take place. The Wehrmacht started to use their home-based, large-scale network of safe telephone and teleprinter links instead of the ENIGMA machines. The "boffins of Bletchley," as the eggheads of the Bletchley Park secret operation were called, could not tap. In other words, less radio meant less ULTRA information.

Afterward when the great role that ULTRA had played in the war against Germany was revealed, it was widely suggested that the reason for the Allied failure to spot the German buildup to their "surprise" attack in the Ardennes was due to the fact that the enemy was not using ENIGMA. Allied commanders, especially Eisenhower and Bradley, had become so used to making their plans on the basis of the ULTRA decodes that they had been virtually lost without them.

But how true was that theory? Was Eisenhower caught completely off guard, with the loss of 80,000 American soldiers killed, wounded, and captured in the subsequent battle of the Bulge, because all he had to rely on as far as German intentions were concerned was conventional intelligence? Were all the German orders and instructions relative to the coming assault relayed by telephone and secure land line so that Bletchley Park was unable to pick them up? The short answer is simple—no!

One thing is immediately clear about the use and non-use of the ENIGMA. That is that the German authorities controlling the movement of troops to and fro across the Reich from the east front to the one in the west and from the various depots and training areas in Northern Westphalia and Bavaria did still use low-level ENIGMA code.

Thus it was that right through November and into December, Bletchley Park was reading the *Reichsbahn* (German State Railway) codes with comparative ease. In particular, they picked up signals indicating that some 5,000 trains were on their way westward during this period, with 800 of them crossing the Rhine River heading for the Western Front. In addition, each time a troop train crossed the great river from east to west, Model's Army Group B headquarters asked for air cover; and again these air force signals were intercepted and decoded by the Allies at Bletchley Park.

The Rhine River proved a bottleneck for the Germans but something of a boon for the decoders. This was due to the limited number and position of the bridges over which the railroad lines ran. These bridges were located at Cologne, Bonn-Remagen, Koblenz, Guls, Bingen, Mainz, and Ludwigshafen. But if the great German river proved a bottleneck for the German State Railway authorities, it provided a very convenient aid for Allied intelligence officers.

For a start, it indicated (by the nature of the German Rhenish railroad system) that all these troops were heading for Hodges's First Army front, say, between Aachen in the north and Luxembourg's Echternach in the south. It therefore gave American intelligence a clue as to which fronts were being reinforced.

The railroad system on the west bank of the Rhine had been designed in the late nineteenth century by the then Prussian authorities, not only to convey passengers and freight, the railroads' primary function, but also troops to the country's border with its neighbors as quickly as possible. To achieve this purpose, the major lines ran along the Rhenish plain between Cologne and Mainz and then down to Ludwigshafen, with branch lines heading straight for the border and the major assembly points beyond the Eifel hills. The theory was that the troops would disembark within virtual sight of the border and march to war. Both in 1870 and later in 1914 and 1940, this had been the major means of transporting troops worked out by the very efficient Prussian and later German General Staff.*

In the fall of 1944, however, American intelligence officers trying to outguess the Germans and their intentions on the First Army's front realized that there were two other pieces of information they needed from the "Bletchley boffins." Where was the new German armor located? And where were the majority of these new German troops being sent across the Rhine going? If they could be given this information they could work out where any attack might come. For it was obvious that the enemy would attack using the main body of his infantry behind this German armor.

For the most part, with all their resources—ground intelligence, ULTRA, and aerial reconnaissance—it was difficult to identify the individual German divisions heading for Hodges's front. But the ULTRA decoders did know that the highest transport priority was given to German armored divisions. When attacked, infantry could abandon their trains. Armor was another thing. The tank crews might jump to safety, but their vehicles on their flat cars would be left behind as sitting ducks for the low-flying Allied fighter-bombers.

In the case of armored divisions moving westward, therefore, they were given priority air cover by the Luftwaffe when they moved by rail. Thus it was that by decoding Luftwaffe signals still transmitted by relatively low-grade ENIGMA, Bletchley was able to learn that the 2nd SS Panzer Division, the feared "Das Reich," was stalled somewhere near Kassel and was thirty-six hours behind schedule. The same signal included the information that the Panzerlehr, the elite training division of the Wehrmacht under veteran warrior Major General Fritz Bayerlein, was also twelve hours behind schedule, as was the 12th SS Panzer Division, *"Hitlerjugend"* ("Hitler Youth") which had held up the British so long at Caes in the summer.

At the same time, ULTRA was also picking up signals that November stating that the army staff at Model's headquarters wanted aerial reconnaissance to be carried out over the areas of

---

*It is stated that the Prussian staff officers first became aware of the use of railroads (several of them in Germany being built by British engineers) for troop movement by studying the use of rail transportation of troops during the U.S. Civil War.

Eupen–Malmedy and Prum–Houffalize, both in Hodges's First Army territory, plus on 29 November, a full-scale reconnaissance on the River Meuse behind Hodges's lines between Liege and Givet. The instructions given to the pilots was to look out for U.S. Army installations in the area, in particular fuel dumps and U.S. tank concentrations. As the decode stated, it was now "a matter of greatest urgency" to photograph some of the bridges across the river and in particular, the road junction off the Meuse at Ciney.* By that date, Allied intelligence at all levels was beginning to identify the general location of these new German arrivals by concentrating on their final rail destination. But after being unloaded from the troop transports, they became virtually impossible to follow.

Following up on the ULTRA decodes of the dispatch and routing of the transports over the Rhine, aerial reconnaissance confirmed the place of arrival of these transports. For the most part, the trains arrived at forward stations on the general line from Blankenheim, Gerolstein–Bitburg, and Wittlich. Some did arrive at Euskirchen and Cologne, but the great majority were unloaded at the Eifel stations. That meant the troops they had unloaded were in a general area of some ten to twenty miles from the line held by Hodges's VIII Corps, commanded by General Troy Middleton. In other words, the weakest part of General Eisenhower's whole front: four divisions, by now mostly green or battle-weary, maintaining a sixty-mile front.

Somewhere the alarm bells should have rung that November, with only weeks to go before the great debacle commenced. But they didn't—at least at the top. Virtually every one of General Bradley's top intelligence professionals from General Sibert downward felt they could explain the new presence of so many German troops in the Eifel facing VIII Corps.

They reasoned the Eifel was centrally located with good railway connections. From that area, Model could switch troops easily to the Saar, in case Patton's Third Army broke through there. Model could also dispatch these men to the north to the general area of Aachen, if Hodges' First Army attacked there towards Cologne and the Rhine. Both attacks were already beyond the planning stage and it seemed feasible to General Sibert, Colonels Koch and Dickson (heads of intelligence at Patton's Third Army and Hodges's First) and

---

* Later to be the furthermost point reached by General von Manteuffel's Fifth Panzer Army.

the like that the Germans knew of the coming American offensives and were preparing to counterattack.

Because they believed what they wanted to believe, that is, that the Germans no longer had the strength to launch a massive new offensive in the West, these intelligence professionals discounted the order for English-speaking soldiers to report to Skorzeny's headquarters. It was the same with the ULTRA decodes dealing with the Luftwaffe reconnaissance flights over Hodges's rear area, in particular, the Meuse. None of them seemed to have asked why a German army committed to the defensive in the West would want urgent information on the state of the Meuse bridges.

Naturally, if these intelligence men had been able to locate the missing German armor in November 1944, they might well have been in a better position to make accurate predictions about the German intentions. In particular they appeared to have been worried about the future Sixth SS Panzer Army, the elite of the Armed SS.* These arrogant young SS men, known for their dash and fanaticism, would, the Allies knew, lead any major German attack. Just as they had held the Allies back in September when everything seemed lost, Hitler would undoubtedly rely upon his Waffen SS to turn the tide once again. As we have seen, the Sixth had been withdrawn at the end of September 1944 when the fighting in the Eifel had ceased and the area had become known to the Americans as the "Ghost Front." But where had the battered SS armored formations vanished to, and more importantly, where were they now?

For the most part they had been retrained, reinforced, and resupplied with new tanks in the great Seonelager area in the north of Westphalia, one of Germany's traditional training schools. Allied intelligence guessed that might be their location back in October. Where else could four elite panzer divisions go, apart from the Russian front; and in the east the Germans were fighting a strictly defensive battle, where infantry and not armor were at a premium.

After October, Allied intelligence differed considerably about the whereabouts of these armored formations. Sibert believed the Sixth SS were still in the same general area, grouped around Bielefeld with its barracks complexes. Koch put the Sixth SS closer to the front in the West. He reasoned they were in the Cologne area, ready to use the Rhenish city's excellent communication system and prepared to

---

*The army would receive its official designation once Sepp Dietrich arrived to take command.

meet an American thrust from Aachen. Dickson put them closer to
the front. He surmised the Sixth was west of the Rhine, between that
river and the River Ruhr already under attack by the First Army. As
SHAEF* Intelligence summed up the confused situation in a report
on 10 December: "There is no further news of the Sixth SS Panzer
Army beyond vague rumors." But there was. General Kenneth
Strong, Eisenhower's chief of intelligence, needed only to have gone
down the corridor at SHAEF headquarters, Versailles, to have
learned what the true situation was on the German side of the line.
"Black ULTRA," restricted to his chief, Eisenhower, would have
enlightened the dark-haired Scottish intelligence expert considerably.

One month or so before, General George Marshall, Eisenhower's
mentor and chief, had found himself in a quandary. Indeed, the
stern-faced southern general, who would not even let President
Roosevelt call him by his first name, was confronted by an agoniz-
ing decision that last week of September 1944.

It was in the form of the threat posed by Governor Tom Dewey,
the Republican candidate for the office of the presidency. Dewey was
about to malign Roosevelt by revealing what he knew of "MAGIC."
MAGIC was the code-name for U.S. decoding operations run mainly from Arlington Hall, Virginia. There, in the former girls' school,
U.S. experts had been reading Japanese codes, mainly their vital
naval ones, for four years. As Dewey saw it, Roosevelt must have
brought the United States into the war by letting Pearl Harbor and
the "Day of Infamy" take place. He felt that although the president
had known, thanks to MAGIC, that the Japanese were going to
attack, he had allowed them to catch America by surprise. As far as
the ambitious young Republican governor was concerned, this dis-
closure about the great secret decoding operation and the cynical
manner in which he felt President Roosevelt had manipulated it back
in 1941 would win him the election.

Marshall was normally above U.S. politics. All the same, he
knew in his heart that he had to do something about the Dewey
threat. For the army chief knew something that Dewey did not. The
same code used by the Japanese in 1941 was still being employed by
Tokyo four years later. If Dewey went public, he would destroy a
war-winning decoding operation that was just as vitally important as

---

* Supreme Headquarters Allied Expeditionary Force

that of ULTRA. What was he to do? Should he try to warn Dewey off? But if he did, he might well have to reveal the secret to a civilian not in the military and therefore beyond his control. It was a very tricky situation indeed.

In the end, without telling President Roosevelt, Marshall sent a colonel as a kind of emissary to Dewey. He told the governor as much as Marshall thought he ought to know about MAGIC. Dewey did not believe the officer. He said he was being given a whitewash; it was a blatant attempt to cover Roosevelt. On 27 September, Marshall tried again. He sent Dewey a handwritten letter explaining his position.

In it, the chief of staff wrote: "Now the point to the present dilemma is that we have gone ahead with this business of deciphering their codes (the Japanese) until we possess other codes, German as well as Japanese, *but our main basis of information regarding Hitler's intentions in Europe is obtained from Baron Oshima's messages from Berlin* [author's italics] reporting his interviews with Hitler and other officials to the Japanese government. These are still the codes involved in the Pearl Harbor events."

Marshall went on to state: "The conduct of General Eisenhower's campaign and of all the operations in the Pacific are closely related in conception and timing to the information we secretly obtain through these intercepted codes. They contribute greatly to the victory and tremendously to the saving of American lives."

Reading the letter in the presence of Marshall's messenger, Dewey exclaimed in anger: "Well, I'll be damned if I believe the Japs are still using those two codes!" He meant the ones used at Pearl Harbor in 1941.

Marshall's envoy reassured the irate former "gang buster of the 30s" that everything was genuine and that one of the two codes "was our life blood" in intelligence. He stated that Churchill regarded this "secret weapon"—the ULTRA decoding operation—as having really saved England in the dark early years of the war.

Dewey grunted that "there is little in his letter that I don't know already. There is one point though. What the hell do Jap codes have to do with Eisenhower?"

As discreetly as he could, Colonel Clarke, Marshall's emissary, told Dewey something of the Bletchley Park–Arlington Hall operation. He added that by early 1944, the reading of Baron Oshima's coded messages from Berlin to Tokyo had become as important for Eisenhower as the Bletchley-generated ULTRA. Indeed, Eisenhower was one of the few recipients of what was known as "Black Book ULTRA." Clarke explained that this "ultra within Ultra" was restricted to a handful of the most important U.S. leaders, Eisenhower in Europe, MacArthur in the Pacific, and Roosevelt himself.

Finally Dewey was convinced. He excused himself, had a brief discussion with an aide in another room, and then returned to tell Clarke: "Colonel, I do not believe that there are any questions I want to ask you, nor do I care to have any discussions about the contents of this letter." The matter was closed.*

"Black ULTRA" had really started in 1940, when the plump but soldierly 54-year-old Baron Hiroshi Oshima had returned to Berlin as his country's ambassador. From 1934 he had spent several years in Germany as the Japanese military attaché, becoming familiar with leading Nazis, including Hitler, and high-ranking officers of the future Wehrmacht, then still the Reichswehr.

By 1939 he had Hitler's ear as a leading exponent of the "Pact of Steel" between the world's three major fascist countries, Germany, Japan, and Italy, and before he had posted back to Berlin he had become a strong advocate of the Nazi philosophy.

A few months before Oshima returned to Berlin to his new post, U.S. Signal Intelligence had broken the main Japanese code he would use in his top-secret communications to Tokyo. Thus it was that from that time onward, the American military could read Oshima's signals and the Japanese ambassador became the main Allied source of Hitler's thinking and intentions in the enemy camp.

Over the years Oshima told Tokyo—*and* Washington—of Hitler's intention to invade Russia; the effect of the Allied bombing campaign; how Germany's industrial production was rising tremendously despite these bombing attacks; plus details of secret weapons such as the jet engine and Hitler's vaunted rocket program.

By the time Eisenhower had become supreme commander in Europe, Oshima was supplying him, unwittingly, with priceless

---

* Dewey never revealed what he knew. Naturally, in later years Marshall denied the whole business, saying—quite truthfully in a way—that he had never had any contact with Dewey until he met the latter at President Roosevelt's funeral in April 1945.

information about the planned French invasion beaches and their defenses of the Atlantic Wall. On 10 December 1943, for example, Oshima radioed home a nine-page report on the German defenses in France. As a former military man, he was able to give an accurate and detailed insight into the German beach fortifications and the divisions holding them, even down to the positions of individual key machine gun posts and bunkers. Indeed, Oshima must have made life a lot easier for a sorely tried and worried Eisenhower, who, to the very last moment as history records, was agitated about whether he should or should not launch the D-day invasion.

After D-day there was a two-month silence on the part of Baron Oshima. The reason why is not known, but one can guess. Germany's Japanese allies were waiting to see the outcome of D-day. Would the Germans cope? Or would they buckle under with the threat to them now being posed on two fronts: the Russians to the east and the Anglo-Americans to the west?

Thus it was with a great deal of anticipation that both Bletchley Park and Arlington Hall received their first new signals from Oshima some time in August, just after the Wehrmacht's debacle in France. They stated that the Japanese ambassador had requested an interview with Hitler for 4 September 1944, and that the request had been granted. Now, the decode experts told themselves, they would soon learn Hitler's true state of mind after the defeat in Normandy.

Even today, so many years later, one can visualize the nervous tension and suppressed excitement at these secret places as the experts waited to find out what Hitler was thinking. He had lost France, his own generals had attempted to assassinate him, and the Anglo-Americans were within striking distance of the unmanned Siegfried Line, the country's last man-made line of defense. Was Hitler finally going to throw in the towel?

They were in for a surprise.

According to Oshima's dispatch to Tokyo, Hitler commenced his discussion with the Japanese ambassador by telling the latter frankly that things had been bad for Germany. He explained about the generals' plot to kill him and the great retreat of the shattered German army from France. But those two problems had been solved. The mass of the Wehrmacht was behind the protection of the West Wall fortifications and were prepared to defend the Reich's border in the West.

Then had come the surprise. Hitler was not only going to defend his territory, but as he told Oshima, he was going to go over to the attack. He had already massed forces southeast of Nancy, soon to be Patton's Third Army headquarters. Soon he would launch these into a counterattack on the Third Army to gain vital territory lost that month in France.

The news that Germany was still capable of attacking must have made those in the know, due to "Black ULTRA," blink with amazement. But they were in for an even greater surprise. Hitler went on, according to the Oshima dispatch to Tokyo, to explain that he was going to launch a major counteroffensive in the West. As the Japanese general summarized Hitler's words: "It was his intention as soon as the new army of more than one million men now being organized was ready, to combine them with units to be withdrawn from the front everywhere and, waiting upon the replenishment of the air force which is now in progress, to take the offensive in the west on a large scale."

According to Oshima, Hitler expected that this buildup would take place under the cover of rainy weather in September and October when the Allies could not make full use of their superior air power. Thus, this planned large-scale attack in the West would take place "after the beginning of November."

That was the last interview that Hitler ever gave to the Japanese ambassador. But for those in the know in the Allied camp it should have been the most decisive. For it was the first indication that, within weeks, Hitler would involve America in its greatest land battle of the twentieth century—its "Gettysburg in Europe."

Naturally, there were some who maintained Hitler was just boasting, trying to encourage Japan to stay in the war on the Axis side. For if Japan got out of the conflict, Russia, which maintained a large army in the Far East to counter a possible Japanese threat, could then throw its whole weight against the battered Nazi empire.

But in the next forty-eight hours, while presumably those in the know discounted the Black ULTRA decodes as just idle talk on Hitler's part, Eisenhower must have taken some action. For when the German Fifth Panzer Army, under the command of General Hasso von Manteuffel, who would figure prominently in the great attack to come in the Ardennes, moved out to advance on the French Lorraine city of Luneville on 18 September 1944, the Americans were waiting for him.

At first the U.S. defenders seemed outnumbered by Manteuffel's two armored divisions and a couple of armored brigades and the diminutive German general gained some ground. But waiting in the wings was Patton's favorite and perhaps best armored division, the "Fighting Fourth," the 4th U.S. Armored, under the command of barrel-chested, no-nonsense General John S. Wood, ably supported by Colonel Bruce Clarke, who was destined to stop von Manteuffel during the battle of the Bulge for seven long, bloody days with his defense of St. Vith.

For nearly seven days the battle raged in the Lorraine area, but in the end the Germans withdrew with a bloody nose and von Manteuffel's Fifth Panzer had to undergo extensive refits to prepare it for what was to come in the Ardennes. It might have been thought that the "surprise" German attack would have worried the Americans. After all, Wood and his 4th Armored had been chasing the Germans ever since Patton's Third Army had gone into battle on 31 July 1944. Now the enemy had actually turned around and attacked. But that wasn't the case. As the official U.S. history of the Lorraine campaign points out: "News of the German attack at Luneburg 'didn't worry' Eddy [the U.S. corps commander] or Patton ... for they were neither greatly concerned." Why should they be? It was obvious that Eisenhower, who had visited them immediately after he had received the "Black ULTRA" decodes, had warned the two Third Army generals of what was to come.

Although Oshima never met Hitler again after that 4 September conference, he did continue meeting other prominent Nazi leaders and reporting on his conclusions to Tokyo. And most of what he sent his masters in the Japanese capital dealt with a tremendous new counteroffensive planned by the Germans in the west.

At Bletchley Park and Arlington Hall, the code-breakers—and presumably in due course, Eisenhower in Versailles—learned that Hitler attached high hopes to this offensive. He hoped, above all, to deal the Western Allies a very severe blow and capture the key Allied supply port of Antwerp on the Belgian coast. The code-breakers were, even at this stage of the business, able to work out some sort of German timetable for the new offensive. For Hitler had stated that he wanted Antwerp captured before the Allies, in particular the British, could clear the port's approaches of mines and the German troops still located on the Dutch Walcheren Islands, blocking the harbor entrances. Thus it was imperative, as far as German thinking went, to start the offensive as soon as the early winter bad weather period commenced. Once the good weather came and the Allies were finally ready to use Antwerp to full capacity the Allies would be able to pour in troops and materiel to halt any future German offensive.

This was a vital clue for the Allied intelligence officers who were in on the "Black ULTRA" secret. They knew from their studies of Western European weather that the rainfall in the Eifel–Ardennes area and Eastern France normally doubled in November. If they placed this information together with what they now knew about German troop movements across the Rhine and their current locations on the border, they could make an educated guess that it would be November when Hitler would launch this counteroffensive in the West, once the weather had broken and Allied air could no longer fly. This seemed to be confirmed when Oshima signaled Tokyo that Hitler had ordered his counteroffensive not to be launched later than the last week in November.

On 16 November 1944, Oshima sent two messages to his boss in Japan. In the first he gave a detailed account of his meeting with German Foreign Minister Joachim von Ribbentrop at Sonnenberg, sixty miles east of Berlin. During their discussions, Oshima reminded the vain German diplomat who had spent his youth in Canada that in September the Fuhrer had promised an offensive in the West. As Oshima stated, "[he had promised] it would be launched after the beginning of November." Now it was already the second week of that month. Had the Fuhrer changed his plans?

Von Ribbentrop, who had offended the British when he had been German ambassador in London by wearing the SS uniform and giving the king the Nazi "Heil Hitler" salute, was evasive. He would not give the Japanese details of the timing. Nor would he be definite about the location of the great attack. He said at first Germany would attack in the east, but then, on the other hand, he admitted it might be in the West.

Oshima pressed him. He mentioned the great German surprise

offensive of March 1918 in France which had sent the British Army reeling back. However, the ambassador added, some historians, he knew, thought the offensive had hastened Germany's defeat. Would it not be a wise plan for Germany to "fight a war of attrition"?

"Absolutely not!" von Ribbentrop snorted. "The Chancellor [Hitler] believes we cannot win the war by defense alone and has restated his intention of taking the offensive to the bitter end."

Oshima came away from the meeting with mixed feelings and perhaps unconvinced. He signaled Tokyo that Ribbentrop's final remark was "one of those instances in which truth from the mouth of a liar reaches the highest pinnacle of deceptiveness." Later that same day he changed his mind. This time he radioed the Japanese capital: "We may take at face value," the intention of the German leadership to attack, for a "Germany whose battle lines have contracted virtually to the old territory of Germany [prior to 1939] ... will have no choice but to open a road of blood in one direction or another." In Oshima's opinion that "road of blood" would lead westward.

In all, between 16 August and 15 December 1944, Baron Oshima sent twenty-eight messages to Tokyo, all deciphered by MAGIC and Black ULTRA, and all dealing with the coming German counteroffensive. In eighteen of those messages, Oshima implied that Nazi Germany was to go over to the offensive as soon as possible. In eight, he maintained the Germans intended to launch a large-scale assault in late 1944; and in two, Oshima stated he was confident that the attack was now soon to begin and although he gave its wrong location, Aachen, he was certain that it was in the west.

If we are to believe General Marshall's statement to Dewey, "the conduct of General Eisenhower's campaign ... [is] closely related in conception and timing to the information we secretly obtain through these intercepted codes," why did Eisenhower not act?

When after the war the German plans for the attack in the Eifel–Ardennes area were discovered and examined, it was found that their key "sitrep" map had identified all the Allied divisions facing them on the Western Front, with the strength of the Allied forces drawn in a line. Wherever the line was thick, it indicated that they were there in strength; where it was thin, it showed a weak Allied front strength. The thinnest stretch of line of all was naturally that of the U.S. VIII Corps under the command of General Middleton.

One might wonder why the Germans, with far fewer intelligence resources than the Allies—no air-to-ground radar reconnaissance, no ULTRA, relying mainly on ground reconnaissance—could produce such detailed intelligence by the end of November 1944 and the Allies, with all their resources, could not.

Or had the Allies really produced a much more detailed picture of German intentions than was admitted later when everything went "pear-shaped"? What about Eisenhower's role? What happened to the information he must have gained from "Black ULTRA's" decodes of Baron Oshima's messages to Tokyo? Did he or did he not pass that information on to his subordinate commanders, especially Hodges and Patton whose armies were certainly going to be effected wherever the Germans struck along the American line between Cologne and, say, Metz?

A lot of questions with few answers. And all the while the Germans prepared for what was soon to come on the Ghost Front.

8

A Plot to Kill Ike?

It is pretty clear that in the half year the Western Allies spent on Germany's border before they broke through to the Rhine they did not get the measure of the civilians on both sides of the frontier. They naturally had a mixed bunch of administrators, civilians in uniforms, who were supposed to oversee the civilians, both friend and foe, who remained in the region of the fighting front. But for the most part, these "Civilian Affairs" officers were hastily and poorly trained and did not speak the local languages. Indeed, the real link between them and the civilians they controlled were their interpreters. And these were mainly ex-Germans and Austrian Jews who had been forced to flee their homeland, and were, therefore, quite naturally embittered and not inclined to do more than was expected of them by their Anglo-American bosses.

In the end the British, with the experience of three hundred years of colonial rule behind them, decided to treat the border people like they had always done the "natives" (naturally for their own good). They evacuated them lock, stock, and barrel over the border deep into Holland where they knew the locals would keep an eye on their former conquerors. Even their animals (if not already scoffed by hungry British Tommies sick of a diet of spam and bully beef) were removed so that the fighting area was officially deserted save for those who did the fighting. Anyone found in civilian clothes could then be automatically arrested or shot on the spot as a German spy— what was called a "front runner" (in German, "Frontlaufer"), a local messenger who carried secret communications to and fro across that dangerous border—in World War I, the "three country corner" ("*dreilandereck*") of Holland, Belgium, and Germany had been the Western Front's espionage hotspot.

The American authorities did not follow the British example though. At least at first. It was only after the bitter experiences of the battle of the Bulge and the subsequent recriminations and accusations, that U.S. Civil Affairs evacuated mass populations from the border. It was done at the behest of the military, who understandably felt they had been betrayed by many of the border civilians they had treated with relative kindness.

It seemed many of the Civil Affairs officers had been brainwashed before they had been posted to Europe by Hollywood's portrayal of the Old Continent at war. A steady diet of romantic and hopelessly ill-conceived war movies à la "Casablanca" with Bogart and Bergman and an assorted cast of monocled Nazis (mostly played, ironically enough, by German Jewish refugee actors) had provided the stereotypes. They knew none of the bitter realities of Occupied Europe with its betrayals, treachery, and double dealings.

Unfortunately in the Eifel–Ardennes area where the fighting took place, the civilians on both sides of the border did not conform to the expected stereotypes. For one thing, on both sides they all spoke German as their native tongue. Whether they were Alsatian, Luxembourger, Belgian from the three East Cantons—Eupen, Malmedy and St. Vith, which had been given to Belgium from a defeated Imperial Germany by the Treaty of Versailles—or Dutchmen from the South Limburg area, they used a German patois, which was very hard for the native speaker of High German to comprehend.

Also there had been a great deal of intermarriage in this community and most of the area's menfolk, who had been declared "*Reichsdeutsche*," i.e., Germans, back in 1940, were serving in the Wehrmacht. So not surprisingly, most of their loyalties were divided. If your husband, son, or boyfriend was serving in the German armed forces, you could not realistically be expected to help and aid those American soldiers who had come to this remote frontier area, possibly to kill your loved one.

Thus it was that though the Our–Sauer Line was apparently impermeable for the Americans in November 1944 so that they could not obtain ground reconnaissance information (or so it was said officially), the Germans were able to move back and forth in this multinational, but German-speaking, community with impunity. How else could they have known the location of almost every American division on Hodges's long front? For although U.S. Army radio communications were surprisingly lax, which in the battle to come the Germans used to their advantage, the enemy, as far as we know, had not cracked the key military codes. So it was that when American Intelligence and Civil Affairs officers started to pick up the pieces after the battle of the Bulge, it would seem to them that there had been German soldiers, often disguised as GIs, wandering about the rear of the U.S. VIII Corps by the scores in those last weeks of November 1944.

Secrecy was now utmost on the Germans's minds. On 7 November, Hitler had decreed that there would be no more patrols in the Ghost Front area in case any German prisoners taken by the Americans might reveal to their captors the great secret. It was for the same reason that all former nationals who had become German citizens in 1940, such as Klaus Ritter's battery sergeant, were transferred elsewhere. *Sippenhaft* (automatic arrest of the "next-of-kin" of any offender) and the death penalty would also be inflicted upon even ordinary soldiers who deserted. (Thus far only high-ranking officers who had defected had suffered this penalty.) Hitler was making absolutely sure that the great secret was not compromised or betrayed.

Even when senior officers such as Field Marshal Model or Colonel-General von Manteuffel, commander of the Fifth Panzer Army facing Middleton, went to visit the front to confer with their subordinate commanders or do reconnaissance of the area they would attack, they hid their true identities. In December, for instance, when the Fifth Army commander decided to observe the positions of the U.S. 28th Infantry Division, the "Bloody Bucket," and the 106th, the "Golden Lions," both destined to suffer grievous losses in the coming battle, he went in the uniform of a lowly colonel accompanied only by a single officer in order not to draw attention to himself.

The only exception to Hitler's November ruling were special formations such as the assault elements of von Manteuffel's 26th

Volksgrenadier Division, Colonel Hoffman's 5th Parachute, Peiper's 1st SS Panzer Battlegroup, and naturally, Skorzeny's new 150th Panzer Brigade. Using guides from the area or Belgian, Luxembourg, and Dutch members of all these formations who were all volunteers, these recon troopers ranged far and wide behind the VIII Corps, even as far as Troy Middleton's headquarters at the sleepy Belgian township of Bastogne.

Later the locals who were French-speaking and lived on the border of the linguistic divide between French- and German-speaking peoples, told Allied interrogators that they had long been expecting the Germans to come. They had seen Germans in that remote area laying out dropping zones for what they presumed to be parachute operations. Why Germans were going to land in that area the civilians didn't know. But all the same they had informed Middleton's headquarters in a former Belgian army barracks. But their warning was pooh-poohed—another example of that old Belgian spy phobia.

Just over the border in Luxembourg at Clervaux, headquarters of the 28th Division's 110th Infantry Regiment, similar reports were spread. Once more they were dismissed by the regimental command located in the Hotel Clarvallis. The men of the "Bloody Bucket" would discover too late to their dismay that the Germans had picked an empty pharmacy in the center of the little tourist town and current 28th Division leave center to install two secret radio operators who would call down fire on the place in due course.

Virtually everywhere in the VIII Corps area Germans in uniform, in civilian clothes, dressed as GIs or farmers and the like were reported to be operating. From St. Vith to Vianden and naturally in Luxembourg, Bradley's own headquarters, there were agents, spies, front runner, and reconnaissance patrols feeding back key information to German intelligence, preparing for the great attack.

But there was one place where these shadowy figures were spotted by the local peasants and farmers that really did not seem important enough for a German to risk being shot as a spy if he were apprehended there. This was the country crossroads on the minor N-31 road from Malmedy to Vielsalm, which ran by stretches of desolate wooded countryside until it came to the one-horse hamlet of Poteau, directly on the linguistic border between French- and German-speaking Belgium.

There on one side of the road that divided "Old Belgium" (the original pre-1919 kingdom) from what the locals called "New Belgium" (the kingdom expanded by the German-speaking East Cantons after World War I) more than once the farmers encountered lone U.S. officers or individual American soldiers who turned away when they realized that the local civilian was French-speaking, though they seemed to be at ease with the German-speaking locals on the other side of the linguistic divide.

Once one of these mysterious Americans offered a farmer at the crossroads a cigar. He accepted it with alacrity. Tobacco was hard to come by—indeed here and there the locals had been forced to grow their own, spraying the leaves after they had dried with "Virginia aroma" to make them halfway smokable—and American cigars were highly prized. It was only later when he came to smoke the treasured cigar that the farmer realized it wasn't American at all. It was made of the same terrible tobacco as his own "homemade" products. It was German.

In particular, it seemed to the more curious of the locals (and in that area with its Maquis and strange linguistic differences, it wasn't wise to be too curious; one could end up dead that way) that these "Americans" were very interested in a deeply wooded area between Poteau and the main road that led from Vielsalm and on across the hills to Huy and the other Meuse cities which possessed bridges over that great natural barrier.

More than once they had asked the way to the "French" or "Napoleon Cross" in the woods, some 250 yards from the nearest road. Why, the locals couldn't guess. What was important, especially for the Americans, about this weathered monument supposedly dating back to the late eighteenth or early nineteenth century? Later, one of the locals who had met the "Americans" in November was accosted by an officer in SS uniform in mid-December who waved to him and asked cheerfully, "Don't you remember me? I gave you a cigar last month!" It was then that the somewhat slow-witted farmer tumbled to it. The cross provided a convenient landmark and rallying point between the two major road systems leading through the Ardennes to the River Meuse. But as the chronicler of that time over half a century ago recorded, he never asked, "A rallying point for what?"

The commander who had sent those mysterious "Americans" to the ancient cross in the woods at the Poteau crossroads was currently at the other end of the Third Reich. Obersturmbannfuhrer Otto Skorzeny, chief of the SS Jagdkommando, was busy, among other things, supervising the training of the 150th Panzer Brigade at the Grafenwohr Training Ground in Bavaria.

There under a guard of SS soldiers who were Ukrainian volunteers who didn't speak a word of German and treated Skorzeny's special troops as if they were prisoners, the brigade was being put through its paces for "Operation Greif." As Skorzeny would have us believe, there were two types of volunteers locked in the remote winter camp: men who spoke some English and would man the three columns of American vehicles, dress in U.S. uniform, and guide the Sixth SS Panzer Army to the Meuse. In addition to this group of some 1,500 volunteers, there was another of about 200 men, who were all supposedly fluent English-speakers, who would dress as GIs and penetrate in so-called "jeep teams" deep behind the U.S. front, spying, sabotaging, and generally disrupting the American lines of communication. It was—and is—this author's belief that there was also a third body being trained at Grafenwohr or perhaps at Skorzeny's headquarters at Friedenthal outside Berlin, that had a more significant and far-reaching mission: one that the scarfaced commando boss would understandably deny after the war when he was an American POW.

Typical of the training of the "jeep team," and possibly of the other more shadowy group, was the learning of common GI slang and idiomatic phrases, plus "the way the American GI lounged and did not take life so seriously as did the German landser," as one of the volunteers remembered after the war. Skorzeny indeed went to great lengths to ensure these special teams, intended for as yet unspecified missions were well-trained and briefed.

As one of them, Sergeant Heinz Rohde, revealed in 1950: "At first we were mostly concerned with learning the idiom of the GIs. The performance of American films, especially war films, played a great role in our training." But apparently the learning of supposed GI phrases as "Go and shit in yer hat" and "Yer old man can't suck eggs either" didn't suffice. Skorzeny sent his men to nearby POW camps dressed as recently captured GIs. As Rohde explained: "Then came short visits to American POW camps where we mixed with GIs and gained the impression that we were developing into perfect Yankees!" It was a daring ploy. There in the great sprawling POW camps, manned by elderly German guards, the supposed GIs could have been quietly disposed of by being drowned in the camp's latrine or something similar.

Unfortunately for some of those "perfect Yankees," they were making a basic mistake right from the start. Skorzeny was allotting four men to each precious captured U.S. jeep. American Army usage, especially that of Patton's Third Army, was three men to each jeep. However, Skorzeny's commandos would realize that afterward. Now this late November everything was going all out in Grafenwohr to prepare the volunteers for this old Trojan Horse operation.

Still the men were puzzled. Rumors circulated on all sides as the volunteers attempted to figure out what their real role was going to be. It was obviously highly secret, for their mail was censured and there were rumors that two men had been executed because they had revealed details of what was going on. Two Dutch truck drivers who had brought supplies to the remote and now snowbound Bavarian camp were also supposed to have been imprisoned, perhaps executed, because they had gotten to know too much during an overnight stay in the place.

At first, as Skorzeny recorded after the war, he attempted to stay the "latrine-o-grams." But in the end he realized that the rumors might well provide excellent cover for the real operation. He let the men whisper the most outrageous theories during their off-duty hours. For he knew his own spies among the spies would report anything to him which came close to the truth about the 150th Brigade's real mission.

Then the event occurred that would start the rumor that would plague Skorzeny for many years to come—one that has not been scotched to this very day. One morning, a young officer identified by Skorzeny only by his rank and first initial, Lieutenant N of one of the jeep teams, asked to have a private conversation with his commanding officer. Skorzeny granted the request and when they were "under four eyes," as the German expression has it, Lieutenant N said excitedly, "Obersturm, I think I know what the real objective is."

The scarfaced commando boss sat bolt upright with shock at the announcement. Officially he and only two other officers in the camp knew of their mission. Had someone spilled the beans? But before Skorzeny could react, the young officer said, "The Brigade is to march on Paris, sir, and capture Eisenhower's headquarters."*

Skorzeny forced himself, according to his own statement, to keep a non-committal manner. Then he frowned, as if he had not liked what he had just heard. The look seemed to convince the lieutenant that he had hit the nail on the head. With all the enthusiasm of youth he said, "May I offer you my cooperation, sir? I was stationed a long time in France and know Paris well. My French is good, too. You can rely on me, sir. This is my plan."

According to Skorzeny, the young officer explained eagerly how the 150th Panzer Brigade would enter the French capital from different directions, posing as Americans. With them they would take German tanks on transports. They would explain that these tanks had been captured by them at the front and they were taking them to the rear to be examined by U.S. specialists for the latest design improvements. All the camouflaged brigade would need was a central rallying point. There they would concentrate for a daring raid on Eisenhower's headquarters at Versailles. They knew all about it, according to the young officer. After all, the Petit Trianon where Eisenhower worked had been the headquarters of Field Marshal Gerd von Rundstedt during his long stay in Paris.

Skorzeny pretended to go along with the excited young officer's scheme (or so he explained it later). He said he knew Paris well and had often sat in the Café de la Paix, sipping a Ricard or Pernod. With that he dismissed "Lieutenant N" (who was never found to substantiate Skorzeny's postwar claim that this wild idea to assassinate Eisenhower had come from the eager young officer). Thereafter even wilder rumors swept the Bavarian camp and Skorzeny would confess after the war that he had lived "to regret ever mentioning that damned Café de la Paix!"

But had that encounter really been the source of the story, which

---

* We know that German intelligence had been trying to follow Ike's movements ever since he had set up his first headquarters on the Continent at the French port of Granville in late August 1944, but how would the young officer know where Eisenhower was that November? After all, it was a military secret even in the Allied camp. That statement about Ike's whereabouts is the first discrepancy in the whole "Eisenhower plot," if there was one.

would later have Eisenhower maintaining that Skorzeny was "the most dangerous man in Europe" and virtually demanding the latter's head on a silver platter? Would a young officer have dared to approach Hitler's favorite soldier, the one who had captured and freed Mussolini the year before and that same fall managed to keep Hungary in the war as Germany's ally by a similarly bold action? It seems unlikely.

The events of that 20 November 1944, when, as Skorzeny wrote, that interview between himself and "Lieutenant N" took place at Grafenwohr, were later dismissed by the German commando leader as "a little stone which spread large ripples" and "evil propaganda ... used by the enemy ... to ensure that three years later I was to face a U.S. military tribunal."

But was it just that? We know that Skorzeny's chief, who had long taken a personal interest in his fellow Austrian, knew little about America. In essence, Hitler was concerned with Europe. If he had known more about the United States and its manpower and enormous industrial potential, he would not have been foolish enough to have declared war on that country.

But if Hitler knew little about American history, he did know something of its politics, and the problems facing an ailing President Roosevelt running for another term in a democratic country with all the difficulties that democracy entails. The Fuhrer felt that the great coalition between the two emerging superpowers, Russia and America, was already looking shaky. It was Roosevelt who was holding it together really, despite the misgivings of the declining third ally (Britain).

As Hitler envisaged it, a German military victory in the West would weaken the Anglo-American bond for a while and perhaps postpone Germany's inevitable defeat at the hands of the great coalition. However, from what his agents had reported, he realized that it was due to the Allied supreme commander in the West, the ever-smiling, cheerful Eisenhower, that the military coalition of the British and American military, plus Churchill,* had been kept together. Thanks to the American with the broad smile, Supreme Headquarters had weathered many bad storms in the last one and a half years.

---

* Churchill, like Hitler himself, always played a great role in directing the efforts of his military. For that reason "Winnie" had always to be taken into consideration when his friend Ike made decisions which affected the whole military coalition.

What, however, if Eisenhower were removed? How would the Western Allies fare if, after suffering a bad military defeat, there was no Eisenhower to weld their shaken, battered armies together? Who would take Eisenhower's place? It couldn't be an Englishman, especially not Montgomery. Not even Field Marshal Alexander, who was too lazy to really assume control of a defeated force.

What American could then take over? Who had the experience? Certainly not Bradley. MacArthur was a virtual dictator in the Pacific. He wouldn't give up all that power to come to Europe with everyone and his son peering over his shoulder. General Marshall himself? Unlikely. He was too old, he didn't know the personalities well enough, and an ailing President Roosevelt needed him too much to control his armies all over the globe.

It must have seemed to Hitler, who had refused to sanction the assassination of political opponents until 1943,* that the murder of Eisenhower would be yet another major factor in his broad plan of keeping the Western Allies out of the firing line up to and into 1945, while the Anglo-American-Russian coalition fell apart and he could achieve a better peace treaty for Germany than the one currently on offer—the no-nonsense, no strings attached "unconditional surrender."

And who else to carry out the dastardly deed than Skorzeny who had achieved his famed scars by facing up to an opponent armed with a razor-sharp sabre and fighting it out, each blow aimed at the head, till the cut which would give the required scar was achieved. Right from the beginning Skorzeny was trained that it was most important to go for the head to achieve the best result.

In his years as Germany's top commando he had carried out that same policy in every operation he had undertaken for Hitler. Unlike the British SAS, on which his Jagdkommando had been based, Skorzeny was not content merely with military operations; they usually didn't achieve longlasting results. He, on the contrary, wanted to influence political events by his missions as he had in the three major operations which he had successfully carried out over the previous twelve months.

Could he—would he—attempt the same with Eisenhower, the Allied supreme commander? For he knew if he failed and Germany lost the war, he would be made to pay for the dastardly attempt on

---

* In 1943, Hitler sanctioned "Operation Long Jump," in which Skorzeny played a role and which was designed to murder the "Big Three"—Roosevelt, Stalin, and Churchill—when they met in November of that year in Tehran.

this key figure, an officer universally admired and respected throughout the "free world."

But his current operation, code-named *"Unternehmen Greif,"* was important and we have Skorzeny's word for it that it had been suggested by Hitler himself. But would it effect the outcome of the war decisively? On the face of it, the mission consisted of two things: a sabotage operation behind U.S. lines and the guidance by the bulk of his 150th Brigade of the spearhead of Dietrich's Sixth SS Panzer Army. Would such a role satisfy the scarfaced giant, vain, arrogant, and spoiled by his sudden elevation from an obscure SS captain on the sick list to the Fuhrer's favorite, who mixed now with the great? Hitler had even informed him of the coming counteroffensive in the West before he had told his three field army commanders—all of them senior generals leading large armies.

On the basis of Skorzeny's past record, it surely would not have. The head of the Jagdkommando would have wanted more, and it was sheer hypocrisy on his part to deny later that he wouldn't have engaged in anything as underhanded as assassinating someone like Eisenhower. For in that very same week when Skorzeny had his supposed conversation with "Lieutenant N," he was summoned to the headquarters of Reichsfuhrer SS Heinrich Himmler. At the village of Hohenlychen not far from his own headquarters, Skorzeny was introduced to the other three men present with Himmler. They were all like himself, high-ranking SS officers, scarfaced, and involved for most of their wartime careers in kidnapping and plain downright murder. And they had come together that cold overcast day to discuss exactly the same subject—murder.

The most senior man there, apart from Himmler, was Dr. Karl Kaltenbrunner, a fellow Austrian. He was then head of the German police apparatus, including the Gestapo, but in the past he had been charged as a criminal himself, involved in political murders in his homeland. Smaller than the two Austrian giants was cunning-faced SD General Walter Schellenberg, head of the SS's own spy organization; the man who had kidnapped the heads of the British Secret Service in 1939, attempted to kidnap the exiled British former king, the Duke of Windsor, and who had had his finger in a dozen different nefarious plots since then. The third, another giant but not scarfaced, was General Hans Pruetzmann, who had made his name—if that was the correct term for such infamy—by leading one of the extermination commandos in the east which had "liquidated" thousands upon thousands of Slavs, Jews, and gypsies. All in all very unsavory company for a man who apparently, according to his own statement, was not prepared to carry out a political murder, even if that assassination would serve the highest purposes of the Third Reich.

Himmler soon got down to business in that prissy, schoolmaster fashion of his. He explained, in view of the fact that sections of the Reich in the east and west had been occupied by the enemy, that action against German traitors was needed. In the west, in particular, the Americans had gained much publicity in the world's press by allowing their new "subjects," the conquered Germans, to state how much better they had it under their U.S. democratic masters than they had had it under Hitler's Nazis. To ensure that, among other things, these traitors were duly punished, it had been decided to form a German resistance movement. Already five thousand enthusiastic young German boys and girls had volunteered for the secret organization and were in training by the SS in several remote sites in the east and west.

This resistance organization called the "Werewolf," a name harking back to Germany's dark medieval history, had already been given a target. It was the new, American-appointed chief burgomaster of the old German imperial city of Aachen, which had been occupied by Hodges's First Army since the end of October. His name was Franz Oppenhoff, a Catholic lawyer who had been a thorn in the Nazi Party's side for years and who had remained behind when the order had come to evacuate Aachen when the Americans had first laid siege to the great border city.

Although the Americans had tried to keep the name of their mayoral appointee secret, it had become known to German spies within the city, and now Himmler wanted to set an example to all those other Germans under American control. Oppenhoff had to be liquidated—and soon. His would be the fate of all traitors to the cause of the Thousand-Year Reich. As Himmler proclaimed to the assembled SS officers, "In the territory where [the Americans] believe they have conquered us, new resistance will spring up behind their backs time and time again—and the werewolves, brave as death, volunteers all, will strike the enemy."

After that rousing statement, the chinless head of the SS peered through his pince-nez at Skorzeny in that severe manner he affected and said, "I think this would really be your kind of work, Skorzeny." Himmler then, for one, naturally supposed that the big Austrian commando leader would not object one bit to leading an organization dedicated to treacherous, stab-in-the-back murder. Then he added, "Or do you have enough on your plate already?"

Skorzeny considered. Again he was being offered a mission that wouldn't gain him the kind of publicity he craved. If he took on the command of the Werewolf Organization, he would be in charge of an outfit that was secret and had to remain secret. Even if his young fanatics did succeed in murdering Oppenhoff,* he would achieve no personal fame for obvious reasons.

In the end, Skorzeny said, "I feel I have enough to do already."

According to Skorzeny, Himmler accepted his refusal without demur and there and then appointed General Pruetzmann to be the head of the new secret resistance movement. Thereafter, Himmler turned his attention to yet another fantastic project: the question of using Hitler's new "vengeance weapons," the V-1 and V-2, against the United States. He asked the big Austrian commando, "Do you think it possible to bombard New York with a V-1?"

Skorzeny answered in the affirmative. "Yes," he assured the Reichsfuhrer, "using a U-boat as a firing base." Himmler concluded the conversation enthusiastically, maintaining excitedly that he'd mention the matter to Hitler and Admiral Doenitz, the head of Germany's U-boat fleet.**

Thus Skorzeny went back to his planning. We know definitely that he had other things in mind for his new 150th Panzer Brigade than mere sabotage and the role of guide for the Sixth SS Panzer Army. Afterward there were too many of his "jeep teams" who were captured and probably forfeited their own lives by revealing the "Eisenhower assassination plot" to their captors to make the matter simply a figment of "Lieutenant N's" imagination.

---

* Oppenhoff eventually was murdered on Palm Sunday 1945 by a Werewolf parachute commando composed of four SS men, its leader definitely from Skorzeny's outfit, a girl, and a 16-year-old boy. The latter, Erich Morgenscheiss, told the author, after that, he had decided he would never join another uniformed outfit, "not even the boy scouts."

** The first V-1s to be fired at coastal installations were used on Christmas Eve 1944, when German bombers launched them from the sea at northern Britain in a kind of early "cruise missile" attack.

One might ask, too, whether the men of the "jeep teams" would have risked their lives, as they did, simply to carry out acts of sabotage. For all of these "jeep team" volunteers were dressed in enemy, that is, American, uniform. If they were caught behind U.S. lines dressed in this manner even the thickest of the German volunteers would have known what their fate would have been. A swift sentence carried out against the nearest wall by a firing squad. This indeed is what happened to at least a score of Skorzeny's men. The Americans showed no mercy even to those who confessed the "Eisenhower plot." They were lined up against a brick wall near the Belgian village of Henri Chapelle (the bullet-scarred wall is still there) and executed forthwith.

Before they had commenced their mission they were told by the German military legal authorities that "the enemy has already violated the laws of war by bombing the civilian population, parachuting units of commando saboteurs to the rear of our lines and fomenting partisan war in the occupied countries. This behavior legitimizes ours. Moreover we advise you not to engage in actual fighting while you are wearing American uniform. Your job is to collect information and to sabotage and disorganize the enemy's efforts. *You are to put on German uniform before you open fire* [author's italics]."

It was an absurd piece of supposed legal advice. Some of the volunteers, at least, would have known that after 1942 Hitler had decreed that any commando, parachutist, or raider, in or out of German uniform, would be shot out of hand if captured on German territory; and it was an order that subordinate German commanders dared not refuse to carry out. As for the business of putting on a German uniform or taking off an American one before engaging the American enemy, it is patently absurd and impossible. How could one carry out such an operation in the heat of battle? Besides, some of the captured volunteers maintained that they had not even been issued a German uniform to hide beneath their American outer clothing.

So would these doomed volunteers have undertaken such risk, which led in a score of cases to their own death as spies, for the sake of turning around a few signposts or misleading U.S. troops by giving them the wrong directions, as is recorded in the literature of the time?

I think not. There was more to "Operation Greif" than mere sabotage. Naturally after the first of Skorzeny's jeep teams had been captured and started to spill the beans, the rumors flew fast and furious. A spy mania broke out right across Western Europe, reaching even to the United Kingdom where a mass breakout of some quarter of a million German POWs in British hands was nipped in the bud.

But why when the battle of the Bulge was over didn't the American authorities open up and give more details about what really happened that dark December? Skorzeny was captured (he said "surrendered") and put on trial. But in the end he was merely rapped on the knuckles and conveniently allowed to escape to Austria with the help of his old comrades of the Jagdkommando. Why?

Again we come back to General Eisenhower, just as is the case with the mystery of "Black ULTRA." What interest would he have in covering up these two possible events: his failure to use the information gained from Baron Oshima and the probability that there was an attempt by Skorzeny to assassinate him? What gain could he obtain from any form of cover-up?

In the first case, he had no need to do anything. The ULTRA operation remained a secret in both the United Kingdom and United States until disclosed by Fred Winterbotham in his 1973 book. What of the second? With hindsight one can only conclude that Eisenhower knew already he was heading for a postwar career in U.S. politics. (Patton certainly thought so; he said of his boss, "Ike is bitten by the presidential bug and he is yellow" and "How can anyone expect any backbone from a man who is already running for president?") Therefore the less made of what was, in reality, a grave failure on his part, the battle of the Bulge, the better.

How would it look if the full account of the measures taken by his staff to guard him from assassination during the Bulge—the tank accompanying him from his office to the mess hall, the double, the battalion of MPs as a personal bodyguard, the week-long blackout on his movements, etc.—ever reached the general public back home? It would not look good at all. In addition, there were those same servicemen who he had put at grave risk in the Ardennes to be reckoned with as potential postwar voters.

No wonder that a year after the events, on 18 December 1945, Eisenhower would write to Robert Patterson, Secretary of War: "I am unalterably opposed to making any effort to publicize at this time any story concerning the Ardennes Battle or even of allowing any written explanation to go outside the War Department."

Patterson was not impressed. He wrote in return the next day: "I believe the main features of this operation—the events leading up to it, the incidents of the fighting and the outcome—should be made known to the American people. Otherwise they will hear nothing but fault-finding and many of them will think the Army is covering up."

But Eisenhower won the day. The army's official account of the battle was toned down sufficiently to become the usual military whitewash job that often follows a scandal.

But at the end of November 1944, confident that they had tricked Eisenhower, the potential target for a Skorzeny assassination squad, the Germans proceeded with their plans. Everything seemed to be running in their favor. No extra measures had been taken to bolster up Middleton's front. Indeed, they thought his defense had been weakened rather than strengthened. For now the VIII Corps commander had two green divisions in the line and behind it, the 106th Infantry and the 9th Armored, and two badly battered ones from the hell of the Hurtgen Forest, the 28th and the 4th Infantry, both of which had lost a third of their strength in that terrible place. It must have seemed to a newly confident Hitler that with only days to go before he launched his great counterattack the Americans were as innocent of his intentions as the day he had dreamed up the whole grandiose plan some two months before.

"*Es geht ums ganze!*" (roughly, "Shoot the works") he had told aged Field Marshal Rundstedt when he had first informed him of the great plan. Then he had said the words with "an almost air of resignation." Now Hitler seemed full of confidence in a manner that he hadn't been since the attempt on his life the previous July. His closest advisers, Jodl, Keitel, Bormann, all noticed it. Perhaps, after all, the last German offensive in the West was going to succeed.

9

The Last Chance

Now the villages of the Eifel on the German side of the Ghost Front were bursting at the seams with the new troops from the German interior. Each new dawn, it seemed to the villagers who had been allowed to remain in the "Red Zone" by the Party big shots, there were other batches of freshfaced kids who had appeared as if by magic in their midst.

In early November at the village of Oberweis on the road from Bitburg to Luxembourg, 16-year-old Hitler Youths had taken over the flak guns intended to cover the key supply road. A little later, girls of a similar age followed. They were to act as loaders and surveyors. That had caused a small sensation in the hilltop hamlet. But by the last week of November, the new arrivals caused no alarm or even interest. As the village chronicler recorded afterward: "In all the sheds and barns there was military equipment and soldiers. Even the gardens were packed with shell cases. Outside there were hidden tanks and armored transports, plus scores of armored reconnaissance cars, and down on the River Prum, the infantry practiced river crossings in their rubber boats.... There were even Russian auxiliaries, hundreds of them, mostly Cossacks who would drive the horse drawn transport." And the chronicler noted that the last time Cossacks had appeared in this region, it had been over "a century before when they had come through the Eifel raping, ravaging and looting and driving Napoleon's retreating troops before them."

Now these exiled Cossacks, who had been captured and had then thrown in their lot with the Nazis, were Germany's allies, part of the great international army that would soon launch itself against the Americans. For contrary to all the propaganda put out by the "Free World," there were many who were natives of "Nazi-oppressed countries" prepared to join in the attack on their liberators. Russians of all races, Ukrainians, Poles, French, Dutch, Belgian, even a few German-American traitors—they were all present in the massed ranks of the "field-greys" waiting for that cynical signal of the German stubble-hopper: *"Marschieren oder Kreprieren!"* ("March or croak!").

By now most of the womenfolk of the remaining male civilians in the "Red Zone" had been evacuated. The farmers were excused even from service with the local Volksturm (Home Guard) and they had time to smoke their evil-smelling, homegrown tobacco and observe the antics of the "foreigners"—the soldiers who had been billeted with them from all over the Reich, men who couldn't even understand the farmers when they attempted to speak High German instead of the local Eifel dialect.

For the most part, it seemed to the local chroniclers of the time that the soldiers were in good heart. Ritter, as we have seen, came to the same conclusion. They played tricks upon one another like happy schoolkids; got drunk on the local schnaps, a fiery firewater made of candied fruits, apple-and-pear pulp, and potatoes when the latter could be spared; and made pets of the small creatures that always lurked in farmyards.

One chronicler in the larger front town of Neuerburg, soon to be totally destroyed, noted that "a tank crew, all boys really, found a mouse eating their bread ration inside their Panther. A great debate took place whether they should kill the culprit or let him go. In the end one of them decided, 'We take him with us, comrades. If we leave him here these Eifel peasants'll let him die of starvation.' So the mouse—Mickey, naturally, after the films—became their pet and they always swore, if we die, Mickey does, too. They and Mickey did—on the first day of the attack over the Sauer."

By the end of November, the German Reichsbahn had secretly delivered 200,000 men, 2,000 guns of all calibers, and 500 tanks to the area between Echternach and Prum that ran on the German side of the Ghost Front. This force outnumbered Middleton's corps by nearly four to one. Although this was a tremendous achievement, the German commanders of the Fifth Panzer Army and the Seventh

Army were worried that the great secret could still be betrayed in the two weeks left before the offensive commenced.

A mini spy mania set in. Suddenly the Red and Green Zones were filled with "chaindogs," German military policemen known thus due to the silver plates and chains they wore around their necks as a badge of office. With them, often in civilian clothes, came the Secret Field Police; and naturally, the Gestapo, the fat, middle-aged regular cops in their leather coats and pulled-down felt hats. Everyone knew and feared them, especially as many of them were local from the Eifel and weren't fooled as easily as "the dumb city folk."

Now the remaining civilians were not allowed to go beyond the village limits. In Neuerburg, for instance, the citizens were allowed to use the outlying paths of the prewar summer resort, as long as they could be seen from the ruined castle which dominated the little town. If they did not, justice could be swift.

In nearby Bollendorf, one day soon to be U.S. General Eddy's headquarters and for a day Patton's too, a civilian was caught listening to "Radio Annie," eight miles up the road in Luxembourg. An officer reported him. The Gestapo came. That was the last ever seen of that poor unfortunate. There wasn't even the usual urn containing his ashes and the official note saying that the "prisoner" had died of pneumonia.

The Gestapo was living up to its frightening reputation right to the bitter end. It routed out so-called "people's parasites," defeatists, and deserters without mercy. It even found Jews, nearly two years since Josef Goebbels had proudly reported to the Fuhrer that *"Deutschland ist jetzt judenfrei"* ("Germany is free of Jews").

Goebbels had been premature. In Berlin, where Goebbels was gauleiter, there were still 25,000 Jews at liberty and the Gestapo were being forced to use Jewish turncoats to betray their co-religionists. There were Jews in the armed forces, the armaments industry, medicine, etc. There was even a "half Jewish" field marshal—the Luftwaffe's Field Marshal Erhard Milch who had planned the bombing of London back in 1940. When his boss, Goering, head of the Luftwaffe, was informed of this, he poked a thumb at the informer (it is recorded) and snapped, "I'll decide who's Jewish around here."

But for those Jews unfortunate to live in small towns and villages after Goebbels's report to Hitler in 1942, there was little chance of survival if they didn't have protective neighbors. An orthodox Jew or even a liberal one who didn't practice his religion, but who conducted a business with a supposedly Jewish name, stood little chance of surviving. Hatred, dislike, even patriotism of a perverted kind would ensure that he or she would be betrayed to the police or Gestapo sooner or later.

By the mid-forties it so happened that there were many Jews congregated in the border areas of the "Red and Green Zones." Many were small businessmen, in particular horsetraders, who plied their trade on both sides of the border with Belgium, Luxembourg, and Holland. A few were those assimilated Jews, whose forefathers had been in Germany and had served the Germans loyally for decades, even centuries. They knew of the persecution of their co-religionists but didn't quite believe it could happen to them. But if danger did come their way, they could slip across the rugged, wooded border there in that region and escape down one of the many escape routes run by natives over the frontier, naturally for money.*

By 1944 most of those border Jews had been picked up or had escaped. But in the small towns just behind the Ghost Front, there were still frightened handfuls of German Jews living "illegally" in what had once been their own country.

Wittlich was one of these towns. Before the war the market town, which had been von Rundstedt's headquarters in 1940 and now was packed with headquarters and troops waiting to be sent to the front, had possessed a small garrison of one infantry battalion and had the highest number of Jews per capita outside of Frankfurt. Both the garrison and the local population cohabitated peacefully with "our Jews" (in contrast with those from elsewhere) despite the fact that there was a local branch of the Nazi Party situated in a dingy pub in one of the side streets.

Indeed the two groups, "Aryan" and "Jew," seemed to get on so well with each other that when, just before the war, the largest

---

* The author knew one Belgian taxi-owner who conducted this kind of human traffic in the Belgian region of St. Vith, where the local border guards often returned escaped Jews to the German authorities for a small tip. In November 1944, his son, a member of the 12th SS Division HitlerJugend, came "on leave" to that part of the world using his father's smuggle routes through the lines of the ill-fated 106th U.S. Division.

Jewish shopkeeper in the market town, Hermann Bach, died, everyone turned out to accompany the funeral cortege to the Jewish hilltop cemetery outside Wittlich. Even the local Brownshirts and SS in uniform went, which caused some of them to be summarily dismissed from the Party forthwith when it came out.

Thus it was when the build-up for the great counteroffensive commenced in the fall of 1944 and, according to Goebbels, Germany had been *"judenrein"* for two years, there was a small group of Jewish men, women, and children still living in the warren of medieval streets near to where the burned synagogue and former medieval ghetto were located. Time and time again they had been warned by locals serving in Russia what was happening to the Jews in the east. But still these relatively humble folks, former small-time horsetraders and so-called *"pluenjuden"** hung on the best they could.

Naturally they possessed no ration cards, indeed no official documentation whatsoever. In the eyes of the authorities they didn't exist. Instead they lived off barter and the goodwill of their neighbors. After dark they would place whatever possession they wished to barter under a stone in one of the ancient tumbledown garden walls that crisscrossed this old medieval place. In the morning, if they were lucky, they would find a new loaf of bread or a piece of scraggy meat in the same place, bought for them by some good neighbor who undoubtedly was just as afraid of being caught as they were.

All this had gone on for months, even years. But now the hour of destiny of these "non-people" was about to strike. The Gestapo and the Field Security Police were beginning to move into the garrison town, now bulging at the seams with troops in force.

Their objective, of course, was to protect the security of the coming counteroffensive. The presence of a handful of Jews wouldn't have been their main priority under ordinary circumstances, save for one thing. Back at the start of the war, the prominent British filmmaker, Alexander Korda, who was Jewish, had secretly circulated many of the more intelligent and important of his fellow Jews on the border area to send him details of Germany's fortifications there and the Nazis's preparations for an offensive in the West.

---

* Wandering peddlers who traveled on foot across the Eifel countryside with huge wickerwork packs on their shoulders, selling clothes and workingmen's overalls on credit to the peasants.

This operation had provided the British SIS, which had lost most of its German agents by this time, with valuable information, especially as the border had become a "no-go" area even for Germans if they didn't possess a special police pass. Although the Korda initiative remained a secret well into our own time, the Gestapo had somehow got wind of it. Now four years after the first Teutonic drive westward, the feared secret police did not want any repetition of the "Jewish betrayal," even though there were not supposed to be any Jews left in the Eifel border area.

The Gestapo "bulls," as they were known behind their backs, went to work with their customary plodding thoroughness, under the command of their boss, SS General "Gestapo" Muller. Most of them were middle-aged ex-cops who had served the Weimar Republic, the Nazis, and as they often boasted in their cups, "even Joseph Stalin when the Commies take over Germany." Somehow in the case of Wittlich, they found a lead to these miserable, cowed fugitives in their own land. Perhaps at last one of the "illegal's" neighbors had betrayed them. Perhaps the Gestapo, who prowled around at all times of day and night (for they were allowed to break the nightly curfew which had been imposed on the whole area and which included both civilians and soldiers), stumbled upon one of the barter transactions being carried out behind the ruined synagogue in Wittlich's Himmeroderstrasse.

We don't know, and after the war those who did weren't talking, for obvious reasons. But abruptly the Wittlich Jews vanished. All they left behind to mark their presence at all and the fact that Jews had lived in Wittlich for nearly three hundred years was the Torah Roll.* Someone, and it was obvious it had to be a local German, had managed to hide it before the Gestapo thugs came.

The arrest of those poor unfortunate Jews and others, including Luxembourgers working in civilian posts in the German administration throughout that same area, seemed to mark the end of German intelligence's concern with the security of the great counteroffensive. They knew from the current disposition of Hodges's troops along the First Army front that the Americans had bought their own concept,

---

*Twenty years ago, when the author first inquired into the fate of these last Jews, his informant disappeared to return, pale-faced and obviously moved, with that precious religious artifact cradled in his arms. As far as the author knows the Torah is still hidden to this day.

namely that the German formations in the Eifel would only counter-attack when the Americans started their drive from Aachen to Cologne. In other words, the American generals were thinking like the German generals had when they had been first informed of Hitler's plan.

The idea of the *"kleiner schlag"* ("small blow"), i.e., a small encircling movement to either side of Aachen, had been accepted by the Americans without any consideration of the Hitler proposal. And his was that of the *"grosser schlag"* ("great blow") which was not to happen around Aachen.

As General Erich Brandenburger, the commander of the German Seventh Army, told his U.S. interrogators after the war:

> The Allies estimated that our available reserves were—at most— sufficient only for local counterattacks. The Allies saw this later view apparently confirmed by the location of the area chosen for the reconstitution of the Sixth Panzer Army. They took the risk of holding the 160-kilometer front between the Hurtgen Forest and the northern flank of the Third Army southeast of Luxembourg. Here they had only two or three divisions in the line and with an armored division thoroughly subdivided into the little "fire depart-ments" located behind the line…. This soft spot in the enemy line and the apparent estimate of the situation made by the enemy were certainly the determining factors which induced the Supreme Command to mount the planned offensive.

The prose is slightly confusing, but what General Branden-burger, an excellent staff officer, was saying to his American interrogators after his capture in 1945 was that, ironically enough, the Allies had conceived the same plan of attack for the Germans as the German generals had done themselves. Unfortunately, as the German generals had already learned, and the American ones would also learn when it was much too late to do anything about it, the man who was directing this great operation was not a staff-trained, conventional regular officer. He was Adolf Hitler. And Hitler hated the *"Monocle Fritzes,"* those arrogant, aristocratic Prussian staff officers, and distrusted them. Their plans were always too conventional, he thought, predictable and based on pre-vious campaigns. His, on the other hand, were never the least bit conventional and more often than not, which was very important, they succeeded.

America's generals, who would fight the battle of the Bulge to come, thought they were opposed by generals like themselves led by that old Prussian wizard, Field Marshal Gerd von Rundstedt. These German generals had attended the same kind of military academies and schools as they had. Indeed, much of conventional prewar U.S. military doctrine was based on the German model. The Americans had studied the same textbooks as their German counterparts; absorbed the same kind of military history; visited the same battlefields and drawn the same conclusions. They thought they could usually guess what the "other feller" (as General Bradley called his opposite numbers in the Wehrmacht) would do under given circumstances. But Adolf Hitler, who had left school at fourteen and had risen to the dizzy height of full corporal in the old Imperial Army, had never done any of the conventional military things: no "war school," followed by "war academy," etc. All the same he thought himself the greatest German soldier of them all, a kind of latter-day Frederick the Great.

General von Manteuffel exemplified the whole concept of Hitler's versus the generals' attitudes to the coming battle when in the final days of the buildup to the Bulge he asked the Fuhrer for searchlights. When Hitler asked why, von Manteuffel replied he wanted to adopt the British idea of artificial moonlight ("Monty's Moonlight") for the first wave of the attack. He would bounce the light of his searchlights off of low-hanging clouds. This would reflect the light downward to aid the first assault companies.

Hitler listened attentively and then asked the little tank general how he knew there would be clouds there in the first place. Von Manteuffel, known for his sharp and witty tongue, replied he knew there would be clouds on that morning of Saturday, 16 December 1944, because, "Mein Fuhrer, you have already assured us that we will have cloudy weather on that day." Hitler could only agree. In the author's opinion, that little episode put everything in a nutshell.

But if the German generals felt that they had succeeded in fooling the U.S. generals into believing that any German attack would come in the Aachen area and were by this last week of November totally convinced that their security was foolproof,* there were still a few brave souls in the Allied camp, mostly of lower rank, who weren't satisfied with that scenario.

But how could these officers of less than field grade rank put their case in front of the top brass, who by now apparently agreed that Germany had accumulated a lot of reserves and might well launch a counterattack in the Aachen region? How could they convince the U.S. generals, Eisenhower, Bradley, Hodges, that they should widen their thinking and consider the "Ghost Front option"—the startling idea (for them) that the Germans would attack the U.S. Army's weakest point, Middleton's VIII Corps?

As most of these young officers were in or connected with intelligence, it would have seemed their obvious approach should have been through General Sibert, Colonel Dickson, and Colonel Koch. But none of these intelligence "experts" seemed to really have the ear of their masters. Bradley's chief of intelligence, General Sibert, in particular, appeared to share his master's somewhat starry-eyed view of German intentions. It was obvious that if Sibert couldn't be convinced, neither could Dickson and Koch; for, in essence, Sibert was their superior officer and they had to respect his opinion.

Therefore there was only one intelligence officer of senior rank in the whole European Theatre of Operations who might have convinced Eisenhower and Bradley at this eleventh hour to rethink the whole situation on the Western Front before it was too late. It was the British officer, whose staff called him (behind his back, due to the fact that he virtually lacked a chin) "the hangman's dilemma."

The "hangman's dilemma" was General Kenneth Strong, the very tall, dark, chinless Scot who had run Eisenhower's intelligence operation since mid-1943. The British brigadier, who spoke fluent Italian, French, and German, had studied the German Army inside Germany from 1935, finishing up prior to the outbreak of war in

---

* The feint devised by General Bradley to convince the Germans the Americans were building up their forces in the Middleton VIII Corps area of Luxembourg had failed completely. As General Brandenburger of the German Seventh Army told his U.S. interrogators after the war: "The American attempt to simulate the presence of the 75th U.S. Infantry Division must be regarded as a failure." Within two days, Brandenburger knew this was simply a simulation exercise. His spies also told him the presence of a large number of U.S. tanks that were really those being repaired in American tank workshops in Luxembourg.

1939 as the assistant British military attaché in Berlin—and somewhat of a minor spy as well.*

Although he would have liked an active infantry command, he
was naturally posted to intelligence in 1939 and would continue to
be connected with that arcane trade until he retired. At that time, he
was one of only three regular officers in his branch of military intelligence and his subordinates, mostly high-ranking ex-civilians and
academics, looked up to him as the fount of all wisdom as far as
intelligence was concerned. As one of his subordinates at the time
wrote of him: "He looked like a beaver—an eager beaver bursting
out of his uniform, with dark hair, a fine forehead, and clever shifty
eyes."

That "shifty" was not quite fair. But it was clear as the years pro-
gressed that he knew, as all regular officers do, that if he wished to
be promoted he would have to hitch his star to some important superior's wagon. So, perhaps as a deliberate act, Strong hitched his star
to Eisenhower's wagon. After mid-1943 he loyally supported the
American general, who like himself had never fired a shot in anger
or commanded troops in battle, and served through the campaigns
in the Middle East, the pre-D-day interim in Britain, and after
August 1944 throughout the battle in Northeast Europe.

But this decision to attach himself to "Ike" (for they were on an
"Ike" and "Ken" basis) virtually ruined his reputation in the British
Army, especially with the Montgomery–Brooke (chief of the British
Imperial General Staff) clique. For they thought, with truth to a cer-
tain extent, that Strong had "gone over" to the Yanks.

For by then Strong had acquired a taste for the American way. In
Eisenhower's great sprawling headquarters in Versailles, where the
staff equalled the size of a whole combat division, he had changed.
As one of his subordinates who had known him back in 1939 wrote:
"I noticed my old chief had changed. By now Strong had the sleek,
well-fed look of a senior staff officer who had adopted the lifestyle
of the American top brass in Algiers. He responded to the generosi-
ty and informality of the Americans and had learnt a lot about the
in-fighting between one headquarters and another."

---

* For several years before his death, the author corresponded with General Sir
Kenneth Strong. I always found him obliging, prompt, and informative. But like
most good intelligence officers he seemed to favor the "oblique approach." It was
only later that one figured Strong was telling you more than you thought he was at
the time, if you were smart enough to comprehend.

And that was really the trouble. At Montgomery's headquarters and the British War Office in London, the staff felt the need for a clearcut decision: one that was basically between Montgomery's "narrow front" strategy and Eisenhower's "broad front" one— "Monty's desire for a full-blooded thrust on a narrow front to Berlin and Ike's advance on all fronts to the same objective."

But Supreme Headquarters could not give a clear decision. Its staff officers spent each day working out compromises. As one critic of the work of the Versailles headquarters had remarked, "It was all balls and rackets." Naturally the Montgomery faction was angered by this lack of straight decisions, as they saw them; while in their turn the officers on Eisenhower's staff were irritated and even angered by Montgomery's constant demands for clarity. As they saw it, with the United States supplying three soldiers for every British soldier, Montgomery was really out for the "narrow front" option as it would give him command over the vast majority of Eisenhower's troops, both British and American.

It was against this background that Britisher Strong tried to steer a relatively clear course. He had thrown in his lot with the Americans, yet as a regular British officer he was dependent on promotion and a professional future in the London War Office. The result—intelligence suffered.

As Noel Annan, who served under Strong in August 1944, put it nearly half a century later: "Intelligence at SHAEF was governed by what one might call the 'Happy Hypothesis.' This was that the German Army had been so shattered in Normandy and battered in Russia that it was only a matter of two or three months before the war would end. When I arrived at SHAEF, I formed the impression that the intelligence appreciations were tuned to justify Eisenhower's policy to attack all along the line. *This policy required intelligence to report the German Army as being incapable of mounting an offensive.* [author's italics]."

This interpretation of SHAEF intelligence seems to be borne out by Strong's own statement that: "Members of intelligence staffs ... were considered defeatist if they predicted anything but Allied successes: if they expressed doubts about the future they were accused of being out of touch with the realities of the war. Such accusations could only be successfully countered by incontrovertible facts and figures." And Strong believed that "intelligence is very seldom able to produce these or predict precise events."

Thus one might think, with hindsight, that the most important intelligence officer in the whole of the five-million strong army commanded by General Eisenhower had fallen into the most elementary trap of his profession. On the facts known to him, he was giving Ike several alternative opinions on what the Germans's options and intentions were. Later he stated he had elucidated on three of these. However, it is generally supposed that the good intelligence officer will outline the various alternatives to his boss but then give him the one possibility which he thinks most likely.

In mid-October, General Strong had received a visit from two former subordinates who were working at Bletchley Park. We do not know who sent them, and it would be futile to guess at this distance of time. In any event, the two, Wing Commander Jim Rose and Major Alan Pryce-Jones, were admitted to Strong's presence despite their lowly rank. Debonair Pryce-Jones parked himself on the edge of Strong's big desk, a daring thing in itself for a mere major, and asked his former boss why he thought the Germans would collapse soon. After all, the Allies had been battering their heads against the Siegfried Line now for nearly two months, incurring terrible casualties, and with little success. Strong replied in that soft Scots burr that he never lost that the Germans were losing a division of men a day. In the light of those kinds of losses, naturally Germany had to cave in soon.

Pryce-Jones wasn't impressed by Strong's theory and he didn't pull his punches. He said straight out: "Sir, if you believe that, you'll believe anything." He then went on to explain that the Germans were replacing losses rapidly and forming a new reserve army, supposedly a million men strong. This they knew from the Bletchley intercept.

Strong had disagreed. But despite the difference in rank and the cocky young major's approach, he did not turn rough. He had dismissed the two and then reported their statements to "Beatle," General Walter Bedell-Smith, Eisenhower's chief of staff, who possessed both flaming red hair and flaming red ulcers, and who always maintained that "somebody has to be a son-of-a-bitch around here."

Four days later Strong had reported to Eisenhower that von

Rundstedt was gathering crack troops (he probably meant the Sixth SS Panzer Army) to act as a "fire brigade." On 19 October he had followed this with a reference to Hitler's wish to launch a November counterattack and put in a "spoiling attack" in the north. Still wide of the mark, as far as the actual location of the coming attack was concerned, Strong's statements went contrary to the prevailing attitude at SHAEF that the Germans were on their last legs.

But by November it seemed General Strong's forebodings had evaporated. On a short leave in London, he told one of his former staff and fellow intelligence officer, Peter Earle of the British Army (who was one of the few staff officers in World War II to be bayonetted by the enemy, in April 1945) that he had concluded: "The original [German] plan for a 'lightning blow' and sudden attack may, with some certainty, be said to have lapsed ... SHAEF thought that none of the German reserve divisions were near the front."

Once back at Versailles, however, Strong was faced with another minor revolt, this time on the part of his own intelligence staff officers, three British and one American. They had worked out, and now told their boss, that if all the German divisions which they already knew were lined up opposite Middleton's front in the Ardennes remained, and if, in particular, one more German division joined them, intelligence could concede that "a relieving attack" in that area was likely.

Strong bought the idea. At conferences with Eisenhower and Bedell-Smith, the details of which were circulated to subordinate headquarters, he suggested that the new formations discovered in the Eifel area might be used for one of three purposes (Strong still was not sticking his neck out and coming to just one option, as a good intelligence officer should): first, these formations might. be sent to the Russian front where the Red Army was exerting great pressure on the Germans; second, they could be used to counterattack a successful Allied penetration in the Aachen-Cologne area (the plan that Hitler's intelligence had successfully sold the Allies); and third, these nine panzer divisions and five infantry divisions definitely identified in the general area of Middleton's Ghost Front might be used to launch a relieving attack through the Ardennes.*

He added to this, as November started to give way to December, that "the enemy's hand is dealt for a showdown before Christmas."

---

* After the war, General Strong wrote that he favored the second option.

He never explained why, save knowing the German tendency to sentimentality, he might have thought that the Wehrmacht wanted to give their hard-pressed Fuhrer a victory for a Christmas present.

While Strong temporized and in a way made the intelligence situation worse for the commanding generals with his three options, specially emphasizing the number two option (the Cologne–Aachen counterattack possibility), his staff and presumably their chief waited. They waited to see if any of the divisions facing Middleton were being moved. They weren't. All right, they must have decided, the clincher is going to be the transfer of another assault division into the area between Echternach (Luxembourg) and Prum (Germany).

Air and signals intelligence were alerted to find out, and then things started to happen. A likely assault division and one that belonged to the Waffen SS as well, the 17th SS Panzergrenadier Division, the *"Gotz von Berchlingen"** was signaled to begin a move. The pro-Ardennes group in Bletchley and in Strong's Versailles must have tensed electrically waiting to find out where. Now it would take only the advance party of this experienced division, veteran of both East and West Fronts, to move into the Eifel and they might well convince Strong at last. He'd have to come off the fence and warn Bradley and his subordinate commanders, Hodges and Middleton, of what was soon coming their way.

But someone, we don't know who after a lapse of over half a century, fluffed it. The report was that the 17th SS Panzergrenadier was moving into the Saar region. In fact, parts of that division, shattered in the battle of Metz against Patton's Third Army, were already in that area and had been for some time, refitting and reinforcing. The movement signal, intercepted by ULTRA, probably referred to "Brigade Kurland," a subordinate formation, which was moving to bring the 17th SS up to strength.

As Bletchley Park correctly interpreted the movement order (in part): the armored infantry had been moved to the area of the Saar township of Merzig in order to take part in the coming attack. Why else should an armored formation be in the area? But the panzergrenadiers were going to participate in the second phase of the battle of the Bulge. They had been selected to lead "Operation Northwind," the assault on the U.S. Seventh Army on Patton's right flank. In due course, the 17th SS would move again closer to their

---

* Named after a celebrated rebel baron of the Middle Ages, whose name was used in a Goethe play to signify "kiss my arse!" It was that kind of a formation.

start-line. But by then the battle of the Bulge would be raging and, as far as the men of the Ghost Front were concerned, they would be fighting for their very lives.

In Strong's case, the movement of the "Kurland" formation was regarded as a false alarm and, although Merzig was only a matter of a score of miles from Middleton's right flank on the Ghost Front, that close proximity was disregarded. The alarmists had been proved wrong. The Germans were not building up their divisions, known by SHAEF intelligence to be facing Middleton by the turn of November/December 1944.

Thus the last chance passed untaken. Since September the Allies had had time enough to come out of that numbing euphoria which had led them to believe that Germany was virtually beaten and victory was just around the corner—that there would be no further trouble from Germany's rabble of an army. But there had been indications enough that the German's *weren't* beaten.

The proof went back to that first terrible week of September when the German armies in the West seemed in full retreat. Exactly then they had commenced their V-2 campaign primarily against England and later Belgium, which was still in full swing. Thereafter had come the U.S. defeat in the Eifel and the stubborn defense of Germany's frontier at Aachen and in the Hurtgen Forest. Try as they may, the Allies had been unable to break through Hitler's "Wall."

The general who had boasted that given the supplies he would go "through the Siegfried Line like shit through a goose" had lamentably failed to do so. Way into December, Patton would still be attacking Metz, which he had maintained he had virtually captured back in September.

On all sides, there were indications that the Germans were defending the Siegfried Line, not only to prevent the Allies from penetrating the Reich, but also to give themselves time to prepare a counterstroke with new supplies of the latest weapons. (In September 1944, Germany's armament production was the highest of the whole war.) Yet even when it started to dawn on Allied intelligence that the Germans might indeed attack rather than just defend, the officers concerned still clung to the vain hope that the

Germans would only respond with an attack *after* the Allies had broken through the Siegfried Line and started heading for the Rhine. In hindsight this seems particularly stupid, when U.S. military doctrine (as exemplified by "Old Blood an' Guts" Patton) always propounded the superiority of attack over defense.

But Allied intelligence had failed to recognize what the German intentions were. They had well and truly been fooled by their counterparts in the Wehrmacht. Indeed, if one concludes that "Operation Fortitude" was the Allies's most successful deception operation of the war—one that made the Germans think the D-day invasion would come through the Pas de Calais area and not Normandy—then one can say German intelligence operations in the Eifel–Ardennes were the Third Reich's greatest deception. With virtually all the facts known through the MAGIC–ULTRA decodes, and aerial reconnaissance, etc., the Allies still believed what they wanted to believe—the Germans would counterattack in the Aachen area. It was a belief that German deception actively encouraged; and the Allies fell for it, hook, line, and sinker.

So the die had been cast. Now only a miracle could save the 60,000 ill-prepared GIs of Middleton's VIII Corps manning the Ghost Front. It was Thursday, 30 November 1944. There were exactly fifteen days left.

DECEMBER
1944

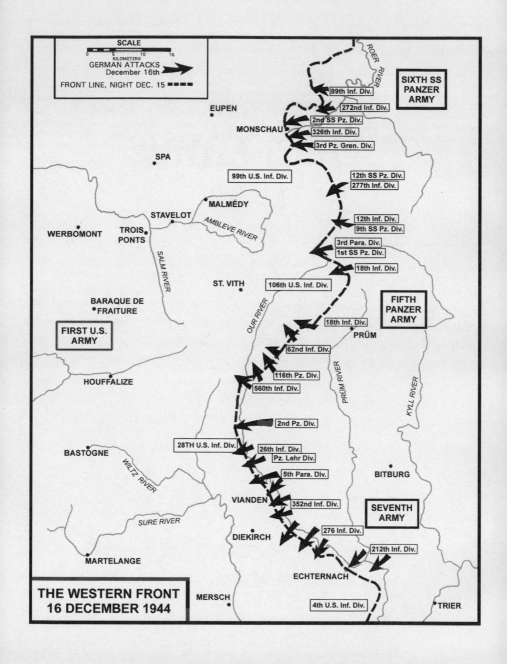

SCALE

KILOMETERS

GERMAN ATTACKS
December 16th

FRONT LINE, NIGHT DEC. 15 ▰▰▰▰

SIXTH SS
PANZER
ARMY

EUPEN

89th Inf. Div.

272nd Inf. Div.

2nd SS Pz. Div.

MONSCHAU

326th Inf. Div.

3rd Pz. Gren. Div.

SPA

99th U.S. Inf. Div.

12th SS Pz. Div.
277th Inf. Div.

MALMÉDY

12th Inf. Div.
9th SS Pz. Div.

STAVELOT

AMBLEVE RIVER

WERBOMONT

TROIS
PONTS

3rd Para. Div.
1st SS Pz. Div.

18th Inf. Div.

SALM RIVER

ST. VITH

106th U.S. Inf. Div.

FIFTH
PANZER
ARMY

BARAQUE DE
FRAITURE

OUR RIVER

18th Inf. Div.

PRÜM

FIRST U.S.
ARMY

62nd Inf. Div.

HOUFFALIZE

116th Pz. Div.

560th Inf. Div.

PRÜM RIVER

KYLL RIVER

2nd Pz. Div.

BASTOGNE

28TH U.S. Inf. Div.

26th Inf. Div.

Pz. Lehr Div.

WILTZ RIVER

5th Para. Div.

BITBURG

VIANDEN

352nd Inf. Div.

SEVENTH
ARMY

SURE RIVER

276 Inf. Div.

DIEKIRCH

212th Inf. Div.

MARTELANGE

ECHTERNACH

THE WESTERN FRONT
16 DECEMBER 1944

MERSCH

4th U.S. Inf. Div.

TRIER

10

Auf Wiedersehen

The Ghost Front was now in winter's firm grip. The snows of mid-November had virtually vanished save for the heights of the "Snow Eifel" ("*Schnee Eifel*"), the area north of Prum. But the air was bitterly cold, with a wind blowing in straight from Siberia, or so it seemed to the bone-chilled GIs. In the mornings the tops of the massed rows of spiked firs marching up the hills on the German side of the Our–Sauer Line were a beautiful crisp sparkling white. Then the cold and warm fronts of that great divide met and the hoar frost would melt. The rest of the day would be grey, misty, and overcast. Noise would be deadened or muted by the steady mournful drip-drip of the melting frost. Time seemed to pass leadenly.

With the winter came a noticeable decrease in activity. On the long American front virtually every armored division was in reserve. This indicated that the top brass were not intending any major thrust into Germany before Christmas. To the north and south of the Ghost Front though, both Hodges and Patton were planning limited offensives again. For three months they had both been attacking—and failing. Perhaps, they hoped, just like the enemy on the other side of the line, to give the "folks back home" a present for Christmas. Thankfully, the "meat wagons" carrying the "stiffs," those poor dead young men packed like cordwood, back to the frontline cemeteries at Henri la Chapelle and Margraten, were becoming ever fewer. The medical problems were chest infections and trench foot. Hospitals at Verviers, Liege, and the like, behind Hodges's First Army front were packed with such unfortunates.

Even so, slowly the thoughts of the men in the line were starting to turn to Christmas—"the last of the war," as the newspapers back home were calling it. The GIs, clad in as much clothing as they could find or scrounge, knew nothing of that. If they ever asked themselves whether the war could conceivably be over in a matter of twenty-five days, they must have reminded themselves they were still in the same spot they had started from back in the heady days of victory of September.

In particular, the survivors of the 28th and 4th Infantry Divisions must have dwelled upon that particularly unpleasant thought—that is, if they were still capable of thinking about anything save sleep, hot chow, and, if they were lucky, finding a willing woman when and if they were finally given a pass to Gay Paree.

The 28th, the "Bloody Bucket," had returned to the Ghost Front on 19 November from the Hurtgen, where it had lived up to its nick-name suffering nearly 5,000 casualties. By 1 December, it had taken in 3,400 replacements but it was still desperately tired and war-weary, short of almost a fourth of its official fighting capacity. On 7 December, the "Bloody Bucket" was followed by the 4th Infantry, the "Ivy League," which similarly had lost over a quarter of its strength in the Hurtgen. Like its neighbor, the 4th, in which Middleton himself had served in World War I, needed thousands of replacements (and the U.S. Army in Europe was running out of replacements) and, above all, rest.

On the Ghost Front, the veterans and the "wetnose" replace-ments seemed to be getting that rest. December was different from September when they had first entered Germany and had been beat-en back at "Hitler's Wall." Now they could move about the line with comparative freedom. Although in some cases, especially in the 4th's area of operations between Echternach and Wallendorf, the Germans were on the heights on the other side of the river, perhaps some 150 yards away, and could see everything the GIs were doing. But on the Ghost Front the Germans rarely fired at them. Occasionally someone would let rip a burst of machine-gun fire from beyond the River Sauer or there would be a minor barrage. But it was never very serious.

The four "Misfits," as they called themselves due to their lack of respect for the authority of their officers, were the tank crew of "Bea Wain II" and veterans of the Hurtgen "Death Factory." They and most of the other survivors of Company B of the 707th Tank Battalion attached to the 28th Infantry Division had come out of that hell feeling even less respect for their officers' bravery and leadership qualities. For they had seen their commanders do some terrible and, in their opinion, downright cowardly things in the Hurtgen.

Now that was behind them, and the crew, under the command of Chicago-born Sergeant Mike Kasovitz, were trying to pick up the pieces. Naturally, so they thought, they were still wearing the same dirty outfits they had worn in the Hurtgen. They lacked ammunition for their Sherman and their CO had not yet replaced the fifth member of their crew who had been killed back in the forest.

All that didn't seem to worry their CO, Colonel Ripple though. He appeared to them to have forgotten the war here in this Luxembourg safe haven. He granted so many officers and enlisted men leave that there were always tanks without crews. Nor did he order maintenance to be carried out on the battle-scarred, worn Shermans, though the "Misfits" were certain that maintenance was badly and urgently needed. At times they were forced to light fires under "Bea Wain II," to get the 30-ton tanks to move, a very dangerous procedure with the Sherman. As one of them, Pfc. John Marshall, reported long afterward: "The tanks stayed idle although we could see the Germans across the river. I never had such a workfree time in camp. It was like a holiday, as though we'd never fight again."

Once, but only once, Marshall thought he might be wrong. Under the command of a young officer, whom the "Misfits" did not trust after the Hurtgen, they were ordered out on patrol along the west bank of the River Our which ran into the Sauer. After lighting the usual dangerous fires under their tanks to get them started, the reluctant Shermans finally moved out. Here the River Our was less than thirty yards across and, although the winter rains had filled the border river, it was running sluggishly as usual save at certain spots. Perhaps that's why they encountered the German patrol when they did. For suddenly there they were, also with some kind of armored vehicles!

As if on sudden, silent command, both patrols stopped in their tracks. What now? The wait seemed to go on forever. Nothing happened. Neither the Germans nor the men of the 707th fired.

Abruptly the platoon leader broke the brooding silence. He gave that classic order that the "Misfits" had heard too often in the Hurtgen. "Let's get the hell outta here!" And they did, to survive to fight the first days of the battle of the Bulge, but by Christmas Day 1944 the 707th would be all but wiped out.*

But for now the Christmas preparations continued. They started to stock up on the local Diekirch beer and the powerful fruit schnaps, Quetsch, made by the Luxembourg farmers and bought on the black market. Others pledged their candy rations to provide parties for the local kids. Cigarettes were too precious, even for the black market. A GI could get a night with a lady of easy virtue for a carton of Lucky Strikes; and down in the dives below the fortifications of the eleventh-century Luxembourg capital, there were whores from the nearby coal and steel towns of the French border who would perform for even fewer cigarettes than that. For the only currency that counted now among Western Europe's debased currency was the American Chesterfield and Lucky Strike.

The top brass, too, now seemed to be more concerned with the coming festive season and its parties than the war. On 15 December, Middleton and his corps staff at Bastogne were going to throw a wingding to celebrate the anniversary of the formation of the VIII Corps in England one year before. The enlisted men for their part were going to have a big dance with the local girls on Saturday, 16 December, in the big rooms of the French Franciscan monastery in the town which had been requisitioned by VIII Corps. The announcement scandalized the more conservative Catholic element in the crossroads town. One day later when the balloon had gone up, the local priest would pontificate against such frivolities at High Mass. He would thunder, "Heaven has already punished those soldiers. As I speak to you, the German troops have reached Clervaux." Not a nice comment from supposed allies. But that was later and by then a lot of things would have changed forever.

Middleton's boss, General Bradley and his staff, some forty air miles away from Bastogne, were also planning to celebrate, but later on Christmas Eve which in Luxembourg takes precedence, in the German fashion, over Christmas Day.

Bradley's chief, General Eisenhower, was still traveling that first

* The last surviving tank of the 707th Tank Battalion is to be found in the castle courtyard of the little 28th Division Museum at the castle in the little Luxembourg pilgrimage township of Clervaux.

week of December. Christmas and partying seemed the furthest thing from his mind. All accounts of his mood at that time seem to indicate that it was foul. Ever since he had commenced his rare visits to the front, or at least to his frontline commanders, he appeared to have grown increasingly angry. Even good news did nothing for his temper. Perhaps it was a personal matter. Naturally the weather was terrible, but if we are to believe his "secretary-chauffeur," who was driving him most of the time now, he had been receiving a lot of "nagging" letters from his Washington-based wife, Mamie (who had good reason to nag); and this upset him greatly. The consequence was, as is so often the case even with great men, that he took his bad mood out on his subordinates.

But as November had closed, Eisenhower had found one important if detested victim upon whom to vent his anger. He was Lt. General "Jake" Devers, the half-Alsatian commander of the U.S. Sixth Army Group, now primarily fighting in French Alsace, with both the U.S. Seventh Army and the French First Army under his command. Neither Bradley nor Eisenhower liked Devers, and the former called the Army Group commander contemptuously, "a .22 caliber general."

Then on the last Friday of November, with Kay Summersby's little scottie cradled in his arms, Eisenhower rode into the headquarters of one of Devers's corps commanders, General Edward H. Brooks, to find that the self-satisfied general was planning a crossing of the Rhine. He and another corps commander were prepared to throw their men across the great river, which Eisenhower had been striving to cross ever since September.

It should have been great news that would please Eisenhower beyond measure. But it didn't. He blew his top. Why hadn't he been informed? He gave a verbal order that the great crossing should be stopped immediately. That night he had a stormy meeting with Devers. The latter assured him he had two companies across already. They had passed through the Siegfried Line defenses without finding a single German defender.

Devers made another try. Eisenhower wouldn't have it. In a heated dinner discussion between the high-ranking generals, he told Devers if he persisted in this course, he'd take away two corps from the Seventh Army. Naturally Eisenhower won. He came out of the heated meeting "mad as hell," while Devers noted in his diary that he "wondered" if he was "a member of the same team."*

Still in a bad mood, Eisenhower undertook his final major journey before the battle of the Bulge. He went to the lair of the "beast," the headquarters of Field Marshal Montgomery in Maastricht. As usual, Montgomery made Eisenhower come to him and not the other way around. It was not something that pleased Eisenhower, especially in the strange mood in which he seemed to be just before the coming battle.

The Maastricht Conference of Thursday, 7 December 1944, epitomized Eisenhower's attitude in the last days prior to the great surprise counteroffensive. Montgomery, who thought that he had convinced Eisenhower of his way of thinking, was in a good mood. Indeed, he had just issued an order to his own armies stating that there would be no offensive operations over Christmas. The men deserved a day of rest. "They shall have opportunities to attend services as desired and to have their Christmas dinner undisturbed." Montgomery was in for a great surprise exactly nine days later.

Over a three-hour lunch—very long for Montgomery—he discovered he was dealing with a very different Ike than he'd known before. Eisenhower was a very angry man who laid down the law. He would not give command of all land forces to Montgomery, as had been the case until 1 September 1944; nor would he assign Bradley's army group to the north for one full-blooded thrust for the German capital. In vain Montgomery said, as long as the thrust went in the north (of the Ardennes), "I would willingly serve under Bradley."

Again Eisenhower wouldn't buy it. He had come up with a new strategy, different from the "broad front" he had advocated for so long. Now Bradley's three-army-strong Twelfth Army Group would be divided into two forces. They would attack in two different directions. Montgomery voiced his concern that if this new plan of attack was implemented in the New Year there would be a gap of one hun-

---

*In the literature of the Battle for Western Europe 44/45, this strange business is virtually never mentioned. Even today it remains a great mystery why Eisenhower did not give Devers his head. As General G. Davidson, the Seventh Army Chief Engineer, who would have been responsible for the crossing, noted decades later: "I have often wondered what would have happened if [Eisenhower] had taken that calculated risk.... Perhaps success would have eliminated any possibility of the Battle of the Bulge."

dred miles in between the two assault groups—that held by Middleton's four-division strong VIII Corps.

Later Montgomery would lament that Ike's plan for winning the war in the West was "quite dreadful…. It will not succeed and the war will go on. If you want to end the war in any reasonable time, you will have to remove Ike's hand from control."

That wasn't to be, especially by someone with Montgomery's personality. For Montgomery was his own worst enemy—a bully, self-opinionated. and egocentric. But all the same he was a product of his times and his nation. None of the U.S. generals had seen and undergone the horrors he had been through ever since he had been abandoned for dead outside a field hospital back in 1914 after the battle of Le Cateau.

But even an angry, pressurized Eisenhower now started to look forward to the enforced rest that Christmas 1944 would surely impose. Like Middleton, he too had a celebration in mind for the weekend of Friday/Saturday, 15/16 December, three days after he returned from London and a meeting with "Winnie," as he now was privileged to call the British Prime Minster, Winston Churchill.

It was to be the wedding of his trusted valet Mickey McKeogh and a diminutive, bespectacled WAC sergeant from Queens, Pearlie Hargrave. Eisenhower had arranged for the pair to be married that weekend at the Louis XIV chapel at Versailles, the first wedding to be held there in that baroque splendor since the eighteenth century.

In the meantime Christmas presents were pouring in for Eisenhower, who was attempting to forget his anger at these "primadonnas," as he called Montgomery, Patton, and Bradley, by whom he was surrounded in his professional life. Sometime before he had stated he liked hominy grits. Now from all over the States good folk were sending him boxes of the stuff. His fan mail was becoming quite a chore, too. Indeed it became a real problem when he decided to sign the replies himself. "Eisenhower" was just a "damned long name" to sign, especially when he had to do so over and over again.

Still, Eisenhower did find the strength in his strained wrist to sign very carefully one of his last letters that week. It was to Prime Minister Churchill, whom he had visited in London on 12 December. It read:

This is just a short note to send you my very best Christmas and New Year's wishes. I hope that 1945 not only brings you personally added success and happiness. While there is scarcely anything that could not add to your national and world stature, yet it is not too much to hope that most freedom-loving people everywhere will gain a much clearer understanding of what they owe to you.

Again my very best wishes to you and your delightful family.

Sincerely,
Dwight D. Eisenhower

Once Churchill had vowed he had not become the "King's First Minister" to oversee the dissolution of the British Empire. Now in indirect consequence of the man who had just sent him such a friendly and flattering Christmas letter that dissolution might commence.

What the half-American Churchill had called the "special relationship" between his two countries, the United States and the United Kingdom, was going to be badly shaken and, in the end, shattered by Eisenhower's lack of grip and perhaps even carelessness this Christmas season. Later some wag would nickname the festive season of 1944 "the Black Christmas" (a pun on the popular Bing Crosby song, "White Christmas") and would hit the nail on the head.

How black it was really to be, no one could ever realize as the generals made their Christmas plans for parties, seductions, leaves, and the usual high jinks indulged in by senior officers when the pressure was off. For now in a matter of days America's greatest land battle of the twentieth century would commence.

But even at that lavish Versailles headquarters, where it was said that each of Eisenhower's most important twenty-six aides had double that number of personal aides themselves, there were still a few of the staff who worried despite the imminent approach of Christmas. Strong was still revising his estimates of German intentions; playing it safe, it seems in retrospect. But one member of his staff felt he had a justifiable worry about the German intentions, in particular, those of Hitler's scarfaced commando chief, Otto Skorzeny.

The staff officer in question was Lt. Colonel Gordon Sheen of the

U.S. Corps of Counter-Intelligence (CIC). This counterintelligence group which had come into being on New Year's Day 1942 when the old Corps of Intelligence Police had been rechristened, was virtually unknown in U.S. Army circles. Even at SHAEF headquarters Sheen and his agents were shadowy figures, fighting to survive in the multitude of intelligence organizations dominated by the CIA's forerunner, the OSS.

Besides Sheen and his men had a bad strike against them. They had incurred the wrath of President Roosevelt; and Sheen, in particular, had probably only been saved from being sacked by being posted overseas to England and then to North Africa. For apparently the CIC had bugged a room occupied by S/Sgt. Joseph Lash, an air corps noncom, who was a personal friend of both Eleanor and Franklin Roosevelt. According to the report, dated 31 December 1943, and later submitted to the president, a sexual encounter between Eleanor and the NCO had taken place in the hotel room.

As the story goes, when the information was passed on to Roosevelt, he flew, understandably, into a towering rage. He ordered Lash overseas within ten hours. After Lash, a suspected communist as well as a seducer, the CIC agents followed. Whatever the truth of the matter, the CIC virtually ceased to exist in the United States and those senior agents who had survived the Washington "bloodbath" were undoubtedly happy to be overseas and out of FDR's striking range.

Sheen must have thought the same, especially when he was appointed to SHAEF and its fleshpots. Now the most senior officer of CIC in Europe, he reported directly to Strong, who was not particularly interested in counterintelligence (at least not yet) and left the rounding up of spies, informers, sleeper agents, etc., to lesser people.

Naturally Sheen had to produce results to justify his position or he might well find himself back in the nation's capital, which might prove fatal to his military career. But he knew he wouldn't impress a high-ranking intelligence expert such as Strong with arresting a few sleeper agents who had gone underground in Paris; and there were plenty of them.* Instead he concentrated on the protection of Eisenhower himself; something which would make the authorities

---

* GIs reported sniping by both French men *and women* from the very day they moved off the beaches in June 1944. It came as a great surprise to many U.S. soldiers that they were not merely tolerated by many French people they had come to "liberate," but were also actively hated.

aware of his lowly presence in a great headquarters where "half-colonels were a dime a dozen."

According to Paris CIC records and those of CIC units attached to army and corps headquarters throughout the U.S. Twelfth and Sixth Army Groups, German troops disguised in American uniforms had begun infiltrating behind U.S. lines as early as August 1944. In certain cases they were also driving captured U.S. jeeps. What their purpose was no one was really able to ascertain, and as far as the CIC was concerned these disguised Germans, sometimes aided by renegade Frenchmen as guides, didn't belong to any overall plans. Their activities seemed to have been directed by local commanders. In addition they were scattered all along the long Allied front, so in the end no great importance was attached to them. However, a CIC commander did note that "six German commandos" had been apprehended in American uniform that August.

In November, however, things had become more serious and Sheen started to worry. On 15 November, he received a report from a subordinate attached to Devers's Sixth Army Group headquarters in France, that a company of the 15th Engineers engaged in frontline road repairs had been surprised by an attack force of some seventy Germans, yelling for reasons known only to themselves, "GI!" All had been dressed in American uniform. Sheen would have been even more worried if he had known that the attack was a try-out for the coming Operation Northwind, the second stage of the battle of the Bulge in Alsace due to start on 1 January 1945.

In the same week, the first of a trickle of German prisoners, who would all repeat the same alarming story, told his interrogators that he had seen a secret order from his headquarters requesting that all captured American uniforms and all English-speaking personnel should be sent to Osnabruck in northern Germany.* There, according to the German POW, special training in reconnaissance and sabotage would be given to these English-speaking German soldiers.

By late November, Sheen naturally had been informed of the Keitel order requesting personnel with the abilities to speak "American-English" and pass as Americans to report to Skorzeny's Jagdkommando at Friedenthal. It didn't take too much mental effort to put two and two together and come up with four. Germans dressed as GIs were obviously already active behind U.S. lines. Now

---

* The author cannot find any connection with the Skorzeny Trojan Horse operation there, but the place was—and is—a large garrison town, housing several barracks.

this danger had been increased by the fact that Otto Skorzeny, the head of Hitler's commandos, had taken them over. But for what purpose?

On the basis of Skorzeny's past record between 1943/44, Sheen didn't need a crystal ball to realize that he was going to use these men in some long-range operation behind the front; and knowing as much as he did of Skorzeny's choice of high-ranking targets—"the Big Three," Mussolini, Horthy's son, Tito—this might well mean that the scarfaced Austrian was after an Allied "big fish." In Sheen's case, the only big fish who mattered in the Paris district was no less a person than Eisenhower himself.

We don't know at this stage whether Sheen communicated his fears and suspicions to General Strong that first week of December. From all accounts of the events there at that time, there seems to have been no noticeable tightening up of security at Versailles. (At the best of times, security at Supreme Headquarters, staffed by personnel from a dozen different Allied countries ranging from America to New Zealand, appears to have been quite lax.) However Major Noel Annan, who worked on Strong's intelligence staff, felt that it was "the Hangman's Dilemma" as to who was to "blame for an episode that turned drama into force"—one that soon would see Sheen "burst into a room at SHAEF headquarters at the Hotel Trianon, crying '*Skorzeny is driving on Paris!*'"

But where was this would-be assassin of Eisenhower, and if we are to believe other sources, Montgomery and Bradley, too?* For the first and second week of December 1944, we can trace Otto Skorzeny's movements somewhat accurately. Thereafter, until he was wounded at the end of that month, we have to rely on his own account of where he was. For like his 150th Panzer Brigade, the mysterious "jeep teams," and the assault formations, Skorzeny was working his way by complicated routes to the front line. And although the Germans, right down to the initial wave, were certain they had fooled the Americans about their intentions, they were still sticking to the strict security procedures laid down by the Fuhrer. They had no alternative. If they slipped up, especially the senior offi-

---

* Bradley took the threat seriously. Each night he slept in a separate room at his Alfa headquarters, left by the kitchen when he had to go to other parts of his command, and changed his helmet with its three stars for one with the lowly single star of a brigadier-general. Montgomery ignored the threat.

cers, it might well cost them their heads. After all, whatever his generals thought, Hitler himself was firmly convinced that the success of the coming counteroffensive in the West might well change the whole future of the long war in Germany's favor.

The first jeep teams reached their start-line a day ahead of Skorzeny's arrival on 13 December. They reached the collecting point of the Blankenheim Forest in the Eifel, just opposite the "Losheim Gap" through which the Sixth SS Panzer Army would drive in three days' time in a raging snowstorm. But they weren't allowed to join the rest of the SS of Peiper's 1st Division, "Adolf Hitler's Bodyguard," already assembled there. Instead they were kept separate from the others until, as Heinz Rohde, a member of one of the teams, recalled in 1950, "several grinning officers appeared and before our tired eyes proceeded to open several sealed cases."

And what cases they were! "The first one cheered us up no end when its contents were revealed," Rohde explained afterward. "It was packed to the top with Ami cigarettes, chocolates, coffee, matches and cans of all kinds." The goodies were subsequently shared out with "Prussian fairness" and then the next case was opened. But this was intended for Rohde's sole use as a jeep team leader.

This second case "made sure we wouldn't lack for anything during our mission. For it was filled with US dollars, English pounds, with which we were to bribe enemy sentries, guards and the like." Soon Rohde would be handed another small fortune in Belgian and French francs, again to be used to bribe people. There was also a plan to bribe Belgian dockworkers at Antwerp, the great Allied supply port, to go on strike at the next convenient weekend as the German armored points of the Sixth SS Panzer Army approached. This would cause even more trouble for the British who were running the port. What Rohde and the rest of the teams didn't know that snowy day in the freezing Eifel forest was that all the notes were forgeries, manufactured by professional crooks and forgers in the German concentration camps.

But the last case to be presented to them by the SS messengers killed their happy mood instantly when they learned of its contents. "It offered a view of numerous lighters of the kind the Amis called 'zippo.' At first there seemed nothing special about these lighters.

They were cheap metal, mass-produced items with no particularly exclusive features. That was until the grinning SS major told us of their use.

"He pointed out that the glass tube, instead of containing lighter fuel, was filled with cyanide ... All we needed to do was to bite into the tube if we were trapped and all our problems would be solved. Guten Appetit!"

That information put an end to the team's appetite for certain, even though they still had the caseful of Ami goodies to enjoy all to themselves—"So we trailed back sadly to our 'wigwams.' For the first time since we had joined Skorzeny we realized what we had let ourselves in for—an Ascension Day Commando! [Suicide mission.]"

Now the top brass were arriving at the camps in the wooded heights of the Schnee Eifel. While the men froze in their forest hiding places, hidden by the snow-heavy firs, unable to talk or smoke or light fires because in some cases they were only a hundred meters away from the outposts of the 99th Infantry Division and that division's link with Middleton's VIII Corps and Colonel Devin's ill-fated 14th Cavalry Group, the top brass conferred.

According to Skorzeny, he had set up his headquarters in a modest house at the outskirts of the village of Schmidtheim and he had taken part in these last-minute discussions of that Thursday. But the author can't find any reference to confirm this. Admittedly it was now that some of the SS's officers learned about the Jagdkommando operation. They were told that the 150th Panzer Brigade would be broken into three formations to accompany the 1st SS Panzer Division. At the same time they had to watch out for the jeep teams in American uniform. They would have certain recognition signals when they met other German troops. They would take off their helmets in such cases and raise them straight above their heads like two middle-aged burghers greeting each other back home. Their vehicles would carry a "Z" mark, which was raised so that it could be traced in total darkness with a person's fingers.

But the lead officers of the SS, those arrogant veterans of a score of battlefields, were not particularly interested in Skorzeny's clandestine operations. They were concerned with the battle that was to come as well as what would become of themselves. Little could Knittel, Sandig, Peiper, and all the rest of them realize just how the next week would transform their lives forever. They would all gain a place in the history of World War II but it would be accompanied by a shame, a smear on their military honor that they would never be able to eradicate until they finally passed away as bitter, foresaken old men, shunned even by their own grandchildren.

Still, despite their complaints about lack of fuel, poorly trained "greenbeaks," and the weather, they were confident. In some cases they were only too eager to close with the Americans. For they felt they had a score to pay back. Only days before, a working unit from the 1st SS had helped to clear up after a terrible American bombing raid on the nearby city of Dueren. Obersturmbannfuhrer Jochen Peiper of the Leibstandarte who had been in charge had been appalled by what he had seen there; and in his time he had seen enough of the horrors of war. Now he felt, as he recalled to the author after the war, "scraping the dead bodies of old men, women and kids off the walls, that I could castrate the first Ami I came across with a blunt piece of broken glass!"

The men who were going out now into the unknown in the "jeep teams" were not so resolute or motivated by such a fierce burning rage. By now all of them knew their fate if they were captured in American uniform behind U.S. lines. Indeed, Rohde, who was going out a day before the counteroffensive commenced, had just been inspected with his men by a young, dashing officer of the 12th SS Panzer "Hitler Youth" in his smart, black uniform.

"He inspected us without asking any questions about our mission. All he did was shake his head, as if he couldn't believe what he saw. Then we were off, heading for a circle of trees, which marked the narrow strip of no-man's land." They were on their way into the dangerous unknown.

As Heinz Rohde commented five years later, "Nobody bothered to say, 'auf wiedersehen.'"

11

The Fateful Fifteenth

On 9 December, General Patton's chief of intelligence, Colonel Oscar Koch, had briefed his chief on the situation in the general area of the U.S. First Army's front; knowledge received from Patton's own intelligence outfit secreted in First Army territory. Koch told his boss that in his opinion trouble loomed ahead on the First Army front, especially in that part held by Middleton's VIII Corps. "In conclusion," he explained later, "the enemy had an approximate two-to-one numerical advantage in the area.... His build-up had been gradual and highly secret. A successful diversionary attack, even of a limited nature, would have a great psychological effect—a 'shot in the arm' for Germany and Japan."

Patton accepted Koch's statement, though the latter had also gotten it wrong again. Koch still felt, like most of those who expected something to happen on Hodges's front, that the real blow would come further north. Once more the U.S. Army from Eisenhower downward had bought Hitler's subterfuge—the counterattack against the Aachen area, the "Fuhrer's Christmas present."

Patton, however, rose and stated categorically, "We'll be in a position to meet whatever happens." Although he was preparing to launch his third offensive, this time in the Saar area, he ordered his staff to look into the need for an emergency force from the Third Army to help out in Hodges's area. By 12 December his staff had come up with a plan to switch at least a corps to the north. This would be the force that Patton would offer to Eisenhower at the celebrated Verdun Conference of 19 December, three days after the "surprise" German attack, and would occasion Eisenhower's annoyed comment: "Don't be fatuous, George!" But Patton wasn't being fatuous and that offer and its subsequent execution as "the greatest switch-around of troops actually engaged in battle (they weren't) in history" made "Ole Blood an' Guts" the great hero of the battle of the Bulge.

But Oscar Koch had come close. He noted the presence of German armored formations, units which would be used in an attack and not defense, in just the right spots for an assault on Middleton's line: "In the area of Trier, Kyllburg, Wittlich, 2nd Panzer and 13 Panzer Lehr Divisions appear to be reforming with 116 Panzer Division reported slated for that area." (These were all assault units of von Manteuffel's Fifth Panzer Army which would break through VIII Corps's line.) But Koch still placed the real spearhead of the German counteroffensive in the wrong place: "In Sixth Panzer Army area, east of the Roer River and west of the Rhine between Dusseldorf and Cologne, 1st SS, 2nd SS, 9th SS, 12th SS, 10th SS and (again) 116th Panzer Division appearing to be reforming." But on the same day that this "Third Army G-2 Periodic Report" was prepared, 15 December 1944, these units were packed up tightly within one mile at the most from the forward positions linking Gerow's U.S. V Corps and Middleton's VIII Corps.

On the same Friday that Koch's staff were preparing their intelligence report, another army intelligence chief took a stab at trying to think the impossible. He was Colonel Monk Dickson, the First Army's senior intelligence officer, stationed at Spa, Belgium.

Dickson was a difficult man to deal with at that time as he was the most experienced intelligence officer on the Western Front and jealous of his position and reputation. He got on with the British allies and made full use of the ULTRA decodes. But he was touchy and tended to fall out easily with his fellow officers, especially if they didn't like or approve his predictions.

In particular, he was at loggerheads with Sibert at Bradley's headquarters; the civilians in uniform in charge of the OSS in Bern, London, and Paris (OSS teams were banned in the First Army area); and especially with General William B. Kean, Hodges's chief of staff. The latter and VII Corps commander, the smart, aggressive Irish-

American "Lightning Joe" Collins, were generally regarded as the officers who really ran First Army.

Kean felt that Dickson was an "oddball," given to impetuous judgments. Back in September, it had been Dickson who had woken Hodges to tell him he'd just heard on the radio that von Rundstedt had ordered the Wehrmacht to disarm the SS and sue for an honorable peace. As we know, the report came from Captain Hans Habe's "Radio Annie," the black propaganda station based on the hill outside Luxembourg's Junglinster. That had not gone down well at all. Now for some weeks, Dickson had annoyed Kean by reporting the Germans were intending an "all-out counterattack" or "an all-out counteroffensive"—two very different things.

On the evening of 14 December he had totally surprised the listening staff officers at Spa's Hotel Britannique by pausing in the middle of a briefing and slapping the sitrep map crying, "It's the Ardennes!" His forecast later would seem (at least in years to come when military historians began to examine the role of intelligence in the battle of the Bulge and what led up to it) to have been based on good information. After all, two days before Dickson had written, "Reinforcements for the West Wall between Dureb and Trier continue to arrive. The identification of three or four newly arrived divisions along the army front must be reckoned with during the next few days ... it is possible that a limited-scale offensive will be launched for purposes of achieving a Christmas morale victory for civilian consumption. Many POWs now speak of the coming attack between 17 and 25 December." All in all a very close approximation of what would happen on the morrow. Unfortunately, the whole effect was spoiled by what the chief of intelligence, a key man in any battle, did next. Colonel Monk Dickson took himself off that very afternoon on what he probably regarded as a well-earned leave.

Dickson's attitude seemed to have been typical of not only the commanders but those officers who were supposed to be closest to the impending disaster. At corps level, Colonel Andrew R. Reeves, Middleton's chief of intelligence at Bastogne, did not appear to take the warnings of what was to come at all seriously either; and he was getting them at first hand from the nearby front.

At the command of General Middleton, Reeves was supposed to send patrols over the River Our every night. According to

Middleton, "some stayed out as long as five days." For there was a standing order that the corps had to take one or more prisoners each night.* In fact, Reeves sent on any of his reports to Sibert at Bradley's headquarters down the road in Luxembourg, where Middleton recorded, "It was not taken seriously."

Despite the fact that Middleton confessed after the war, "We expected something in the way of an attack from the Germans before December 16," the corps commander did not appear unduly worried. That Friday he prepared himself for the evening's "wingding" and devoted his morning to dealing with the affairs of Louisiana State University, where, prior to his return to the service, he had been the prewar dean of administration. As he wrote in a letter enclosed in the last mail to go out of APO 308 before the deluge broke: "Colonel E. Monnot Lanier came to my headquarters today and left me a file of correspondence and his reply regarding the Louisiana State University William Helis oil lease." Lanier, whoever he was, had apparently requested that the corps commander responsible for the lives of 60,000 young men in the front line cast his eyes over the details of a commercial lease dating back to 1941. This Middleton did. Thereupon, Troy Middleton, who would return safely to become president of the university and die in bed of old age, probably rubbed his arm—he was suffering from bursitis of the elbow— and concentrated his thoughts on the anniversary party to come that night. After all, Friday night parties had always been the high point of the week in dull garrison towns such as Bastogne.

Naturally the men on the lines knew nothing of this that Friday. How could they? They had to believe that their commanders and fellow Americans would do their best for them. After all, *they* were doing the fighting and dying. Besides the top brass were protected by sycophants at all levels, who made sure they weren't exposed. So they waited that Friday in Middleton's VIII Corps unaware of what was to come on the morrow. A few, as we have seen, were veterans. But so many were novices, totally new to battle; they were the thousands of replacements to the battered 4th and 28th Infantry Divisions and the greenhorns of the 106th, where only one senior officer had actually had any taste of combat—and that had been a

---

* The author has been totally unable to find evidence of patrols staying out on the other side of the River Our for five days. Indeed there is little evidence of VIII Corps patrolling at all in this final pre-attack period.

quarter of a century earlier as a doughboy in the trenches in World War I.

"The Golden Lions," as the ill-fated 106th Infantry was nicknamed from its divisional patch, had come into the line only five days before. They had crossed France, packed in open "deuce-and-a-half" trucks in bitter rain and had arrived at the front in the Bleialf area where the 4th Division had battled in what seemed now another age. Numb, frozen, miserable, they hadn't been cheered by what they had first seen of the abandoned battlefield and the frontline positions of the "*Schwarzer Mann*" ("Black Man") section of the U.S. captured Siegfried Line.

But over the intervening days they had discovered this Ghost Front wasn't so bad as they had thought at the beginning. They were not going to live in damp freezing foxholes as they had anticipated. Instead they were housed inside the heated West Wall bunkers or wooden squad huts which their predecessors of the 2nd Infantry Division had constructed from the plentiful timber of the area. S/Sgt. Petersen, for example, of a 422nd Regiment mortar team, found his new domicile in a big concrete bunker "almost homey." There were tables on which to write and eat. Steel bunks were hanging from the walls and there was a woodburning stove in the corner. To the 20-year-old NCO, it looked "almost like a Boy Scout camp back home." He was soon to be disillusioned.

Pfc. Martin, who although blind in one eye was to man a machine gun, thought the same as Petersen. He was almost happy to be there. "It was like being in a Boy Scout camp and not the frontline. We had three good meals a day, served by the company cooks." These were "Marmalade" Martin and "Peanut Butter" Rosen and both cooked well. Not only that, but the 19-year-old private, glad to have escaped from a claustrophobic home life, had heard that there was never any fighting on this Ghost Front and in due course he would be sent on furlough to "meet foreign women," the kind his father, a GI in the "old war," had warned him against.

Nights were hairy for the newcomers. Naturally they saw German infiltrators everywhere—and sometimes they were real. But when they reported their findings to intelligence they were pooh-poohed; they were letting their imaginations run away with them, the old hands thought. After all, General Walter Robertson had assured General Alan W. Jones of the 106th, when the latter had taken over from Robertson's 2nd Infantry: "Take it easy, General. The Krauts won't attack even if they were ordered to."

The mood of quiet complacency also reigned along the 28th Division's front to the 106th's right flank. The 28th, as we know, was an experienced division, commanded by no-nonsense "Dutch" Cota, who had won an award for his bravery on the D-day beaches and believed in keeping a firm grip on his troops.*

Cota and his surviving, experienced officers organized the 28th Division's defenses better than those of the 106th. Cota made his own alterations, unlike Jones who was too new (after a quarter of a century in the U.S. Army, he'd still never been in combat) to make the attempt. Keeping just outposts on the River Sauer which ran the length of his front, he ordered the men to "come home" at night to their billets in the villages behind the line; he maintained permanent strongpoints in a series of Luxembourg villages running along what the GIs called "Skyline Drive." All the same, too many of his men were reinforcements, worried like the "Golden Lions" by night duty, and relying very much on their experienced officers in emergencies.

Not that Cota or his men expected emergencies. His division seemed solidly established, with no apparent danger looming on the horizon. At his headquarters in Wiltz, the commanding general was more concerned with getting through the frivolities of Christmas and then concentrating on making the old "Bloody Bucket" a top-class fighting outfit once more. Perhaps they'd have more luck than usual in their next combat assignment.

Up on the Skyline Drive, with the Germans hidden in the heights on the other bank of the River Sauer, some of the officers of the 110th Regiment guarding that section of the line were not so sanguine as headquarters. Captain Frederick Feiker, commanding the 110th's "K" Company which had been in the village of Hosingen ever since they had returned from the Hurtgen, was one.

He knew this was regarded as the Ghost Front and perhaps his fears, which he kept mainly to himself, were in reality ghosts, too. But he had a definite feeling that everything was not right up there in the mile-long village that extended along both sides of the Skyline Drive. During daylight hours he kept patrols on the steep slopes that

---

* It would be one of General Cota's men, Private Eddie Slovik, who would become, in January 1945, the only U.S. soldier to be shot for "desertion in the face of the enemy" since the Civil War.

led down from Hosingen to the river far below. But once darkness fell these patrols were withdrawn and then the valley was supposedly no-man's land. But Captain Feiker did not quite believe that. He felt that there was something going on. But what?

The villagers, although they spoke German and many of their younger menfolk were serving in the German Army, were friendly. They had welcomed the weary, filthy veterans of the Hurtgen the month before with warm beds, hot baths, and even fresh linen from their own resources. All the same, Feiker noted that the locals would be engaged in deep conversations which would cease as soon as he or anyone else in American uniform appeared. Why?

There had also been a few mysterious disappearances of lone Americans using the dead straight road running along the heights. Once a jeep with three doctors had been ambushed. The Germans had left the bodies of the three dead MOs behind. But they had been stripped to their underclothes and their jeep stolen. Again Feiker had no answer. And what could he make of the persistent rumor that had been passed on by their predecessors here that the Germans had some way of passing underneath the river to the American side?*

In any event, Captain Feiker was concerned that his young men did not lower their guard. He knew that his fellow company commander, Captain Jarrett of Company "B" of the 103rd Combat Engineer Battalion which also garrisoned Hosingen, did not share his fears. He was more prepared to allow his young soldiers to enjoy their time at this Ghost Front. For as one of them put it, after the Hurtgen: "Hosingen was heaven.... There was even running water. Apart from the odd spot of guard duty, there was plenty of time for reading, relaxing and writing letters home."

But Feiker ordered his own infantrymen to be on their lookout and never mind the easy-going attitude of the combat engineers. He told them he did not want them to be surprised like those unfortunate and now dead medics. And sometimes it wasn't just the chill wind that always blew on the heights of Skyline Drive, winter and summer, that made Feiker give a little shudder. It was that strange, childlike irrational feeling of being watched by something or someone unknown.

---

* The men of the Fifth Parachute Division and the 26th Volksgrenadierdivision, who would attack in this area, both used culverts to do this before and during the assault.

Meanwhile the 707th Tank Battalion, which would soon attempt to come to the rescue of the two companies in Hosingen and would fail lamentably, also was taking it easy. Colonel Ripple still was not making much effort to get his battalion back in shape. The tanks were still yet to be repaired and fully ammunitioned and the "Misfits" still had not changed the dirty uniforms they had worn throughout the battle in the Hurtgen. Not that the men minded much. If Ripple wanted it that way why should they buck it?

For now they were actively preparing for Christmas in their base, the little village whose name most of them never learned. They were hoarding "suds" and "hooch" and were preparing for their own Christmas wingding. The natives were still friendly, especially the women, though they seemed, like those further up the line at Hosingen, to be becoming more secretive and nervous. No one knew why or even bothered to find out. Why should they? This was going to be a good Christmas; they felt they deserved it, too. For most of them had not spent one at home since 1942. As Pfc. Marshall, the only one of the "Misfits" to survive what was to come, recorded many years later: "It was a fun time—while it lasted!"

Even further down the line, right on the Germany–Luxembourg border at the pilgrimage town of Echternach, the men of the 4th Division's 12th Infantry were enjoying their time out of war on this so-called "Ghost Front" even more. They were quite happy with their new home. They had come out of the Hurtgen a week before to be billeted in what appeared to be an empty town. For just across the river with its shattered medieval bridge was located the second biggest bunker of the whole Siegfried Line. Seven-stories deep, it dominated the whole area. With its guns and those of the surrounding German batteries it could make life hell for anyone who lived in Echternach below. Thus the town had been evacuated, leaving it empty for the newcomers.

The weary, grubby veterans of the Hurtgen had grabbed at the chance with both hands. It might be dangerous to live in the ghost town, but it had its compensations. The cellars of one of Luxembourg's largest tourist towns were still full of the kind of goodies that soldiers liked, mainly the liquid kind. In addition there was plenty of fruit, canned, bottled or otherwise stored in those virginal underground vaults for those whose stomachs still had room after the plentiful champagne, schnaps, and wine.

Admittedly, the Germans still infiltrated the ghost town from across the River Sauer in daytime, but at night, Company E of the 4th's 12th Infantry Regiment battened down the hatches. No one moved out of his billet without orders and whenever the GIs heard the slightest suspicious noise it called for an immediate burst of machine-gun fire and a swift grenade lobbed in that direction.

Otherwise it was a good life for the men of the "Ivy League" Division and they grabbed at it. They received three good meals a day from the company kitchen set up in the garage of the Hotel de Luxembourg; their duties were limited; and for the lucky few who received a pass the women beneath the bridge in Luxembourg City awaited them.

On that Friday, 15 December, before it all started, a Captain Paul Dupuis of the Regiment's 2nd Battalion stationed at nearby Consdorf decided he'd take a day off and visit the "big city [Echternach]." Perhaps he'd strike lucky like the GIs already stationed there had. For Dupuis was going on pass to "Gay Paree" and he'd heard that there was a 1937 Plymouth located in Echternach. According to his informant, it was without a battery and there was a hole in its gas tank. But he thought he could have it patched up and his CO, Major Dorn, had agreed he could borrow the Plymouth for this weekend pass in Paris if he could get it started. It wasn't an offer to be passed up.

So he set off in the battalion headquarters jeep, probably watched by keen eyes from the "Cat's Head" bunker on the heights beyond. For the men up there watching had plans of their own for this coming last weekend before Christmas.

Arriving in Echternach he found the celebrated Plymouth and together with the "instant experts," who gathered around in the garage where its Luxembourg owner had hastily abandoned it, he concluded that the prewar automobile could be repaired. That decided, as it was getting dark early, Captain Dupuis chose to spend the night at the headquarters of the local company. It was a fatal decision. Like so many others who had plans for the coming weekend, he would never realize them. He would not see Paris or the Plymouth ever again. What he would see was bloody battle alongside what was left of Company E, fighting for its very life.

The final hours of the celebrated Ghost Front, with which the Allies had fooled themselves for so long, had commenced.

Ten or fifteen miles away on the other side of the line on that last day, equally humble German soldiers waited, too. They knew what was to come, unlike the Americans who would die with them—perhaps some 15,000 on both sides before the coming week was out. But they did not like that knowledge.

Well could the Fuhrer pontificate to his generals on 12 December that Germany was faced with "a dying world empire, that of Great Britain, and on the other hand a 'colony,' the United States, anxious to take over the inheritance." It, in its turn, was being challenged by the "ultra-Marxist state, Russia." It was inevitable, therefore, that "if Germany can now deal out a few heavy blows, this artificially united front [Russia, Britain, and the United States] will collapse at any moment with a tremendous thunderclap."

What did that matter to the thousands of ordinary *landsers*? Oh, there might well be a few of them and certainly more officers, especially those of the SS, who looked forward to the coming battle. They believed implicitly in Hitler as "the Great Captain of All Times."

Klaus Ritter, the "old hare," who had seen his native Eifel destroyed over the last three months since he had returned and wrangled his way into the 18th Volksgrenadierdivision, now ready for the attack on the unsuspecting greenhorns of the U.S. 106th Division, was one of those who swayed between hope and despair. He was sheltering this night in the cover of a bunker with his crew just outside the "Verdun of the Eifel," Brandscheid, which the 4th Division had failed to take in September 1944.

A young officer appeared. He was unknown to the crew of the captured Russian gun. But he was enthusiastic. He gave every two men a bottle of Moselle wine and then gave them a pep talk to go with the unexpected gift. Then he was gone, with a cheery, "See you in Paris!" down the winding road where the People's Grenadiers were already assembling for assault on the sleeping 106th stationed in Bleialf.

Ritter would have liked to believe that the enthusiastic young officer was right. Somehow he felt though that they would never see

Paris again. But he dare not say that to his comrades. These days you couldn't trust anyone. So he drank his share of the free wine out of his aluminum canteen cup and stared through the darkness at where Bleialf was waiting. How often had he visited the place with its cobbled square between the fine church with its great bulbous Baroque tower and "Cafe Zwicker." God only knew what had happened to it since the Amis had taken it over three months before. He savored the golden wine and stared ahead, while the others chatted softly around him in the freezing, damaged bunkers.

But Ritter did not listen. His mind was on what was to come. Here and there a flare sailed effortlessly into the dark sky, hung there in a burst of garish, unreal light and then came bumbling to the ground like a fallen angel. Far off, he could hear the muted sound of machine-gun fire. He didn't know it then, but it was Hodges's last attack on the Siegfried Line in 1944: an attempt to capture the crossroads above Malmedy that the GIs called—with good reason—"Heartbreak Crossroads."

So he sat there and ruminated. Soon, he knew, the searchlights behind him on the ridge would click on. They would focus on the low clouds and illuminate the battlefield. In their ghostly light the infantry of the 18th Volksgrenadier would rise. For a long while, or so it would seem, there would be a heavy brooding silence. Then would come the heavy, slow tick-tick of the old-fashioned Ami machine guns. There would be shouts of anger yells of pain. The infantry would increase their pace and then stumble forward through the mist-bound fields that separated them from Bleialf—and the killing would commence.

Behind Ritter and his comrades, the artillery waited. Perhaps they made their final adjustments to their cannons—all 2,000 of them. Some might even have prayed for themselves and aid from St. Barbara, the patron saint of the artillery. To their front the tankers and crews of the assault guns, all 980 tanks, would be making their final preparations too, hoping against hope that their engines would start up once it all began.

The second wave would be roused and ready now, shivering in the cold, stamping their feet, urinating too often, a sure sign of nerves. Still Ritter, the old hare, knew there was something even magic about a first attack. A kind of fearful exhilaration that was beyond description. But it was there all right, taking these callow "greenbeaks" out of the prosaic world of greenpea soup and sausage and the pettiness of military routine.

Their equally young officers would feel it too, as with their machine pistols slung over their shoulders, they read out Field Marshal Gerd von Rundstedt's eve of battle message to the men:

> Soldiers of the Western Front!
> Your great hour has come. Large attacking armies have started against the Anglo-Americans. I do not have to tell you more than that. You feel it yourself. *We gamble everything!*
> You carry with you the holy obligation to give all to achieve superhuman objectives for our Fatherland and Fuhrer!

It was midnight in the Ardennes on 15 December 1944.

Combat Engineer Ralph Obuchowski and a buddy from the U.S. 28th Division's 103rd Combat Engineers were on guard duty that midnight hour. "We were standing next to the church at Hosingen where the two roads meet in the shadow of a small chapel. It was full moon and freezing cold."

What they were talking about so long ago is forgotten, but Obuchowski, today an old man, still remembers vividly "the lone soldier coming from the direction of the village itself." They stopped him and found he didn't know the password. "In the Hurtgen Forest we would have taken him to the CP immediately, but here we decided not to for three reasons: he came from inside the village and knew where he was; he spoke perfect English and he had a good reason to be about after curfew; he'd been called to do an urgent repair on a signal wire."

So Obuchowski and his buddy let him go about his business. With a hurried thanks, he was off, disappearing into the silver darkness along the Skyline Drive. Slowly the two buddies followed, heading for the guardroom and relief. Thereafter they'd hit the hay and, with a bit of luck, be able to sleep in longer on the morrow. After all, it was Saturday and there was nothing pressing to be done a week before Christmas.

Ralph Obuchowski, whose life was going to be totally transformed within the next few hours did not know that—as far as we know—he had just made first contact with the attack force that would wipe out the 28th's 110th Infantry Regiment.

For the unknown signalman without the password was a German soldier probably from the 26th Volksgrenadierdivision of Manteuffel's 5th Panzer Army, doing a final reconnaissance of Hosingen. Already the *fusilierregiment* of that division had not stuck to the von Manteuffel timetable. At that very moment hundreds of them were scaling the valley heights to either side of the Skyline Drive village. They hoped to surround it, isolate it, and cut the main highway before pushing on to the 110th's headquarters at Clervaux, where two of their signallers were concealed in the local pharmacy, next to the ruined castle housing the American garrison. They would bring down the 26th's massed artillery fire and prepare the way for the crossing of the next river, the Clerf, and push on to Middleton's corps headquarters at Bastogne, only a matter of kilometers away.

But in Hosingen nothing was known of this. The three-hundred-man garrison slept on, save the handful of weary, frozen GIs on guard duty. One of these was a green 19-year-old—his name unrecorded—who had the "graveyard shift." The nameless GI, who might well have been killed before Hosingen and its garrison surrendered in two days' time, was posted on the top of Hosingen's watertower on the side of the Skyline Drive that overlooked the valley and Germany beyond—the way the Germans would come, if they ever did.

There the young sentry carried out his boring assignment, waiting for the dawn that seemed as if it never would come. We have no knowledge of what thoughts went through his head that night as time passed on leaden feet. But time and time again he must have peered to the east for the first sign of the new dawn.

But at five-thirty that morning, it was not the dawn he saw. Instead the young soldier was startled out of his lethargy by what he reported to Captain Feiker a few minutes later as "pinpoints of light" everywhere down below by the river. For a second or two he was dumbfounded, at a loss to explain them. Below, a whole circle of yellow and bright red lights, totally noiseless, spread around the curve of the river.

Suddenly, startlingly, this lone sentry was assailed by the belching thunder of a huge artillery barrage—that of the 554 assorted cannons of the German XLVII Panzer Corps's twenty-nine batteries of artillery. The air trembled. The tower shook like a live entity. On all sides, shells and mortar bombs began to slam into the fortified villages of Skyline Drive. The days of the Ghost Front were over. Right to the very last moment the Germans had deceived the Americans. Now they were attacking, all 200,000 of them in the first waves. America's greatest battle of the twentieth century had commenced.

The Deceivers and the Deceived

FIELD MARSHAL WALTHER MODEL

Field Marshal Model, defeated in the Ruhr Valley by the U.S. Ninth and First Armies, was last seen outside his small staff group at the race course at Dusseldorf, once the most elegant German city in the west, now a sea of ruins. He was traveling in a DKW Meisterklasse sallon car (which one day an irate General Omar Bradley, the conqueror of the Ruhr Pocket, would commandeer for himself as a legitimate prize of war) with a dozen or so key staff members in an assorted mix of vehicles, including an eight-wheeled armored car.

The field marshal, who had just surrendered an army of nearly half a million men to the Americans but had refused to surrender himself, paused to consider what he should do next. Like Field Marshal Paulus, who had surrendered to the Russians at Stalingrad, he had that choice. But Paulus had been disgracefully used by the Russians and Model had no intention of being "placed in a lion's cage and displayed to a jibbering group of peasants."

One of his key advisers that pleasant late April day in 1945, with only a few days before Germany was finally defeated, was Colonel Michael, who ironically enough would be in the pay of the CIA before the decade was out. There in what would soon be named "Truman Park" by the occupying U.S. 94th Infantry Division, the staff decided they would break out of the U.S. ring around Dusseldorf. They would then head for the vast woods. There they would come to their final conclusions on what the fugitive field marshal should do.

By this time General Bradley knew his old opponent was on the run. He decided to do something about the commander who had fooled him prior to the battle of the Bulge. Officially, as he explained in his memoirs, he gave other reasons for his determination to capture Field Marshal Model: "Remembering how the chilly Prussian had blocked our advance through the Siegfried Line in September, I told G-2 to give a medal to the man who brought him in." The award of that Bronze Star would undoubtedly have pleased the G-2 exceedingly as well. For he was no less than General Sibert, who had been so badly fooled by that same missing field marshal (and the man incidentally who would ensure that Model's current fellow fugitive, Colonel Michael, went to work for the fledgling CIA in due course).

On 20 April 1945, after they had successfully broken through the American ring, Model and his staff gathered expectantly around a little radio in a wooded glade. This was a special day; for 20 April was Hitler's birthday, an event which had been celebrated throughout his Thousand-Year Reich for the last twelve years. Eagerly the fugitives waited to hear what the Fuhrer had to say about the war and Germany's future.

They were to be disappointed. It wasn't Hitler who spoke to the nation but Goebbels. "The Poison Dwarf" pointed out that it was not time for the traditional greetings; the news was too grim. Instead he said somberly: "We have to thank [Hitler]—and him alone—that Germany still exists today and that the West, with its culture and civilization, has not been completely engulfed in the dark abyss which yawns before us."

The information did not please Model and his people. What came next pleased them even less. For Goebbels, the Minister of Propaganda and Public Enlightenment, who would murder his own children, all five of them, by the end of April and then kill himself together with his long-suffering wife, now continued with an attack on Model's old army. He condemned the *Ruhrarmee* as a treacherous force, whose surrender by Model to the Americans had helped to bring the Third Reich to its knees.

Now Model decided, perhaps influenced by Goebbels's reference to the "treacherous Ruhr Army" to make an end of it. In 1946 when Colonel Michael was interrogated, he claimed that Model had decided to commit suicide because "he had been accused of being a war criminal by the Russians." Who had told him that? None other than Michael. He said that he had warned Model that the "Western powers would hand [Model] over to the Russians."

But why Michael should have told Model any such thing is something of a mystery. But then the whole business of Model after the surrender of his Ruhr Army is something of a mystery and continues to be one to this day.

Back in 1943, Model had proclaimed that a "German field marshal does not surrender.... Such a thing is not possible." Now he had to make a fateful decision. What was he going to do? To his chief of staff General Wagener, he remarked that day, "In ancient times they took poison."

Saturday, 21 April 1945, things took their final course. Model did not say much that morning. He gave one of his adjutants a few of his personal items to deliver to his wife. Then around midday he took a stroll with his adjutant, Colonel Pilling, in the woods. Neither man made conversation. Both were buried in a cocoon of their own thoughts and apprehensions. Finally the two of them paused near an old oak. Then, according to the statement that Pilling made to the police in 1951, Model said, "Anything's better than falling into Russian hands." He drew his pistol and clicked off the safety. He then added, "You will bury me here."

Now Model took what the German officer class called "the traditional way out." Previous German senior officers who had attempted to kill themselves in the last few terrible months of the war had made a hash of it. Not Model. He put the pistol muzzle to his right temple with a steady hand. While Pilling watched, he paused and then pulled the trigger.

Later Pilling fetched Michael. No words of explanation were needed. Together they dug a shallow grave beneath the big oak tree. Pilling wrapped the field marshal's body in a greatcoat and then the two of them piled the earth above their former commander. No attempt was made to put a cross on the spot. The two staff officers were going to ensure that Bradley would be unable to award that Bronze Star to some lucky GI.

But someone—no one ever discovered who—came back later to where Model's unmarked grave lay in that lonely forest glade and started to carve something on the oak. It appeared to be a rather crude attempt. Perhaps the unknown person had only a bayonet or trench knife with which to work. But in the end the mark was legible enough. In 1955 young Hans-Georg Model, who had last seen his father at the forest lodge headquarters during a snowball fight just before the battle of the Bulge, recognized it easily enough and got on with what he had come there secretly to do. It was a simple letter "M."

Thus Model, who had given Giskes his strange orders back in that autumn that had begun the great deception, disappeared himself for a whole decade. Perhaps for some people on the Allied side it was fortunate he did. But the "Model mystery" did not quite end there. His son, who back in 1944 had been an officer cadet and who, in a conversation with the author, remembered looking back at his father as he returned to his unit and feeling, "I would never see him again," decided in 1955 it would be safe to attempt to find his father and rebury him in a more appropriate place.

With help from a handful of ex-staff officers who knew the location of Model's woodland burial place, he found the "M" carved on the tree in the von Spee wood. Overnight the son and his friends drove the corpse—a bag of bones still wrapped in a tattered field marshal's uniform—across the Rhine to that remote battlefield which had once been called by Bradley's GIs "the death factory."

There in the Hurtgen Forest at the German "Heroes Graveyard" (*Heldenfriedhof*) at Vossenack where some of the bitterest fighting had taken place, the bones were re-interred among the dead of Army Group B; there with the gray ranks of stones that marked the graves of the men his father had once commanded. Like the Pattons, the Model family wanted the dead field marshall to be buried among his fallen soldiers. So just as sixty miles away "Ole Blood n' Guts" lay among his thousands of Third Army dead at Luxembourg military cemetery at Hamm, outside the principality's capital, Model rested for another three decades under a simple stone tablet. It was marked modestly, "Walther Model—FM."

But Model was not to be allowed to enjoy the peace of his remote final resting ground in that old battlefield.* Someone decid-

*In both the Vossenach and Hamm, dead *landsers* and GIs are still being interred yearly from where they have been found by local farmers, etc. The superintendant of the U.S. cemetery told the author that in 2000, at least three GIs who had been killed nearly six decades before were found and buried in his cemetery with full military honors, at peace at last.

ed otherwise. In the mid-1990s, the grave was robbed. Not that it would seem that there was anything worth robbing. His Knights Cross and other medals had long gone. But the little field marshal's remains vanished that day and up to the present time they still have not been recovered. Yet another mystery, well over half a century after those more significant mysteries which conceal the truth about the battle of the Bulge.

COLONEL HERMANN GISKES

Surprisingly enough, Giskes, the brain behind "Operation Heinrich" which fooled the Allies totally and reinforced, as it were, their own prejudices, seemingly was never very proud of his role in foiling intelligence before the battle of the Bulge. He should have been. After all, not only did he convince Sibert and Strong, and their masters, Bradley and Eisenhower, that the Germans would attack in the Aachen area, but he also bamboozled the OSS and the very sharp Captain Hans Habe, also attached to "Radio Annie."

In later years when he was allowed to talk and write about his role in the German Abwehr during the war, Giskes concerned himself mainly with his Operation North Pole: the great deception in Holland between 1942 and 1944 which trapped at least fifty agents working for the British Secret Intelligence Service. This was surprising, for Giskes did have the lives of several dozen agents indirectly on his hands and he had been fortunate to fall into the hands of British intelligence at the end of the war. The Dutch might well have executed him if they had caught him first. The British "humiliated" him, as he complained later, stripping him naked and subjecting him to hour-long interrogations under the command of "Ton-Eye" Stephens, a monocled Rhodesian colonel in charge of the SIS's Lachtmere House Interrogation Centre in the Surrey village of Ham; but they did not shoot him.

Finally Giskes was released back to the British Zone of Occupied Germany, without ever having even mentioned "Operation Heinrich" to his captors. Middle-aged and without a profession—he had been a wine salesman in the Rhineland when he had been recruited into the Abwehr in the late thirties—he drifted back into the "great game," albeit with a new master. This new boss was not one who paid in cigarettes, the only valid commodity in postwar

Germany worth anything. No, Giskes's employers were not even German and they paid in the mighty U.S. greenback. For Giskes was recruited by America's top intelligence chief in Europe, General Reinhard Gehlen, once the head of Hitler's military intelligence agency, Foreign Armies East, during the war. Secretly working for America virtually since the day World War II had ended, Giskes, who had so cleverly misled General Sibert in the Ardennes, was, due to that same U.S. general, protecting the U.S. Army's interests at the army's key port of Bremen. The wheel, it appeared, had come full circle.

GENERAL EDWIN SIBERT

Back in November 1944 while Giskes had been busy fooling Sibert, at Bradley's headquarters in Luxembourg, Sibert had been contacted by one of Allen Dulles's rather dubious assistants in Bern, Switzerland, the German-American Gero von Gaevernitz. The latter, who had Dulles's ear, had suggested to Sibert he might break the impasse of the Siegfried Line by getting the German generals to help him. Using German military intermediaries in Allied hands, Sibert could convince the German frontline commanders down the road on the Our–Sauer Line to surrender.

Sibert, a novice to the treacheries and double-dealings of the "great game" (he had joined Bradley only in March of that year) soon found enough German officer POWs of senior rank in the various Allied cages to do this. Only weeks before the "surprise" offensive started, Sibert radioed the War Department in Washington asking for permission to form a committee of German POWs under the leadership of Major General Bassenge, a former Abwehr officer from the Luftwaffe. This committee would first be attached to SHAEF headquarters or Bradley's as an advisory formation.

Washington hurriedly turned Sibert down. With Russia as an ally, a committee of that kind would be far too much of a hot potato for the State Department. Besides, the nation's capital was riddled with high-ranking spies at top level.* The Russians would soon learn of any attempt of this nature to approach the Germans in the West.

Thereafter had come the battle of the Bulge and the "German committee" had been hastily forgotten, especially as Washington

---

*The so-called "Venona" spies, whose identifies have only been released in the last decade, and even then not all of them.

was now demanding an inquiry into Sibert's lack of foresight. The inquiry was duly carried out, with Sibert generally being regarded as the scapegoat for the intelligence failure which had cost 80,000 American casualties alone during the battle of the Bulge.

In the end Sibert was rehabilitated by the War Department, where he had influential friends, soon to include both Bradley and Eisenhower.

After the war had ended, out of the Alps came a certain General Gehlen, who claimed he had hidden all his documentation on the Russian war machine gathered over four years in the East. He, Gehlen, was prepared to do a deal with the Americans; and in the summer of 1945 there were few Germans who had the nerve to make a suggestion of that kind to their American conquerors. He would put the material and the whole of his massive organization at the disposal of the U.S. military in exchange for his freedom and that of his key officers—and naturally coin of the realm!

Sibert was astounded by this barefaced lie, but he was impressed, too. He shared, in addition, Dulles's conviction that now that Germany was defeated, Russia had become America's greatest enemy and that in order to safeguard the U.S.'s interest it would be necessary to use the former enemy, Germany, to defend the country against the former ally, Russia. As Sibert recalled later, "I had a most excellent impression of [Gehlen] at once."

According to Sibert, he then broke the customary use of "channels," i.e., putting proposals forward through the next senior officer and then on upward till it reached the officer who could approve or disapprove of whatever was being suggested. In this case, it would have been Eisenhower's chief of staff, Bedell-Smith, and naturally General Eisenhower himself.

Instead he went ahead on his own and pursued the Gehlen proposal in secret and, if we are to believe his own statement that "only later did I inform General Bedell-Smith, Chief of Staff to Supreme Headquarters, of Gehlen's value to us," risked his military career to do so—a highly unlikely act, in the opinion of this author.

Then, as the Sibert account goes, he did inform Bedell-Smith. The latter, not wishing to compromise Eisenhower, talked it over with other intelligence officers and finally forwarded the proposal to Washington. Apparently the reaction was lukewarm there. But by

September, Gehlen was in Washington, in a German general's uniform, selling his ideas and having them bought by those who wished
to see the back of the U.S.'s own intelligence agency, the OSS. By
October, Sibert and one of Gehlen's key staff officers, Colonal Baun,
were touring the U.S. Zone of Occupation recruiting ex-officers of
Gehlen's organization. Soon the OSS would be disbanded. In its
place would appear the CIA, with both Bedell-Smith and Allen
Dulles as its chief at various times. For years, Gehlen and all those
agents who had fooled and tricked the Americans during the lead-
up to the battle of the Bulge worked full out for their former enemies. The Cold War had commenced and in the end no one would
really be able to clarify who was the deceiver and who was being
deceived.

COLONEL OTTO SKORZENY

Like Gehlen and his staff, Otto Skorzeny, too, had gone to
ground at the end of the war, hiding like most of the Nazi war criminals in the high Alps on both sides of the German-Austrian border.
The scarfaced giant had good reason to go into hiding. The man who
Eisenhower had named "the most dangerous man in Europe" was
not only on the Allied wanted list for "automatic arrest," he was also
featured on several thousand posters plastered all over the U.S.
Zones of Occupation in Germany and Austria.

For several reasons, all bogus, Skorzeny later explained that he
had actually written a note from his mountain cabin hiding place
offering to give himself up to the Americans and they did not react; so
he decided to surrender in person. But the French officers who were
present at that momentous occasion weren't interested. He had just
announced proudly, "I am Obersturmbannfuhrer Otto Skorzeny. I am
ready to surrender and also surrender 300 members of my Jagdver-
bande," when a French captain interrupted him, saying, "Well I can
see you are too tall to be Adolf Hitler and not fat enough for Goering.
But right now, I don't have time to handle the surrender of every SS
officer who walks in here. Just be patient. Your turn will come."

In the end, Skorzeny did find some Americans to surrender to
and immediately became the darling of the U.S. Press Corps. After
all, he was excellent copy. They flocked to Salzburg in Austria to
interview him. But first, it seemed, he had to be vetted by the U.S.

counterintelligence authorities before he was allowed to talk to the correspondents.

Later Skorzeny always thought that the U.S. colonel who did the first interview on 18 May 1945, in Augsburg, Germany, was the head of counterintelligence in the U.S. Seventh Army. But in reality this officer, who as Skorzeny recorded "was one of the most decent and fairest of all my interrogators," was none other than Colonel Sheen of the CIC, who had burst into Ike's headquarters crying in panic, "Skorzeny is driving on Paris!"

For six long hours he grilled Skorzeny. He told the latter of all the rumors which had circulated at that time, down to a French pharmacist reporting from Toul that Skorzeny had bought a packet of aspirins from him to cure a headache during his drive on Paris. Naturally, he put the words into Skorzeny's mouth that it was just one "hell of a wild rumor." Naturally, Otto Skorzeny, who knew that if the Americans handed him over to the Russians his fate would be sealed, agreed.

Later, the *New York Times* reported dutifully that, "Handsome, despite the scar that stretched from ear to chin, Skorzeny disclaimed credit for leading the mission to murder members of the Supreme Command."

A week or so later, Colonel Sheen gave an interview carried in the U.S. forces paper, *Stars & Stripes*. In it he stated that there "had never been a German intention to attack General Eisenhower's headquarters." It had been just another of those "wild rumors" which had circulated during the battle of the Bulge.

Was Sheen right? Or had Otto Skorzeny bought his freedom from a trial as a war criminal by toeing the Sheen line? Or had he been blackmailed with the threat of being handed over to the Russians? One might ask, too, in this context, why Sheen had rushed to interview Skorzeny before the scarfaced giant could talk to the U.S. press? Why had he posed as the head of counterintelligence for the U.S. Seventh Army, which he wasn't? In addition, it could be asked, why his questions (or at least the form he gave them to the press) were always phrased in a way that related to an attack on the "Supreme Headquarters," and never on that headquarter's supreme commander, General Eisenhower?

A lot of questions without answers.

GENERAL DWIGHT "IKE" EISENHOWER

Back in that week of the "Black Christmas," when Sheen really thought that General Eisenhower was seriously under threat and ordered he had to be guarded against "Skorzeny's killers" at every move, Commander Harry Butcher, former radio executive and Ike's spin doctor, remarked to the heavily guarded Eisenhower: "Now you know how it must feel to be President and always under the watchful eye of the Secret Service."

Later, when Butcher prepared to publish his hugely popular *My Three Years with Eisenhower*, his former boss insisted that it had to be heavily censored before publication. It was. But that particular reference to the presidency somehow escaped. It did, however, tie in with Patton's remarks on the same subject made in that same year and so we can assume that it was widely expected by the people in the know that one day General Eisenhower, like Washington and Grant before him, would assume his country's highest office.

Accordingly, General Eisenhower's record and reputation had to be protected, especially in regards to the battle of the Bulge which had cost so many lives. As Eisenhower himself wrote to Secretary for War Patterson in December 1945, when the question of reviewing the battle of the Bulge publicly was raised: "I have been informed that many of the Army's sincere friends are considerably disturbed by certain implications and insinuations that occasionally appear in the press concerning the so-called Battle of the Bulge."

Eisenhower went on to state, "I consulted with my principal subordinates concerning the probable effects of a German offensive ... since I had received warnings from my intelligence system that there were indications that such an attack might take place."

Eisenhower then admitted he knew of whatever warnings about the coming battle which intelligence had cared to pass on to him, though he made no mention of his own secret source, the Oshima transcripts forwarded from Washington via the "Black ULTRA." Then, Eisenhower goes on to maintain that "General Bradley actually traced on the map, many days in advance of the attack the line on which he estimated the Germans could penetrate if they succeeded in concentrating considerable forces under conditions of very bad weather. The line he traced coincided in remarkable detail with the one they actually reached."

I will leave the reader to make what he will of this statement, which indicates, or so it seems, that Eisenhower and Bradley knew what was going to happen and had taken measures to deal with the attack, if and when it materialized. But it does appear to be, with hindsight, all very pat, too cut-and-dried. But one thing emerges from that long communication one year after the battle of the Bulge: intelligence was very much on Eisenhower's mind.

As has always been the case, victory excuses everything. Who concerns himself with the failures prior to the achievement of victory? What do they matter? Victory is the thing; leave the defects, the mistakes and the like to the Johnny-come-latelies; the nitpicking academic historians, who in their ivory towers away from the sound and fury of battle have time enough to consider such unimportant failings.

But in Eisenhower's case, he knew in the years to come he would not just be seen as a general, one who had achieved a victory out of a potential defeat, which he did. He would also be subjected to the scrutiny of a wider public, that which voted on his suitability as a person aiming to become the president of the United States. And Eisenhower was a sensitive, shrewd man (who else but Eisenhower could have kept that difficult Allied coalition together in 1944–45?). He must have known already in late 1945 when his future was in doubt (where else could he go in the U.S. Army after he had achieved the office of chief of staff, the army's most important office?) that his record prior to the Bulge would be examined by the media and the electorate.

He would realize, too, that his great weakness that "Black Christmas" was in the field of intelligence. Had he known what was going on, thanks to the Oshima transcripts? Or had he been fooled by his own wishful thinking, namely that the Germans were beat and were not in a position to attack? Or had he accepted the deception plan, launched (unknown to Eisenhower naturally) by Hitler himself, that if he did move westward it would be in the form of a counterattack to stop the Allied drive from the Aachen area?

That year nearly sixty years ago now the problem was partially solved for Eisenhower by the strange disappearance of both copies of the top SHAEF intelligence bulletins from both Frankfurt and London where they were kept. As General Strong wrote the author, it was "twenty-five years before I found out that Bedell-Smith had launched a secret inquiry into the pre-Bulge Intelligence business. I was even more surprised to discover that by some mistake or other, both copies of these Intelligence summaries had been shredded or burned by some strange oversight."

One wonders whose.

Allied to the confused pre-Bulge intelligence set-up, which foiled the Allies in such a disastrous fashion, there is also an even more mysterious matter: the question of whether Eisenhower knew of the wartime attempts at making contact between the U.S. Army and the German generals, presumably mainly those defending the German side of the Ghost Front.

Back in August of 1944, it is clear from recently released British evidence* that Reichsfuhrer SS Himmler, both Giskes's and Skorzeny's boss, made a deliberate peace offer to Churchill. Churchill would not buy it. Of the 15,000-odd ULTRA transcripts that went through the prime minister's hands in World War II, this was the only one that he kept. But not for long.

On the first day of that month, the ULTRA signal had been forwarded to Downing Street by "C," the mysterious head of the British Secret Service. That same day, "C," or Sir Stewart Menzies, to give him a name, received a handwritten note back from Churchill. In it the prime minister stated, "Himmler telegram kept, and destroyed by me."

Three weeks later, on 18 September 1944, when Gerow's V Corps had just launched its first attack on the West Wall, a German intelligence signal was intercepted which read: "Himmler forbids by W/T [wireless traffic] all contact with English since their offers are bluff." About two weeks after that, General Walter Schellenberg, Himmler's smart, ex-lawyer head of the SS's own secret service, the SD, began to make his first tentative contacts with Allen Dulles, the head of the OSS and friend of General Sibert, located in Berne, Switzerland.

The rest we know, including Sibert's recruitment of the Gehlen Organization as the future main source of Soviet intelligence in Europe for the CIA. But back in 1944/45 could all these contacts with the enemy, in particular, the executor of the holocaust, Heinrich Himmler, have gone unremarked by Eisenhower? If nothing else, the

---

* January 2001, British Public Record Office. Article in *The Times* dated 19.1.01.

military contacts with the Germans should have gone through the right channels, which meant, in Europe, *Dwight D. Eisenhower*.

Perhaps one day we shall learn more of what happened on that remote frontier in that autumn/winter of 1944, though it is doubtful. Yet one thing is certain. That silent front, where nothing happened for three months until all hell broke loose on Saturday, 16 December 1944, is still inhabited by more ghosts than those of the hundreds of young men who died violently there that day. Those deep silent wooded valleys and steep mountain sides, where the mouldering fox-holes and rusting fragments of jagged metal still remain to remind one of the great tragedies which took place there, retain their secrets. The Ghost Front is still with us.

Sources

Annan, N. *Changing Enemies*. HarperCollins, 1995.

Barrett, R. (York), interview with author.

BBC Reports, BBC 1945.

Bradley, Omar. *A Soldier's Story*. Ballatine, 1948.

Brombeeck, Herr W. (Dunkirk), correspondence with author.

Cole, H. *The Lorraine Campaign*. Department of Defense.

Colljung, P. *Bollendorf Heimat im Grenzland*. Eifelverein.

Dahman, Herr (Bleïalf), interview with author.

Denniston, R., interview with author.

Dickinson, Tom, Correspondence with author.

Downs, Hunter, interview with author.

Ed. *Weihnachten brannte die Westeifel*. Rudolf Hofmannverlag, 1999.

Eisenhower, D. *Eisenhower*. MacMillan, 1980.

Giskes, H. *Inside North Pole*, Kimber 5I.

Giskes, H., interview with author.

Habe, H. *Im Jahre Null*. Heyne Verlag, 1977.

Hartel, F. *Erinnerungen*.

Hausser, P. *Waffen SS im Einsatz*. Munin Verlag, 1969.

Heimatkalender, 1995. Bitburg, Prum. Landkreisverwaltung.

Heimatkalender, 1997. Bitburg-Prum.

Hemingway, Ernest. *Collier's* 1944/45.

Hinsley, F. & A. Stripp. *Code-Breakers*. Oxford, 1999.

Hoffman, Herr, interview with author.

Infield, G. *Skorzeny*. Military Heritage Press, 1997.

Information Office, Junglinster.

Kessler, L. *The Iron Fist: A History of the SS Panzer Divisions*. Futura, 1977.

Koch, O. *G-2. Intelligence for Patton*. Shiffer, 1999.

Lahlud, J.P. *The Bulge, Then and Now*. After the Battle, 1992.

Lehmann. *Die Leibstandarte*. Vol I-IV. Muninverlag.

MacDonald, Charles. *Company Commander*. Ballatine, 1953.

MacDonald, Charles. *The Seigfried Line Campaign*. Department of Defense, 1977.

Marshall, John, correspondence with author.

Meyer, K. *Panzermeyer-Grenadiers*. Schildverlag, 1973.

Milmeister, M. (Luxembourg), interview with author.

Milmeister, M. *Ardenneschladt*. Luxembourg: Editions Saint Paul, 1993.

Model, Gen. Walther, interview with author.

Newspapers: *Grenzecho; Trier Volkszeitung; Aachener Nachricten; Welt am Sontag*.

Nobusch, J. *Bis zum bitteren Ends*. Bitburg, 1978.

Pallud, J *Ardennes Offensive, Then and Now.* After the Battle, 1992.

Peiper, J., interview with author.

Piekalkiewicz, J. *Spione, Agenten, Soldaten.* Sudwestverlag, 1969.

Price, F. *Troy H. Middleton.* Louisiana State Press, 1974.

Province, Charles. *The Unknown Patton.* Hippocrene Books, 1983.

Ritter, K., interview with author.

Ritter, K. *Prummer Bote.* Eifelverein.

Ruyter, Rob de, interview with author.

Skorzeny, Otto, correspondence and interview with author.

Skorzeny, Otto. *Wir Kampften, wir verloren.*

Spiegel. Letters Column, 1950.

Sprott, Hans, interview with author.

Stober, H. *Die Styrmflut und das Ende.* Munin, 1970.

Strong, Kenneth, correspondence with author.

Strong, Kenneth. *Intelligence at the Top.* Cassell, 1968.

Tammerman, J. *De Belgische Parachutisten.*

Thorpe, Professor James, University of Maryland, correspondence with author.

Tree, W. (Aachen), interview with author.

Volkischer Beobachter. October 1944.

Winterbotham, F., interview with author.

Whiting C. *The Last Assault.* Sarpedon, 1994.

Index